How to Write a Master's Thesis

Third Edition

Yvonne N. Bui

San Francisco State University

SAGE

Los Angeles | London | New Delhi
Singapore | Washington DC | Melbourne

FOR INFORMATION:

SAGE Publications, Inc.
2455 Teller Road
Thousand Oaks, California 91320
E-mail: order@sagepub.com

SAGE Publications Ltd.
1 Oliver's Yard
55 City Road
London EC1Y 1SP
United Kingdom

SAGE Publications India Pvt. Ltd.
B 1/I 1 Mohan Cooperative Industrial Area
Mathura Road, New Delhi 110 044
India

SAGE Publications Asia-Pacific Pte. Ltd.
18 Cross Street #10-10/11/12
China Square Central
Singapore 048423

Library of Congress Cataloging-in-Publication Data

Names: Bui, Yvonne N., author.

Title: How to write a master's thesis / Yvonne N. Bui, San Francisco State University

Description: Third Edition. | Los Angeles : SAGE, [2019] | Previous edition: 2014. | Includes bibliographical references and index.

Identifiers: LCCN 2019006833 | ISBN 9781506336091 (Paperback : acid-free paper)

Subjects: LCSH: Dissertations, Academic—Handbooks, manuals, etc.

Classification: LCC LB2369 .B75 2019 | DDC 808/.066378—dc23
LC record available at https://lccn.loc.gov/2019006833

Acquisitions Editor: Leah Fargotstein
Editorial Assistant: Claire Laminen
Production Editor: Astha Jaiswal
Copy Editor: Deanna Noga
Typesetter: C&M Digitals (P) Ltd.
Indexer: Wend Allex
Proofreader: Lawrence W. Baker
Cover Designer: Karine Hovsepian
Marketing Manager: Shari Countryman

19 20 21 22 23 10 9 8 7 6 5 4 3 2 1

How to Write a Master's Thesis

Third Edition

To M. & O. with all my love

Brief Contents

Sara Miller McCune founded SAGE Publishing in 1965 to support the dissemination of usable knowledge and educate a global community. SAGE publishes more than 1000 journals and over 600 new books each year, spanning a wide range of subject areas. Our growing selection of library products includes archives, data, case studies and video. SAGE remains majority owned by our founder and after her lifetime will become owned by a charitable trust that secures the company's continued independence.

Los Angeles | London | New Delhi | Singapore | Washington DC | Melbourne

Detailed Contents

List of Students' Master's Theses

By Student

Cheryl Gomes: Chapters 7, 9

Lindsey Henderson: Chapter 8

Lori Hess: Chapter 9

Amelyn Ho: Chapter 6

Diana Iniguez: Chapter 8, Appendix G

Robin Irey: Chapters 7, 8, 9

David Kendall: Chapters 7, 8, 9, Appendix G

Michelle Kornhauser: Chapter 7

Sara Mireles: Chapter 8

Barbara Nixon: Chapter 7

Shain Rau: Chapters 8, 9

David Stephens: Chapter 7

Aprille Williams: Chapters 7, 8, Appendixes E and F

By Chapter

Chapter 6:

- Ho
- Iniguez

Chapter 7:

- Williams
- Kendall
- Irey

Preface

The purpose of this book is to teach and model how to write a master's thesis. The book is intended for graduate students who will write a thesis as part of the requirements for a master's degree as well as for university faculty who are teaching and advising students pursuing this goal. As a former faculty member at the University of San Francisco and now at San Francisco State University, a major part of my role has involved teaching and advising graduate students pursuing their master's degrees. This time has been an enjoyable, fulfilling, and educational experience. Most of my students are employed professionals working and going to school full time, caring for families, or assuming other responsibilities that require their attention. As the culminating experience of their graduate program, some see the master's thesis as an opportunity to research new solutions to problems they have encountered in their course work or in their professional work. Behind their enthusiasm, however, there is often fear and uncertainty about how to conduct the research and write the thesis.

Based on my experiences in advising and teaching master's students, I have undertaken the task of demystifying the process of how to write a master's thesis. In writing the book, I assumed that you are familiar with the content in your field or discipline. However, I did not take for granted that you know the *process* of writing a master's thesis because the only way to know how to write a master's thesis is to have already written one! Thus, my goal was to provide a useful, straightforward, and practical book that goes beyond informing what "should" be done. In addition to the "should dos," the organization and structure of the book is designed to offer guidelines on how to research and write the master's thesis, step-by-step.

There are 10 chapters in the book, and each one begins with a detailed outline of the content in the chapter. Chapter 1 provides an overview of the master's thesis. Chapters 2 and 3 focus on how to select a research topic and search the existing research literature in electronic databases and Internet search engines. Chapter 4 discusses the ethical issues when conducting research and the process of applying for approval from the Institutional Review Board (IRB). Chapters 5, 6, 7, 8, and 9 introduce how to write the main components of each of the five chapters in a traditional master's thesis: Introduction, Literature Review, Methods, Results/Findings, and Discussion. Chapter 10 focuses on editing and formatting citations, references, tables, and so on, using the writing style from the American Psychological Association (APA). Within each chapter, I describe and explain what is expected within a specific section in the thesis, give tips and strategies on how to prepare and write the section, and provide sample excerpts adapted from students' completed master's theses to illustrate my suggestions. There are also numerous figures and captured "screenshots" from relevant websites to enhance the text.

At the end of each chapter, there is a *Resources* section that can be used to deepen your understanding or to tailor information in the text to your particular thesis. The resources are suitable for use by individual students or in group and/or class settings. The *Resources* section includes Common Obstacles and Practical Solutions, Reflection/Discussion Questions, Try It Exercises, Key Terms, Suggested Readings, and Web Links. In the Common Obstacles and Practical Solutions section, I discuss problems that students typically face and make suggestions that may help prevent or alleviate these frustrations. In the Reflection/Discussion Questions, I offer broad questions that may help synthesize the information in the chapter. The Try It Exercises are opportunities to practice what was discussed in the chapter to prepare for or write sections of the thesis. The Key Terms are critical concepts that were defined in the chapter and are included in the Glossary. In the Suggested Readings and Web Links, I offer recommendations for additional readings and websites on the Internet to supplement your understanding of the information in the chapter. Taken as a whole, the book is full of detailed explanations, examples, and supplemental materials that I have successfully used to advise students to complete their master's theses.

Important changes have been made to this third edition. First, every chapter has been carefully edited and updated with new citations. Second, the suggested readings and web links at the end of each chapter have also been updated to reflect the most current electronic resources. Third, due to advances in technology, new sections on conducting Internet searches and screenshots have been added to Chapter 2. Fourth, more details and updated examples are provided to illustrate the funnel writing strategy and the three parallel ladders strategy. Fifth, there is more information about qualitative research and mixed methods and data analysis in this edition. Finally, sections were added on how to read and use the book and prepare the master's thesis for presentation and publication.

Writing a master's thesis is a complex task, and I would be less than honest if I suggested that all you need to do is read this book and the task will be easy. You will work hard in doing your research, and you will spend long hours writing the thesis. I have great respect for you as you undertake this important and admirable task to fulfill a worthy goal, both personally and professionally. Your master's research will cause you to think and write differently, give you confidence in your professional role, and open new doors for you. In the absence of not having the opportunity to work with you personally, I hope that this book serves your needs during your journey and that you benefit from it as much as I have from working with students like you.

Acknowledgments

I would like to acknowledge and express my appreciation for the individuals who helped make this book a possibility. I would like to thank the following reviewers for their comments and suggestions on how to strengthen the book:

- Andrew Vorder Bruegge, Winthrop University
- Margaret K. Chojnacki, Barry University
- Joel M. Cox, Liberty University
- Michael Dreher, Bethel University
- Tavis Jules, Loyola University Chicago
- Hsin-I Liu, University of the Incarnate Word
- Jonathan Mercantini, Kean University
- Dr. Julie Norflus-Good, Rampao College of New Jersey
- Linda Smetana, California State University, East Bay
- Libby Smith, University of Wisconsin-Stout
- Elizabeth Tolman, South Dakota State University
- Cheryl Young-Pelton, Montana State University Billings

To Leah Fargotstein, my amazing editor at SAGE Publications, I cannot thank you enough for your guidance, patience, and support. To the editorial, production, and support staff at SAGE Publications, thank you for your assistance throughout the entire process. To my students, thank you for all that you taught me and for sharing your master's theses with others. To my devoted friends and colleagues, thank you for providing sustenance and comfort. To my life mentors and confidantes, Edward Meyen and Larry Brewster, thank you for your eternal wisdom, encouragement, and insight. To my loving parents and siblings, thank you for believing in me and supporting all my endeavors. To my beautiful family, you are my heart and inspiration. Thank you for your unconditional love. I am grateful to you all.

About the Author

Yvonne N. Bui (PhD, Special Education, University of Kansas) is a Professor and Chairperson of the Department of Special Education, Graduate College of Education at San Francisco State University. She has taught master's- and doctoral-level courses in Special Education, Research Methods, Master's Thesis, Statistics, Grant Writing, and Dissertation Proposal Development. She has served as the chairperson and committee member for students' theses and dissertations. She is the coeditor of *Exceptional Children in Today's Schools: What Teachers Need to Know*. Her research interests include developing curriculum for students with disabilities from culturally and linguistically diverse backgrounds and international special education. Her personal interests include reading, writing, hiking, backpacking, camping, traveling, and spending time with her family.

Overview of the Master's Degree and Thesis

*As it has for more than two centuries,
progress will come in fits and starts.
It's not always a straight line. It's not
always a smooth path.*

—Barack Obama

I f you are reading this page, congratulations! This signifies that you have already successfully completed a bachelor's degree in your field, a major accomplishment. Now you are ready to embark on the next phase of your educational journey: completing a master's degree. Why congratulations and not condolences? Because whether or not the master's degree is the highest professional degree in your field or a gateway to doctoral studies, completing the degree will open many doors for you, both personally and professionally; it is up to you to find them and walk through.

The Master's Degree

There are a vast number of types of master's degrees in a variety of disciplines and specialty areas. The two main types of academic degrees at the master's level are the Master of Arts and the Master of Science. The **Master of Arts (MA)** degree is typically awarded in the disciplines of arts, sciences, social sciences (e.g., education, psychology), and humanities (e.g., history, philosophy, religion). The **Master of Science (MS)** degree is typically awarded to students in technical fields such as engineering, nursing, mathematics, and health care management but can also be in the social sciences.

In some fields, the **master's degree** is referred to as a *professional degree* or *terminal degree*. A **terminal degree** is the generally accepted highest academic degree in a field of study. For the purposes of this book, no distinction is made between the MA, MS, or professional degrees, because all are referred to as the *master's degree*.

A **master's degree program** is a graduate-level, postbaccalaureate program in a specific field or discipline that typically involves a culminating activity, project, exam, or thesis. Depending on the discipline and the institution, there may be several pathways to obtain the master's degree. In some cases, students may take a certain number of units through coursework and complete a fieldwork project at the end of their studies. For example, graduate students may submit a project related to a particular topic such as a curriculum unit, a handbook or manual, or a visual arts performance. In other cases, students may take courses and pass a comprehensive oral or written exam at the end of their studies. In still other cases, the degree may require coursework and a research study. There may be a combination of the options mentioned involving coursework, an exam, and a final project or study. Although each discipline has its own specific requirements for the master's degree, they all share a commonality of having a cumulative experience or final activity to show that students have "mastered" the necessary content. Thus, before you proceed in your studies, it is best to find out the requirements for the master's degree within your own discipline, field, and institution of higher education.

In addition to many tangible benefits, a major benefit of obtaining the master's degree is the amount of personal satisfaction that it brings. I always tell my students (especially when they are on the verge of giving up), "Yes, it is a tremendous amount of work; yes, I know you have not seen your partner in a week; and yes, I understand the dog is angry at you. However, when you are done and you have completed your master's degree, no one can take that away from you." This usually keeps them going for about a week. The point is although it will seem like a long (and virtually endless) journey, and it will not always be easy to see the finish line, once you complete your culminating experience, a unique sensation will overcome you (unrelated to the fatigue). This sensation comes from knowing that despite the adversity and hurdles, you have accomplished your own personal goal, acquired by only a small proportion of the general population.

What Is a Master's Thesis?

For the purposes of this book, I only address the master's thesis option. The **master's thesis** is an empirically based research study that is an original piece of work by the graduate student. An **empirically based** research study is based on data that are produced by experiment or observation (rather than opinion). The thesis must be an original piece of work because it represents the student's culminating research and writing abilities. Thus, this book focuses on the research process and a traditional five-chapter thesis rather than an artistic performance or production. Completing a thesis demonstrates your ability to conduct original research, review the existing literature, collect data, analyze the data, report the results, discuss conclusions, and draw implications from your research findings. Moreover, the completion of a thesis represents your perseverance, discipline, and scholarly writing. Just like there is more than one way to skin a catfish, each discipline has slightly different specifications and requirements for the thesis. Some institutions may also require that there is a final presentation of the study. It is important for you to find out what the requirements are for the components, format, and process for completing the thesis. Usually the graduate division, college, school, or department will offer these guidelines.

If you are preparing to write your master's thesis, most likely you are at the end or toward the end of your master's degree program. Although master's degree programs are not typically designed to teach students how to write a thesis, the course of study and experiences from the program benefit you greatly as you go through the research and writing process for the thesis. First, the master's thesis process provides you with multiple opportunities to learn the critical core content in your field or discipline. This content knowledge will help you as you select an appropriate topic to study—one that is both relevant and significant to your field—and frame your research interests. Next, most master's degree programs require students to take a research methods course. The thesis experience will help you research the literature, analyze and synthesize research articles, develop answerable research questions, and create a rigorous, yet feasible, design for your study. Thus, throughout the thesis writing process, you will be constantly relying on the content knowledge and experiences that you gained from the master's degree program to demonstrate you have "mastered" the content and associated research skills in your field or discipline.

The Benefits of Writing a Master's Thesis

As mentioned earlier, there are many options to obtaining the master's degree—with the thesis as one of them, perhaps the most challenging and time-consuming. You are probably thinking, then, "Why on earth am I choosing this option?" Besides the feeling of euphoria that will wash over you when you copy and bind your final draft, there are some tangible benefits of choosing a thesis that make it a worthwhile choice.

First, completing a master's thesis can inspire you to continue study within your discipline. Conducting academic research or pursuing an academic career is not for the weak of heart. The thesis can help prepare you for the next level of research practice within your discipline and/or candidacy for a doctoral program. Not only will you have evidence of research potential (and practice in conducting research), you will have the opportunity to discern early if an academic career is a good fit before committing to pursue further degrees.

Second, the thesis writing experience provides a rare opportunity for mentorship and guidance with a faculty member, an expert in your discipline area. During this process you will meet and work individually with a faculty thesis advisor and committee members who will give you detailed advice and push you to a higher level of thinking and writing. The faculty thesis advisor can also be a great reference for future jobs, internships, or the next graduate-school application. To this day, I still maintain a close relationship with my former thesis students, and they know they can always come to me for support.

Finally, the skills you acquire in writing a thesis will benefit you in any career you choose. For example, you will learn how to pose a problem, present data to support an argument, organize your thinking, communicate through scholarly writing, manage a large project and your time effectively, and receive constructive feedback. All these skills will enhance your performance in any chosen career path.

The Difference Between a Master's Thesis and a Term Paper

One of the biggest hurdles for students when writing the master's thesis is adjusting from the writing style of a term or research paper format, a common expectation at the undergraduate level. There is a qualitative (and often quantitative) difference between the master's thesis and a term paper. As mentioned, the master's thesis is based on original research on a particular topic conducted by the student. In comparison, the term paper is a major written assignment about a particular topic (representative of a student's achievement during a term) (https://www.merriam-webster.com/dictionary/term paper). In the term paper, there may be a subject or question that will be answered using examples from books, journals, articles from newspapers, and so on, to support the findings. However, the student is not conducting a research study to answer a research question. For example, a term paper may consist of presenting the argument that the use of social media technologies (e.g., blogs, social networks) has actually decreased rather than increased the quality of relationships within society. The student would cite research and other sources to persuade the reader and support his argument. For a master's thesis, on the other hand, the student would conduct a full literature review on the topic and then develop a research question. Then he would collect data, perhaps administering a survey to 200 people at random to find out their perspectives about their social media usage and the quality of their social relationships. Finally, he would analyze the data, report the results, and discuss the conclusions and implications of his findings (based on the data that were collected).

The Difference Between a Master's Thesis and a Doctoral Dissertation

In some cases, you will hear the word "*thesis*" used to refer to both master's and doctoral degrees. More commonly, universities use the term *thesis* to refer to the requirement for a master's and a dissertation for the doctorate. A **dissertation** is typically the culminating requirement for a doctoral degree. The difference between the thesis and the dissertation depends on your particular discipline, specialty area, and institution. In many instances, there are more similarities than differences between the two, especially when considering the "traditional" research form of a master's thesis. For example, both the thesis and dissertation studies should follow a *systematic* process where there is a researchable problem, literature to support and contextualize the problem, data collection methods (e.g., sampling, measurement instruments), analysis of the data, and discussions and conclusions based on the results of the study.

However, at every step of the process, the dissertation may require the student researcher to go into more depth or breadth. For example, the dissertation usually includes a theoretical rationale or conceptual framework that relates to the problem. Sometimes the purpose of the dissertation could be to develop or to refine an existing theory. This is not commonly required for a master's thesis. The dissertation may also require a larger sample size or complicated sampling plan, more measurement instruments, and complex statistical or rich qualitative analysis of the data. Thus, the length of the dissertation study (both in time spent collecting data and page numbers) may be significantly greater than that of the master's thesis.

Another distinction between the dissertation and the master's thesis is the number of people involved in the process. For the dissertation, most institutions require that the doctoral student form a committee with a chairperson and two, three, or sometimes four other faculty members who serve as readers. Students have to "defend" their dissertation proposal to the committee members before they are allowed to proceed with the study, with a final defense after they have completed the study. For the master's thesis, it is more common for the student to work with her assigned faculty chairperson and one other faculty member throughout the process.

Finally, another important distinction between the two is the focus or purpose of the study. The master's thesis may have a narrow practical focus, whereas the dissertation may have a broader and more theoretical focus. Although both have practical implications, the master's thesis may be more directly related to a present or immediate problem. Thus, one way to differentiate between the two is to think of the dissertation as a more complex and sophisticated master's thesis. In fact, when I advise students on their master's theses, I am constantly reminding them that this is to prepare them for their doctoral dissertation!

Selecting a Thesis Chairperson and Committee

One of the most important parts of the thesis process is selecting a chairperson and committee member(s). A critical benefit going through a master's degree program is getting to know the different faculty in your program or department. By this time, you will have a better sense of which faculty would be the most compatible in terms of working style and research interests to select as your chairperson. The **chairperson** is the faculty member who is assigned to or selected by the graduate student to advise him throughout the master's thesis process. Keep in mind that your chairperson may be different from your faculty adviser or the department chairperson. At some institutions, the program selects the chairperson for you, while in others you can select the chairperson as well as the other members of your committee. Typically, there are two faculty members on your master's thesis committee: the chairperson and one committee member. However, it is best to check with your institution because this number can vary from two to five members. Most commonly, it is required that the chairperson be a faculty member within the degree program, while the committee members could be faculty from within or outside the program and department. Again, it is a good idea to check with your institution regarding the specific criteria for the selection process.

If you are allowed to pick your own chairperson, there are a few things to keep in mind. First, your chairperson is not the coauthor of the master's thesis. In other words, she will not be writing the thesis *with* you (or *for* you). Rather, the role of your chairperson is to guide and direct your study. This does not include writing, editing, conducting research, or collecting and analyzing data. The chairperson will assume that you have all the necessary skills to complete the thesis—she will help facilitate the process. One factor to consider when selecting a chairperson is her area of *expertise*. Having a chairperson who is familiar with the topic of your thesis is helpful because she can offer suggestions on critical research literature. The chairperson may also have expertise in a particular research design that you want to use in the study. Another factor to consider when selecting a chairperson is *fit*. Here, you should evaluate whether or not you could have a positive working relationship with the faculty member. Keep in mind that you are not trying to make a new friend, but you do want someone who will offer insight and constructive feedback on your work. Finally, make sure to consider whether or not the faculty member is *accessible*. The role of the chairperson is time-consuming (especially when it comes to the giving feedback part), so do not pick a person who is already overwhelmed with her other responsibilities.

Once you have selected a chairperson, set up an initial meeting to discuss how you will work together. Each chairperson will vary on how she will want to work with graduate students, so it is critical for you to know and follow her expectations. See the *Resources* section at the end of this chapter for a list of possible questions to ask at your initial meeting. These questions will help you and your chairperson get off to a great start with a mutual understanding of your working relationship.

How to Read and Use This Book

The intent of this book is to give you a blueprint of the research process as well as to provide you with step-by-step guidance on how to write the actual thesis, one chapter at a time. This is not a *New York Times* best-selling novel, so unless you are an insomniac like me, there is really no need to read the book from front to back cover in one sitting. Rather, it might be helpful to read the book as you would a reference book—skimming the entire book and then probing deeper into specific chapters as you need more detailed information. As noted with the beginning quote, everyone's writing process will differ. While the book is written in a linear fashion for organizational purposes (and because I'm a pretty linear person), some of you may want to start with writing Chapter 2, and then go back to write Chapter 1. Others may want to start with writing Chapter 3 and so on. This is really a matter of personal choice (and that of your advisor). Clearly the only chapters you cannot start with are Chapters 4 and 5! The key point is that you start and keep reading and writing; use the book as a reference guide to keep your progress and momentum going forward.

Keep in mind that this book is not written as a research methods book (and should not replace one) that teaches in depth how to conduct different research designs and data analysis methods. While I cover these topics briefly, I highly recommend that you supplement this book with actual research methods books (and courses) that fit your selected design. There are many excellent research methods texts available, and there are some suggested throughout this book. Your faculty advisor will also know which research methods books to recommend.

At the end of each chapter there are also additional resources: common obstacles and practical solutions, reflection/discussion questions, try it exercises, key terms, suggested readings, and web links. The resources are a compilation of helpful advice, suggestions, and activities I have used with my former masters students. The resources give you a chance to practice and apply the content that is covered in each chapter and get feedback to make sure you're on track. I find that it always helps to think out loud some of the ideas (with a colleague or your faculty advisor) before you have to commit them to paper.

Components of a Master's Thesis

For the purposes of this book, the master's thesis structure will consist of five distinct chapters. Each chapter has a specific focus and objective. The titles of the five chapters are (a) Introduction, (b) Literature Review, (c) Methods, (d) Results or Findings, and (e) Discussion. The structure of the five chapters is the same whether you are conducting a qualitative, quantitative, or mixed methods research study (although some of the subsections may be different). Each chapter is described briefly here. There is a more comprehensive discussion of how to write each chapter of the thesis in Chapters 5 through 9. To avoid confusion, I refer to chapters of this book with numbers (e.g., Chapter 1, Chapter 2) and chapters of the master's thesis with their word forms (e.g., Chapter One, Chapter Two). Keep in mind that your school or program may use a different chapter format for the thesis or use other terms, such as "sections," to refer to the different components of the master's thesis.

Chapter One, Introduction

Chapter One introduces the topic of the thesis to the reader. The critical part of writing Chapter One is to establish the statement of the problem and research questions. Basically, you are justifying to the reader *why* it is necessary to study this topic and *what* research question(s) your study will answer. Usually, the topic is based on a particular problem area you want to focus on (I discuss how to select an appropriate topic in Chapter 2). For example, if your master's degree is in social work, your topic of interest may be homeless single women with children, and the specific problem may be that these mothers are not able to find jobs because they lack appropriate child care or educational services for their children due to their frequent transitions. However, before you introduce the reader to the specific topic and problem, you have to first provide the reader with the broader context (the general problem) and consequences related to the topic. In other words, before you discuss the specific problem, you need to contextualize your topic within the larger problem. For example, you would first discuss the problems related to homeless families with children in general and use national or state data and statistics to support your claims. This part would include the consequences related to the social and emotional effects on the mothers and their children.

Chapter One of the thesis includes a section on the *Statement of the Problem* (information about the specific problem), *Background and Need* (the background literature related to the problem and gaps that still remain), the *Purpose of the Study* (the focus and goal of the study), *Research Questions* (what questions the study proposes to answer), and other significant sections. In this chapter, you need to support all your claims and positions using citations from empirical research studies, government reports and data, websites, and theory and opinion papers. How to write Chapter One and its major sections is discussed in great detail in Chapter 5.

Chapter Two, Literature Review

Chapter Two introduces the reader to the research literature related to the topic. The critical part of writing Chapter Two is to identify the most relevant and significant research related to your topic rather than to conduct an exhaustive search. Basically, you are informing the reader of the *critical* studies that have been conducted related to this topic. This provides the reader with the background information that she needs to understand the problem(s) related to your topic. The literature review also provides the justification for your study as you indicate the gaps and weaknesses in the existing research. Chapter Two provides credibility to your study because it shows you have done your "homework" in reading the research for this topic and your study is "grounded" in the research. In other words, your thesis did not simply appear from thin air; instead, it was developed because there was a need to conduct the study, and it will contribute to the body of research related to this problem.

To organize Chapter Two, you first start with an introduction about the general problem and your topic. Then you provide an advance organizer, which indicates what will be covered in the literature review. For the purposes of this book, you will cover three areas that are related to your problem. The **advance organizer** explicitly states the three areas of research that are addressed and the order of the discussions. This helps structure the literature review and manage the research articles that you find. For example, in the social work example, three areas related to the problem could be (a) homelessness and its effect on children's development, (b) quality of parental interactions between homeless mothers and their children, and (c) collaboration of school and social agencies. Where did these areas come from? Do not worry; the three related areas will emerge as you read the existing literature and develop the *Statement of the Problem* and the *Background and Need* sections in Chapter One and the literature review in Chapter Two.

After you have introduced the three related areas, you will locate and synthesize three to four research articles (with empirical data) for each of the three areas related to the topic. Each section should start with a brief introduction about the area and end with a summary paragraph to recap the main points and limitations within the area. At the end of the literature review, there should also be a summary that ties together all the literature related to the topic. How to write Chapter Two and the three major sections are discussed in great detail in Chapter 6.

Chapter Three, Methods

Chapter Three explains the research methods and design that were used to conduct the study. The critical part of writing Chapter Three is to describe the actual procedures that were used to conduct the study. Basically, you are informing the reader of *how* the study was conducted. Thus, you need to include detailed descriptions about every aspect of your study. Chapter Three will include the following components: (a) *Setting* (where the study took place), (b) *Participants* (the individuals who participated in the study and how they were selected), (c) *Instructional* or *Intervention Materials* (any materials or instructional strategies that were used to conduct the study), (d) *Measurement Instruments* (the tools you used to collect data), (e) *Procedures* (how you collected the data and/or implemented the study), and (f) *Data Analysis* (the statistical, qualitative, or mixed methods techniques that were used to analyze the data). Enough detail should be included so that another researcher could replicate your study (for a quantitative study). How to write Chapter Three and the major sections are discussed in great detail in Chapter 7.

Chapter Four, Results and Findings

Chapter Four reports the results or findings of the study. The critical part of writing Chapter Four is to present the results or findings from the data collection and data analysis process in Chapter Three. Basically, you are informing the reader of *what* was discovered. This chapter integrates a narrative, numerical, or tabular presentation of the outcomes of the study, depending on whether you have conducted a qualitative, quantitative, or mixed methods study. In Chapter Four, you report the results or findings from the data analysis for each variable, participant, and measurement instrument that was discussed in Chapter Three. For example, if you conducted a qualitative study, you would provide a narrative description of the findings in relation to the research questions. If you conducted a quantitative study, you could include descriptive statistics for each participant or for the entire group (or both). Descriptive statistics are the basic level of statistical analysis for a data set from a sample group. Typically, reported statistics include the mean, median, mode, variance, and standard deviation. If you conducted an intervention for a large group or more than one group of participants in the study who received different treatments, you could apply inferential statistics to indicate any differences observed in performance before and after the intervention or between the two groups (if appropriate). Inferential statistics is the higher level of statistical analysis where inferences are made from a sample to a population. Inferential statistics may also include hypothesis testing and set probability levels to test for statistically significant differences between groups (or treatments). How to write Chapter Four and the major sections are discussed in great detail in Chapter 8. For the purposes of this book, quantitative, qualitative, and mixed methods are discussed separately in Chapter 7 (Methods) and Chapter 8 (Results and Findings) since these are the main areas where the distinction between the three methods is the greatest.

Chapter Five, Discussion

The last chapter in the thesis, Chapter Five, discusses the results from Chapter Four and draws conclusions about the study's results or findings. The critical part of writing Chapter Five is to discuss the significant results or findings in relation to the statement of the problem and the research questions that were identified in Chapter One. The discussion section includes the researcher's interpretation of the results or findings. You may also discuss the relationship of your study's results or findings to previous research conducted in the literature. In addition, Chapter Five includes a section on *Limitations*. This section discusses the limitations or weaknesses of the study's design or findings. Another section in Chapter Five is the *Recommendations for Future Research*. In this section, you make recommendations for future areas of research that should be conducted related to your study (e.g., follow-up). Additional recommendations could include those for actions, policies, or procedures. Finally, the last section of Chapter Five is the *Conclusions*. In this section, you identify the critical conclusions about the results (e.g., lessons learned) and their implications. How to write Chapter Five and the major sections are discussed in great detail in Chapter 9.

Quantitative, Qualitative, or Mixed Methods Research?

Thus far, I have briefly mentioned quantitative, qualitative, and mixed methods research, assuming you know the difference between the three types. Because you are reading this book, it is likely that you have taken or are currently taking a course in research methods, so I do not go into too much detail about the different research approaches and designs. However, since the type of study you conduct, whether quantitative, qualitative, or mixed methods, informs the writing of the five-chapter thesis, I briefly distinguish the broad approaches and give examples of possible topics from different disciplines. Although quantitative and qualitative approaches will be described separately, it is important to keep in mind that these approaches fall on a continuum rather than on polar opposites (Newman & Benz, 1998). Neither method is considered better or more important than the other, and they each have their strengths and weaknesses and advantages and disadvantages. What drives a researcher to conduct either a quantitative, qualitative, or mixed methods study is not so much a match to the personality of the researcher (although this is important) but rather the research question(s) that need(s) to be answered. In addition to the type of study a researcher chooses to conduct, she must also select a specific research design within quantitative, qualitative, or mixed methods studies. Research designs are types of inquiry or "strategies of inquiry" (Denzin & Lincoln, 2011). A few examples within each type of study are offered below.

Quantitative Research

In a **quantitative research** study, the emphasis is on **numerical data** (i.e., numbers) that can be collected using objective measures and analyzed with statistics (descriptive or inferential). The results from the data analysis (of the sample group) are then used to generalize findings across groups of people or to explain a particular phenomenon (Babbie, 2016; Mujis, 2010). Some of the more common quantitative research designs include experimental (e.g., true experiments, quasi-experiments, single-subject design) and nonexperimental (e.g., causal-comparative, correlational, survey) (Creswell & Creswell, 2018; Mills & Gay, 2019).

In quantitative experimental studies, the researcher can measure the outcome of cause-effect scenarios with single or multiple independent variables. The **independent variable** is the variable that is deliberately manipulated (e.g., cause) by the researcher to produce a change in the dependent variable. The **dependent variable** is the variable that is observed to see if there is a change (e.g., effect) in response to the independent variable. The researcher cannot manipulate the dependent variable. In quantitative research, **deductive reasoning** is often used, which is moving from the general to the specific. Typically, a quantitative researcher has a set hypothesis (prior to conducting the study) based on a theory that he tests to support or not support the given **hypothesis**. In quantitative studies, a hypothesis involves making assumptions or predictions based on probability distributions or likelihoods of events.

In quantitative nonexperimental studies such as correlational designs, the researcher is trying to measure the degree of association or the relationship between two or more variables or sets of scores. Survey research provides a description of trends, attitudes, behaviors, and opinions of a population based on a representative subset (i.e., sample) of the population.

Data are often collected with one or several measurement instruments. **Measurement instruments** are data collection tools (e.g., surveys, observations, tests) that are used to measure changes in dependent variables or variables of interest. The data are recorded in numerical format such as a percentage score, grade point average, mean score, or rating. After the data are analyzed, the hypothesis is either confirmed or unsupported. Quantitative studies typically have large sample sizes and can also have multiple groups within the sample. In addition, the researcher may have limited direct interactions with the participants in the study. Once the data are collected, descriptive or inferential statistics are applied to analyze the data. Some of the strengths of quantitative methods are that the researcher has control over many aspects of the study and, given a large sample size, the results of the study can be generalized to a broad population.

Quantitative studies can be conducted in many different disciplines and topics, again depending on the research question(s). For example, in counseling, a study could be conducted on the effects of parents' divorce on children's social and emotional behavior for 4-year-olds at one preschool. In criminology, a study could be conducted surveying adolescents whose parents are incarcerated to assess their attitudes and perceptions toward law enforcement. In organization and business management, a study could be conducted on the relationship between employees' use of self-care strategies to mediate stress (e.g., exercise, yoga, meditation, acupuncture) and their level of productivity. In social work, a study could be conducted on the effects of having aging parents on sibling relations within Asian American families. Finally, in education, a study could be conducted on differences in math scores between female and male high school students in coed or same-sex classrooms. As you can see from the examples mentioned, there is no limit to the topics and studies across the disciplines that can be conducted using quantitative methods. Notice that all the mentioned potential studies would require numerical data collection using surveys, tests, or observation checklists.

Qualitative Research

A **qualitative research study** delves into a particular situation to better understand a phenomenon within its natural context and the perspectives of the participants involved (Mills & Gay, 2019). In general, qualitative researchers attempt to explore, describe, and interpret human behavior based primarily on nonnumerical data (e.g., words).

Studies that use qualitative approaches collect nonnumerical data to answer the research question(s). **Nonnumerical data** are narrative data (i.e., words). There are many different kinds of qualitative research designs. Some commonly found approaches in the social and health sciences literature are narrative research, phenomenology, grounded theory, ethnography, and case study (Creswell & Poth, 2018). Unlike quantitative researchers, qualitative researchers do not start their study with a hypothesis that they set out to find support for or to test. In qualitative research, **inductive reasoning** is often used, which is moving from the specific to the general. A qualitative researcher starts with specific situations, finds patterns or themes in the data, establishes a tentative hypothesis, and then develops theories or conclusions. Data are often collected through extensive and detailed field notes, observations, interviews, and focus groups with the participants in a natural setting (i.e., the researcher does not control or manipulate the environment). Qualitative studies typically have small sample sizes, which allow the researcher the time and opportunity to have extensive interactions with the participants. Once the data are gathered, they are coded, analyzed, and organized or categorized according to the themes and patterns that emerge. This provides the researcher with findings in a narrative format. Some of the strengths of qualitative methods are that the researcher (a) has investigated a topic in depth; (b) has interpreted the outcomes based on the participants', not the researcher's, perspectives; and (c) has created a holistic picture of the situation.

Qualitative studies can be conducted in many different disciplines and topics. For example, in counseling, a study could be conducted on the perceptions of single-parent Latinas on using mental health services. In criminology, a study could be conducted on how incarcerated teenage mothers cope with raising their children in juvenile detention centers. In organization and business management, a researcher might be interested in how volunteerism affects employee motivation and satisfaction at a nonprofit organization. In social work, a study could be conducted on the factors that promote resiliency within domestic violence victims. Finally, in education, a researcher could conduct an ethnographic study on the experience of first-generation African American college students. As you can see from the examples mentioned, there are certain topics that require using qualitative methods such as interviews and observations to answer the research question(s).

Mixed Methods Research

A third type of study, mixed methods research, resides in the middle of the continuum of qualitative and quantitative approaches because it incorporates elements of both. The **mixed methods research** study has gained in usage and popularity over the past few decades. "In mixed methods, the researcher collects and analyzes both qualitative and quantitative data rigorously in response to research questions and hypotheses, integrates (or mixes or combines) the two forms of data and their results, organizes these procedures into specific research designs that provide the logic and procedures for conducting the study, and frames these procedures within theory and philosophy." (Creswell & Plano Clark, 2018, p. 5)

Three core mixed methods designs are convergent design, explanatory sequential design, and the exploratory sequential design (Creswell & Plano Clark, 2018). The different designs illustrate the phases of data collection and interpretation with subsequent results building on each other or offering further explanation. In the convergent design, the researcher typically collects both forms (QUAN+QUAL) of data at the same time and then integrates the information for data analysis and interpretation. In the explanatory sequential design, the first phase is quantitative and the researcher analyzes the numerical data; the second phase involves qualitative research (QUAN→qual). In the exploratory sequential design, the order of phases is reversed with the first phase as qualitative research and the quantitative research as the second phase (QUAL→quan). While it may appear that the researcher is simply "adding" phases of research together, there is actually an integration of information that should occur to create new knowledge greater than the sum of the parts such that 1 + 1 = 3 (Fetters & Freshwater, 2015).

Researchers can conduct mixed methods studies in all disciplines when they find that in answering their research question, one data source may be insufficient. In some ways, mixed methods research is a researcher's dream—you are not restricted to certain types of quantitative or qualitative data collection tools, and you can provide more evidence to study the research question(s) in depth. However, keep in mind that mixed methods research does require extensive research skills and also the time and resources to conduct the multiple phases of data collection and data analysis.

Style Form

In addition to selecting a research type and design, you also need to adhere to a style form. All scholarly writing such as books, journal articles, reference materials, dissertations, and theses must comply with a style form. Style form refers to both writing style and editorial style. The **editorial style** is a set of rules or guidelines that writers must adhere to for publishing manuscripts, books, and so on. Some of the critical elements include how to format headings, citations, references, tables, figures, and so forth. The style form developed by the **American Psychological Association** (referred to as *APA style*) was selected for this book and the master's thesis because it is commonly used in various social science disciplines such as education, psychology, sociology, business, economics, nursing, and social work. Specifically, I follow the sixth edition of the *Publication Manual of the American Psychological Association* (VandenBos, 2010). The APA manual is a reference book that has the rules and guidelines for the APA writing and editorial style. As new issues arise, the manuals are revised or updated on the APA website (http://www.apastyle.org), so make sure that you are following the most current edition. The APA style is widely accepted in the behavioral and social sciences, but the particular style form varies by discipline or academic departments. Other common references include the *Chicago Manual of Style* (17th edition, 2017) from the University of Chicago Press and the *Modern Language Association* (MLA) (8th edition, 2016), which is widely used in the humanities. Check with your chairperson for the one that applies to your thesis.

The thesis must be written in a format that complies with a style form, so it is always helpful to be familiar with the style form as you begin to write. However, the style form is not a research method. Rather, it is a tool to use in communicating your thesis. In this book, Chapter 10 is devoted to helping you comply with the APA style. The placement of the chapter late in the book does not diminish its importance. If you have used the APA style for previous papers or are familiar with the style form, this chapter will be a review for you. If you have not used the APA style before, I recommend referring to Chapter 10 as you proceed through the data collection and writing process for each chapter.

SUMMARY

Congratulations on getting through the first chapter of the book (only nine more to go)! You should now have a sense of the overall thesis and feel energized, empowered, and ready to embark on this educational adventure. Thank you for allowing me to be your tour guide. In the next chapter, I discuss how to select a research topic and questions. I wish you all the best of luck and will lead you to the finish line (and pull you through if I have to)! Here is a summary of the most critical points from Chapter 1:

- The master's degree is a postbaccalaureate degree conferred by a college or university on candidates who complete 1 to 2 years of graduate study.

- In some fields, the master's degree is referred to as a *professional degree* or *terminal degree*, meaning that the program or degree is the highest academic level for that profession rather than a gateway to the doctoral degree.

- The master's thesis provides you with multiple opportunities to learn the critical core content in your field or discipline and research methods.

- For the purposes of this book, the master's thesis is an empirically based research study written in five distinct chapters.

- Chapter One introduces the topic of the thesis to the reader and establishes the statement of the problem and research questions.

- Chapter Two introduces the reader to the research literature related to the topic and identifies the most relevant and significant research.

- Chapter Three explains the research methods and design that were used to conduct the study and describes the actual procedures.

- Chapter Four reports the results or findings of the study from the data collection and data analysis process in Chapter Three.

- Chapter Five discusses the results or findings from Chapter Four in relation to the statement of the problem and the research questions that are addressed in Chapter One and draws conclusions about the study's results or findings.

- What drives a researcher to conduct either a quantitative, qualitative, or mixed methods study is not a match to the personality of the researcher (although this is important) but rather the research question that needs to be answered.

RESOURCES

Common Obstacles and Practical Solutions

1. A common problem that students face at this stage is feeling overwhelmed with the magnitude of the thesis. Words that come to mind are, "What did I get into?" If you are feeling anxious because you have never conducted research or written something like a master's thesis, do not panic! This book (and your chairperson) will help divide the parts into manageable and feasible chunks and guide you through the entire process. However, it might be helpful for you to review the text and notes from any research methods course that you took.

2. Another common obstacle that students face at this stage is trying to decide between conducting a quantitative, qualitative, or mixed methods study. Instead of putting pressure on yourself to make that decision now, it is better to let the design emerge as you read the existing research and develop your research questions.

Reflection/Discussion Questions

Before you delve into the thesis, it is a good idea to take some time to make the "mental shift" from the type of conceptualizing and writing that was required in your undergraduate years and the type of conceptualizing and writing that is required for the master's thesis. In addition, now is a good time to think broadly about the issues and problems in your discipline and whether they would be amenable to quantitative, qualitative, or mixed methods research. The following reflection/discussion questions will help guide this process.

1. What are the similarities and differences between quantitative, qualitative, and mixed methods research?

2. Brainstorm and discuss critical research problems in your specific field or discipline. What would be the best approach(es) to address these research problems? Provide the pros and cons of selecting each type of research approach.

Try It Exercises

The following exercises (Activities One and Two) will help you identify potential faculty to serve as your chairperson and committee members as well as prepare for that first critical meeting with your chairperson. Activity Three is designed for you to research the professional and personal benefits of receiving a master's degree in your field or discipline. This knowledge will help keep you motivated as you progress through the thesis knowing that when it is all done, you can reap the rewards!

1. Activity One: For this activity, focus on the faculty within and outside of your master's degree program.

   - Make a list of all the professors and/or instructors from whom you have taken a course.

   - Make a list of all the professors and/or instructors with whom you have worked on projects outside of coursework.

   - Review the professors' and/or instructors' curriculum vitae (usually available on the university website) and list the professors and/or instructors with whom you have common (research) interests.

   - Make a list of potential professors and/or instructors who could serve as your faculty chairperson and additional committee members.

   - Create an e-mail message that gives a general overview of your research interest(s) and ask one of these professors or instructors if she would be willing to serve as your master's thesis chairperson or committee member. Set up an initial meeting.

2. Activity Two: The first meeting with your chairperson is very critical. This meeting sets the tone for future meetings and also clarifies the expectations for the relationship between you and your chairperson.

   - Make a list of questions that you would ask at the initial meeting with your chairperson. Keep in mind that you may only have 30 minutes with your chairperson, so the questions should be succinct and related to your thesis. You should also be prepared to answer questions that your chairperson might have related to his expectations of you. The following is a list of possible questions that may be included in your list:

     1. How often should we meet—weekly, biweekly, as needed?

     2. Which days and when are the best times to meet—mornings, afternoons, evenings?

     3. What is the best way to contact you if I have to schedule or cancel an appointment?

     4. In which format should I present drafts—electronically by e-mail or with hard copy?

     5. What is the typical turnaround time to receive feedback for my drafts?

     6. What is the typical turnaround time you will want me to return the next draft?

7. What are some tasks I should be doing while waiting for feedback?

8. What resources are available on or off campus to help with writing, editing, and data analysis?

3. Activity Three: For this activity, focus on personal and professional benefits of receiving a master's degree in your field or discipline.

- Imagine that you have completed your master's degree and have been asked to give the keynote address at your graduation. The department chair has asked you to conduct research in your field or discipline related to how the degree will enhance and/or further your career goals. You have to write a 5-minute speech that addresses the professional and personal benefits of receiving your master's degree (as well as thanking everyone who supported you along the way). Knowing *why* we want to do something can be just as important as how.

Key Terms

advance organizer 10
APA style 16
chairperson 6
deductive reasoning 13
dependent variable 13
dissertation 5
editorial style 16
empirically based 3
hypothesis 13
independent variable 13
inductive reasoning 14
Master of Arts (MA) 2

Master of Science (MS) 2
master's degree 2
master's degree program 2
master's thesis 3
measurement instruments 13
mixed methods research 15
nonnumerical data 14
numerical data 12
qualitative research 14
quantitative research 12
terminal degree 2

Suggested Readings

Creamer, E. G. (2017). *An introduction to fully integrated mixed methods research.* Thousand Oaks, CA: Sage.

Creswell, J. W., & Creswell, J. D. (2018). *Research design: Qualitative, quantitative, and mixed methods approaches* (5th ed.). Thousand Oaks, CA: Sage.

Creswell, J. W., & Plano Clark, V. L. (2018). *Designing and conducting mixed methods research* (3rd ed.). Thousand Oaks, CA: Sage.

Creswell, J. W., & Poth, C. N. (2018). *Qualitative inquiry and research design* (4th ed.). Thousand Oaks, CA: Sage.

Dane, F. C. (2018). *Evaluating research: Methodology for people who need to read research* (2nd ed.). Thousand Oaks, CA: Sage.

Drennan, J., & Clarke, M. (2009). Coursework master's programmes: The student's experience of research and research supervision. *Studies in Higher Education, 34*(5), 483–500. doi:10.1080/03075070802597150

Ercikan, K., & Roth, W. M. (2006). What good is polarizing research into qualitative and quantitative? *Educational Researcher, 35*(5), 14–23.

Fatima, N. (2009). Investment in graduate and professional degree education: Evidence of state workforce productivity. *Florida Journal of Educational Administration and Policy, 3*(1), 9–35.

Fletcher, K. M. (2005). The impact of receiving a master's degree in nonprofit management on graduates' professional lives. *Nonprofit and Voluntary Sector Quarterly, 34*(4), 433–447.

Labaree, D. F. (2003). The peculiar problems of preparing educational researchers. *Educational Researcher, 32*(4), 13–22.

Little, S. G., Akin-Little, A., & Lee, H. B. (2003). Education in statistics and research design in school psychology. *School Psychology International, 24*(4), 437–448.

Mills, G. E., & Gay, L. R. (2019). *Educational research: Competencies for analysis and applications* (12th ed.). Upper Saddle River, NJ: Pearson.

Modern Language Association. (2016). *MLA Handbook* (8th ed.). New York, NY: Author.

Morrow, S. L. (2007). Qualitative research in counseling psychology: Conceptual foundations. *Counseling Psychologist, 35*(2), 209–235.

Patenaude, A. L. (2004). No promises, but I'm willing to listen and tell what I hear: Conducting qualitative research among prison inmates and staff. *Prison Journal, 84*(4), 69S–91S.

University of Chicago Press. (2017). *The Chicago Manual of Style* (17th ed.). Chicago, IL: Author.

VandenBos, G. R. (Ed.). (2010). *Publication manual of the American Psychological Association* (6th ed.). Washington, DC: American Psychological Association.

Yauch, C. A., & Steudel, H. J. (2003). Complementary use of qualitative and quantitative cultural assessment methods. *Organizational Research Methods, 6*(4), 465–481.

Web Links

APA Style

http://www.apastyle.org/

Glossary of Master's Degree Programs

https://study.com/article_directory/Glossary_of_Master's_Degree_Programs.html

Modern Language Association (MLA)
https://www.mla.org/

Modern Language Association (MLA) The Style Center
https://style.mla.org/

Purdue Online Writing Lab (Chicago Manual of Style 17th Edition)
https://owl.purdue.edu/owl/
research_and_citation/
chicago_manual_17th_edition/
cmos_formatting_and_style_guide/
chicago_manual_of_style_17th_edition.html

The Chicago Manual of Style Online
http://www.chicagomanualofstyle.org/home.html

The Princeton Review: Find Your Grad School
https://www.princetonreview.com/grad-school-search

Selecting a Research Topic

Writing is making sense of life. You work your whole life and perhaps you've made sense of one small area.

—Nadine Gordimer

Now that I have covered the basic overview of the master's thesis, it is time to start the work! As in most writing projects, the first step is to select a topic. This is often a difficult task because there are many interesting unanswered research questions to study. Obviously, the topic that you choose for your thesis should be important to your field or discipline. However, keep in mind that your study should address a *research problem* and *questions* that you want answered because they are important to you and you have been unable to find meaningful and validated answers. Your research problem and question could address original research (a new question) or be a replication of a previous study. For example, if I am earning my master's degree in college counseling, then I may want to study some aspect of college counseling that is important to the process of counseling, the issues and challenges related to counseling, or the people involved in counseling. I also have to focus on a research question, or a few, that my study will attempt to answer. For the college counseling process, perhaps I want to find out the differences in participation and satisfaction during group or individual advising sessions. For the issues or challenges related to college counseling, my research question could examine the differences in retention and graduation rates for first-generation students or students of color. Finally, for the people involved in counseling, I could research the differences in college experiences for immigrant or refugee students. Framing research questions is an important part of planning your thesis. Later in this chapter, I discuss research questions in depth.

Important Factors to Consider When Selecting a Topic

A common question asked by graduate students is, "Where do I start?" Often, students feel anxious about selecting a research problem because it is like making a long-term commitment to someone you have not met! Selecting a research problem should not be like going on a blind date or a random act. Instead, it is a systematic process that requires time, reflective thinking, discussion, and, of course, research. You want to select a problem that has significance and is in need of attention. You should also select a problem that you can research within the time that is available for your thesis. I discuss four important factors to consider when selecting a research problem: (a) personal significance, (b) critical issues in the field, (c) the existing research literature, and (d) ethical considerations.

Personal Significance

The first place to look for a research topic is within. The research problem that you select should be first and foremost meaningful to you. There was a reason why you chose to enter your particular field or discipline, and hopefully you have an affinity or passion for what you are studying. This is where all the course work and experiences in your master's degree program should come in handy. Through your course work, you reviewed research and are familiar with several studies. Some of these studies may have caused you to think about additional research problems. Perhaps there was a topic, theory, or problem from a course, reading, something an instructor said, or fieldwork experience that intrigued you. Keep in mind that your research study and thesis may take 1 to 2 years to complete, so the topic should be meaningful and something you are passionate about since you will be devoting a lot of time and energy to it. Selecting a topic based on personal interests will also keep you motivated to continue and persevere, especially when you feel like quitting (which will be often).

When I pursued my master's degree, I was having problems selecting a topic because there were so many educational problems that I was interested in. Most of them were broad, societal issues that were important for students with disabilities, but none were within my reach. When I finally sat down with my chairperson and rattled off 10 ideas, he said, "What is important to you? Where do you come from? Who can you give a voice to that so few others can?" I was stunned. Important to me? Why would anyone want to hear about what is important to me? I replied, "Well, there are a lot of recent Vietnamese refugees who have children with disabilities who emigrate to the United States, and I wonder if they know much about special education services since they do not speak the language and there are few special education services in Vietnam." Thirty minutes later, I walked out of his office with a research problem and questions in hand and excitement in my heart! I had just been given permission to conduct a research study that was personal and meaningful to me. Conducting a study on a topic that was personally significant changed my entire perspective about the process. Instead of viewing the data collection process as a burden, I was excited to meet different families and was truly interested in their perspectives and experiences related to obtaining special education services for their children with disabilities. When I completed my study and presented the findings at a national conference, I was absolutely amazed by the roomful of people who wanted to hear about the perspectives and stories of refugee Vietnamese families with children with disabilities—I guess I was not the only one who thought this was important after all. Thus, the lessons learned here are to select a topic that you are passionate about and get guidance from your chairperson who will help you focus on the critical issues. After all, you cannot go wrong if you follow your heart (well, most of the time).

Critical Issues in the Field

The second place to look for a research topic is right in your own backyard. In other words, what problems or issues are you and your colleagues currently facing in the immediate environment, whether it is at a university, school, classroom, clinic, juvenile detention center, foster home, business, or nonprofit organization? Often, the research opportunity calls to you because it is an issue or problem that you have been grappling with and need some help to find solutions. For example, maybe you are interested in finding out how to retain and engage donors for nonprofit organizations. At the school setting, maybe you are concerned that the level of cyberbullying has increased over the past few years. Perhaps you are interested in mental health issues for young adults in the juvenile justice system.

If you are not sure about the problematic issues in your field, a good idea is to talk to your colleagues, instructors, administrators, and your chairperson. They will have a plethora of ideas, and it is always helpful to bounce your ideas off another person, especially someone who is familiar with the issues in the field. The research problem could be something that has a direct relationship and implication to what you do or see in your professional setting. However, keep in mind that the goal is to focus on one problem, not all the problems in your field (or obtain world peace).

Existing Research Literature

A third way to find a research topic is by doing good, old-fashioned research of the literature. Conducting research through the Internet or at the library is often a good method of finding a topic because it gives you a sense of the broad and critical issues in your field. This is very important because your study should make a contribution to the research literature. As is the case with most research studies, you want to be able to add to the existing knowledge base in your field. In other words, a "personal" concern must also be a concern for the larger academic community" (Machi & McEvoy, 2016). Conducting research gives you a general sense of what studies have already been completed, the best practices, and the gaps that still remain. Based on your findings, you may choose to replicate an existing study, implement a previously validated practice with a new population, or conduct a study that fills one of the gaps in your field.

An often overlooked resource for finding existing research is clearinghouse websites and reports from government offices. These websites list research studies that were often funded by grants and are published in many different fields and disciplines. This is a good place to start your research because they are indicators of the major issues and problems in a particular area. For example, the National Institute of Justice (Office of Justice Programs, U.S. Department of Justice) hosts a clearinghouse website called CrimeSolutions.gov. The website posts research studies conducted on a variety of practices and programs related to criminal justice, juvenile justice, and crime victim services. Experts in the field rate each program's effectiveness (e.g., Effective, Promising, No Effects) based on the strength of the evidence presented in the study. An example of a clearinghouse website in education is WhatWorksClearinghouse, which is hosted by the Institution of Education Sciences. Advantages of looking at clearinghouse websites and government reports is that they are usually readily available, free to the public, and provide a broad overview of the existing research in a particular area.

The process of conducting research of the literature has changed dramatically over the past 15 years. When I conducted research for my master's thesis, I had to actually walk into the library (yes, in the snow), first locate the books and periodicals through the card catalog, then find and take books and periodicals off the shelves, and finally bring rolls of nickels and dimes to feed the copy machine. Sometimes I had to figure out how to use and make a copy from the microfiche! Now, with modern technology, conducting research of the literature involves sitting comfortably in front of your home or library's computer in a plush chair with a cup of coffee and a half-dozen donuts.

Search Engines

Through the Internet, there are many available search engines to help you with your research of the literature. A **search engine** is a computer system where information is stored and organized for easy retrieval. The most common search engines search for information on the World Wide Web through the Internet. However, when searching the Internet, you want to make sure that your research is guided rather than general. **Advanced search** is setting specific parameters (e.g., date, author, and subject) around your search to narrow the pool of resources and results. This helps you avoid reading thousands of article abstracts. One place to start your research is Google Scholar (https://scholar.google.com) (see Figure 2.1 for Google Scholar search screen). The Google Scholar search engine will locate thousands of research articles in many discipline areas in less than a few seconds. Note that this is different than researching a topic in the regular Google search engine (which would be like trying to find a penny dropped in a well). For example, pretend I want to conduct a study on cyberbullying. When I typed "cyberbullying" into Google Scholar and clicked on the magnifying glass icon (or hit enter) to search, I retrieved over 37,300 articles! To narrow my search, I can use the Advanced Scholar Search (see Figure 2.2 for Advanced Scholar Search screen). In the Google Scholar screen, you need to bring the cursor to the top left side and click on the menu bars for the Advanced Scholar Search box to appear. In the Advanced Scholar Search, you can find articles about a topic using specific search terms and where they appear, and by author, publication, or date. When I used the Advanced Scholar Search and asked for articles where "cyberbullying" is "in the title," I retrieved 4,640 articles (see Figure 2.3 for Advanced Scholar Search screen using title of the article). I further narrowed my search by putting a 5-year limit on the dates and retrieved 2,670 articles. Finally, I added "social media" in the "exact phrase" box and guess what—I only have to read 62 articles (see Figure 2.4 for Advanced Scholar Search screen using exact phrase and date limits). That is quite a big difference from the 37,300 that I started with! Narrowing your search fields and conducting an advanced

Figure 2.1 Search engine Google Scholar search screen.

Figure 2.2 Advanced Scholar Search screen in Google Scholar.

Figure 2.3   Advanced Scholar Search screen using the title of the article.

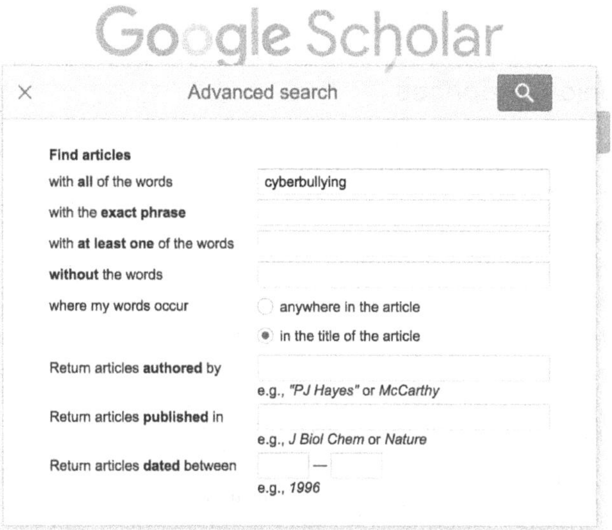

Figure 2.4   Advanced Scholar Search screen with exact phrase and date limits.

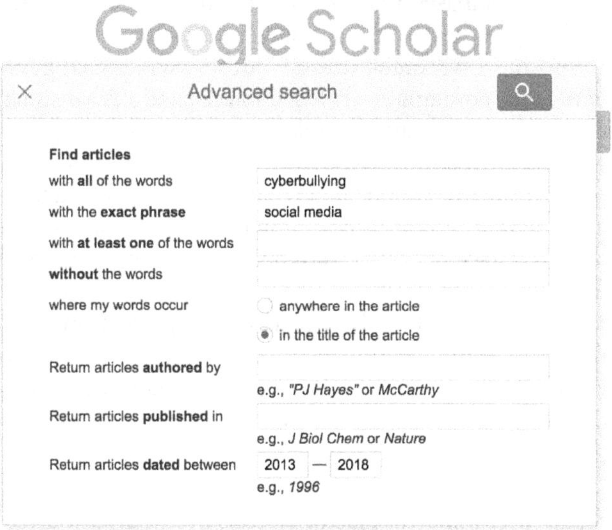

search will help you sort through the information and cull out the research that is important, but not specific enough to your research problem. Your chairperson is a good resource if you need help shaping your search terms to conduct the advanced search. A 15-minute meeting with your chairperson could save you hours and hours of being lost in cyberspace.

Electronic Databases

Searching through electronic databases is another method to find a potential research topic. An **electronic database** is an electronic collection of information (e.g., books, journal articles, reference materials) where an individual can research and retrieve resources.

Electronic databases can be interdisciplinary or organized around a particular subject area or field. In electronic databases, you can find citations and summaries to journal and newspaper articles, dissertations and theses, books and book chapters, technical and government reports, and tests and measures related to your field. Sometimes, if you are lucky, you can even get the full article from the database (that always feels like winning the lottery!). The library at your institution subscribes to a variety of electronic databases, and as an enrolled student, you may be able to access the databases for free. Typically, you can search these databases by subject or alphabetically. For example, PsycINFO (http://www.apa.org/pubs/databases/psycinfo/index.aspx) is a very popular and helpful database that has resources related to psychology and related fields such as nursing, sociology, education, linguistics, anthropology, business, and law.

If you do not have access to your institution's library, there are other electronic databases that are free to the public, although some of them may charge a small fee for their articles. For example, Education Resources Information Center (ERIC) (http://www.eric.ed.gov) is a huge digital library that contains over 1.2 million citations, abstracts, digests, peer-review, and full-text articles related to education from 1966 to the present. ERIC is sponsored by the Institute of Education Sciences, U.S. Department of Education. Once you enter the electronic database, the process is very similar to a typical search engine. Again, you will want to conduct an advanced search with set parameters regarding topic, author, dates, and so on. However, an advantage of an electronic database over a general search engine is that most of the resources in the electronic database will be directly related to the field of study. I discuss how to search for research through electronic databases and the Internet in more detail in Chapter 3.

Ethical Considerations

Finally, another important factor to consider when selecting a research topic is ethics. For example, it would be unethical to ask a group of volunteers to deliver electric shocks to another person (against their conscience) if directed by an authority figure, right? This study was actually conducted at Yale University by Stanley Milgram in 1961. Thus, before proceeding in selecting your topic, you should ask yourself these questions: Will my study on this topic and the methods used to answer the research question(s) jeopardize the participants' (a) physical well-being, (b) emotional well-being, (c) academic well-being, (d) economic or financial well-being, (e) spiritual well-being, (f) social well-being, or (g) privacy? If you can respond with a definitive "No" to these questions, then most likely your study will pass muster on ethical considerations. If you are unsure whether or not your study will violate an ethical consideration, do not worry; every institution of higher education requires that graduate students submit their master's thesis study proposals through the **Institutional Review Board (IRB)** for approval *prior* to conducting the study. The IRB is a group that has been formally designated by the institution to review and monitor research applications involving human subjects. I discuss ethical considerations, the IRB process, and how to write an IRB proposal in more detail in Chapter 4.

How to Narrow and Refocus Your Topic

Once you have selected a potential research topic, you will probably need to narrow it down. Often, students select topics that have met the four criteria above—personally significant, critical issue in the field, contributes to the existing research, and meets ethical standards—only to discover that the topic is still too broad and outside the scope of their immediate surroundings. This can be somewhat frustrating, but fortunately there are ways to make your research study more concrete and manageable. Sometimes students will select significant problems to study, but because they did not narrow and refocus the study prior to starting, they eventually feel overwhelmed, helpless, unmotivated, and finally quit altogether. To avoid these pitfalls, schedule an appointment with your chairperson early in the process to discuss ways to narrow your study but still keep the essence of what interests you. Investing this time at the beginning will save you time and frustration later and could make the difference between completing or not completing the thesis within the allocated time. As I often reminded my students, "The 'best' master's thesis is the one that is completed!" In addition to getting advice from your chairperson, you also have to draw on your own personal research skills and knowledge about research methods and designs. Throughout this process, it will help to access research methods textbooks and academic journals in your field to use as references. In this section, I discuss three factors to consider when focusing and narrowing the scope of your study: (a) feasibility, (b) accessibility, and (c) time and resources.

Feasibility

Often, students will be so excited when they find a topic of personal and professional interest that they may choose a problem that is not feasible to study. **Feasibility** refers to how realistic it will be to access data or participants and the time needed to complete the study. For example, the topic of study may be the stress levels of high school students on applying for college admissions in a school district, and I want to measure students' perceptions using a survey and some follow-up interviews. However, because the problem is so broad, it would require a team of experienced researchers with sizable resources to make this a feasible study to complete.

One method to increase feasibility is to limit the sample group. The **sample group** is the group of participants in a study. They are the group that the researcher collects data from or about. How to reduce or shape your sample group will depend heavily on your research question(s), but this is one of the best ways to make your study more feasible and manageable. For example, in the study above, rather than measure the perceptions of *all* high school students in the school district, I could study the perceptions of high school students at *one* high school within the school district. However, if it is like the public high school I went to, the sample group would be 2,400 students! That is still too large for one person to manage. One method to further reduce the sample size would be to randomly select a certain number (50) of students from each of the grade levels. This would still give me a "representative" sample of the entire school, but I would only have to manage 200 surveys rather than 2,400. Another method to reduce my sample size would be to measure the perceptions of students from *one grade level*, such as the juniors. This shows only one slice of the high school, but perhaps this is the group most affected by the college admissions process. Again, this could be 600 students, so taking a random sample from one grade level would also be another possibility to narrow the study. By limiting my sample size, I have made the study more feasible, which increases my chances of successfully collecting the data (and completing my thesis).

Another method of narrowing the study and increasing feasibility is by reducing the number of research questions. (I discuss how to develop research questions in more depth later in the chapter.) Keep in mind that the more research questions you have, the more data you will have to collect and analyze (and possibly include more participants). The intent of the thesis is not to study everything with regard to your topic; often, it is better to study one or two things in depth. By limiting the amount of data you collect, you gain more control over the process. In many ways, conducting a study is like cooking (something I have never been able to master). If you select a recipe with 10 ingredients (some of which you have to buy in specialty stores), the cooking process becomes more complicated than if you had a recipe with five ingredients because there are more factors outside of your control. If done correctly, you could end up with a mouthwatering dish and get rave reviews from friends and family. However, with so many ingredients to mix, blend, blanch, or puree, there is an increased chance of making mistakes, burning something, cutting yourself, over- and undercooking items, and basically losing your sanity in the process.

Accessibility

Another related factor to consider when narrowing your study is accessibility. **Accessibility** refers to the ability to gain access or entry to the research site and participants. This is related to feasibility because without access to the research site or participants, it will be impossible to conduct and complete the study. Keep in mind that some places of business, schools, detention centers, hospitals, and clinics do not allow individuals outside of the organization to conduct research at their sites. If they do allow outside researchers, the application and approval process may take weeks or months to complete, so you need to plan accordingly. Thus, before you finalize your research plan, it is best to get a letter of permission to access participants from the administrator at the research site (some IRB applications require this for the proposal). This will ensure that you can at least get through the front door.

If you do gain access to the research site, another factor to consider is ease of access and proximity. Basically, you need to determine how easy it will be for you to collect the data for your study. For example, I want to conduct a study on the parenting skills of teenage mothers in juvenile detention centers. I measure their parenting skills by conducting observations while they are interacting with their children. The administrators at the detention center have given me permission to access the participants for my study. The center is 15 miles away from my house, and the visiting hours for mothers and their children are Monday through Friday from 12:00 p.m. to 2:00 p.m. In the morning from 8:00 a.m. to 12:00 p.m. and in the afternoon from 2:00 p.m. to 6:00 p.m., the children are at the onsite child care center. However, my normal work hours are from 8:00 a.m. to 1:30 p.m., which means by the time I get to the center, I will be able to observe the mothers and children for only 15 minutes! This is not enough time to collect rich observation data for the study. Even though I had access to the research site and participants, because of other external factors outside of my control, I did not have access in terms of ease and proximity. Thus, when considering your study, make sure that you will have true access to collect data for your study. One way to increase true access is by conducting the study at a setting where you already spend a good deal of time such as at your place of employment, volunteer site, or training or school site. For the example study above, since I could not quit my job but was able to access the children at their child care center in the afternoon, I could refocus my topic to study the effects of incarcerated teenage mothers on children's social and emotional development. By refocusing the topic, I was still within the broader area of teenage mothers in juvenile detention centers, but I made the study's participants truly accessible by observing the children rather than the mothers.

Time and Resources

In addition to feasibility and accessibility, you must consider available time and resources before starting a study. **Time** refers to the researcher's time that is available to devote to the study as well as the duration (length of study) and frequency (how often the researcher will interact with participants). **Resources** are tangibles such as materials and finances necessary to conduct a study but also include nontangibles such as personal health and energy. Make sure you have the time and resources to complete the tasks required by the study such as traveling to the research site, implementing an intervention if required, purchasing or developing materials, collecting data, analyzing the data, and reporting the data. Keep in mind your "team" of researchers will consist of yourself, a computer, and a supportive spouse, partner, friend, pet, or family member if you are lucky. Thus, before you start, it is critical to narrow and refocus your study so that you are not overcommitting and stretching yourself too thinly.

For example, your school district has required all teachers to receive in-service training on research-based practices to improve students' state-wide reading test scores. Since you are in a master's degree program for education, your principal has asked you to conduct your thesis on this topic. She wants you to lead 20 hours of professional development sessions at the school site with 15 kindergarten through 5th-grade teachers, collect data on the teachers' implementation of the research-based practices, and report on the students' outcomes. The in-services would start in January after the winter break, the state assessments start in April, and you would have to develop and provide all the training materials. To be fair, the principal has given you a $300 budget and two 50-minute periods of release time per week from your 3rd-grade class. Should you do it? You have access to willing participants, some release time, a small budget, and the support of the principal, so it should be feasible, right? WRONG! Clearly, this study is above and beyond what you have available regarding time and resources. First, the allocated time is much too short. Three months is not enough time to research and locate materials, conduct 20 hours of in-service trainings, conduct observations for 15 teachers, and collect student data—all this on top of your normal teaching responsibilities. Second, there are no curriculum resources available, so this means your $300 budget would be quickly spent or you would have to develop your own materials (in your spare time) for the trainings. Thus, even though it may have seemed like a good study to conduct because of the accessibility, this is an unrealistic study because of the demand on your time and resources. Some suggestions I would make to narrow the focus of the study would be to start much earlier in the school year, reduce the training from 20 to 10 hours per week, limit the responsibilities so that you would only provide training and observation to one grade-level team, and ask the principal to increase the budget for materials and release time. By making the parameters more realistic (both in length of the study and time to devote to the study) and having resources available, you have increased the feasibility and quality of the study.

Developing Answerable Research Questions

Once you have selected and narrowed your problem, it is time to develop the research question. A **research question** is related to the problem in a study and is the question the researcher attempts to answer. Good research questions narrow the topic and focus of your research study. They also guide the type of data that will be collected or how the data should be collected. For example, I want to conduct research around the problem(s) related to neighborhood violence and young children's development. The broad problem is "neighborhood violence," and the research problem within this topic is "How violence within neighborhoods affects young children's cognitive development." Once I know my research problem, I need to generate a research question(s) that will guide my study. Some programs or disciplines may use different terms to refer to the research questions, such as research hypothesis or null hypothesis. Always check with your chairperson to make sure you are using the appropriate terms.

Answerable Questions

The most important consideration when developing a research question is whether or not you can *answer* the question (i.e., the question is researchable). That may seem a bit strange—after all, aren't all questions answerable? Not necessarily. An **answerable research question** is one where the researcher is able to collect data or information (using a measurement instrument) to answer the question related to the problem. There has to be some measurement instrument and method that can be used (e.g., survey, observation, test, interview) to collect data or information from the participants in the study. In other words, if you cannot *measure* the research problem in some way, then you cannot answer the research question. For example, for my research problem of "neighborhood violence and young children's cognitive development," the research question is about the effects that violence within a neighborhood has on young children's cognitive development. Thus, one possible research question is, "What are the effects that neighborhood violence has on young children's academic performance?" This is a possible research question because I can collect data to measure the effect or outcome of the problem on my participants. However, the research question is not very clear because there are several ambiguous terms. These ambiguous or subjective terms must be *defined* before I can determine what exactly is being studied. For example, what constitutes neighborhood *violence?* Who are considered *young* children? What is meant by *academic performance* and which indicators will be used? When considering whether or not a term is ambiguous, ask yourself if you and a complete stranger would have a different definition of the term or if the term would be unfamiliar to a person outside of your field; if so, it is best to define the term.

Defining Terms

There are three ways you can define terms related to your research question and study: by dictionary, by example, or operationally (Fraenkel & Wallen, 2015). A **dictionary definition** is a definition that is offered in a dictionary to define ambiguous terms related to the study or research question. This may not always be applicable to your study, especially when it is a compound word or if the terms represent a concept or idea such as neighborhood violence. For example, when I look up *neighborhood* in the dictionary, the closest definition is "the people living near one another" ("Neighborhood," n.d.). Then, when I look up *violence*, the closest definition is "exertion of physical force so as to injure or abuse." When I put the two together, my definition of neighborhood violence would be "exertion of physical force so as to injure or abuse by people living near one another." This is close to what I am thinking of but does not really capture what I want to research because it is vague regarding the parameters of the neighborhood and type of violence.

Another way to define terms is by giving an example definition. An **example definition** is a definition that uses examples to define ambiguous terms related to the study or research question. For instance, for neighborhood violence, an example definition would be an area where violent crimes such as shootings or stabbings, home and auto theft, and gang-related activity such as fighting, muggings, and so on, occur regularly. This gives the reader a better idea of what I want to study, but there is still ambiguity about the size of the area and how regularly the violent crime must occur in the neighborhood. Perhaps the best way to define terms is to give an operational definition. An **operational definition** is a definition that describes attributes or characteristics of the term that need to be present to measure it. For example, a neighborhood could be determined by the area within a given zip code or group of city blocks, and neighborhood violence could be limited to violence committed with weapons such as guns and knives. In this study, a *young child* could be a child between the ages of 6 and 9, and *academic performance* could be the child's performance on a standardized achievement test. By operationally defining the ambiguous terms in my research question, it is now clear to me and to the reader the exact phenomenon I am studying. I have also defined the terms in such a way that I can now collect measurable data to answer the research question.

There are at least three types of questions that would *not* be good research questions: philosophical/rhetorical, value/moral, and hypothetical (Fraenkel & Wallen, 2006). The first kind is philosophical or rhetorical in nature and resembles questions asked by 4-year-olds that leave you scrambling for an answer. For example, "Why was I born? Why did our dog have to die? What is the meaning of life?" are all nonresearchable questions. A **nonresearchable question** is a type of question where the researcher cannot collect measurable data to answer the question, or where the "answers" are based on philosophical, spiritual, or personal beliefs. The second kind of nonresearchable question involves making a value or moral judgment. For example, "Should plastic bags be eliminated at grocery stores? Should all children be vaccinated? Does electroconvulsive therapy help or hurt patients?" are not researchable questions because the answers to the questions can be influenced by personal values and biases. The third type of nonresearchable research question is based on hypothetical situations. For example, "What if there was no war? What if everyone grew their own food? How long would humans live if disease were eliminated?" are all nonresearchable questions because you cannot collect data in a setting that exists only hypothetically. Additionally, there would not be any measurable outcomes.

Look at these questions from my example study and decide which type of nonresearchable question they are:

- Why are neighborhoods plagued with violence?

- What is the best way to save children from neighborhood violence?

- Should handguns be banned to reduce neighborhood violence?

- What would happen to children's development if they did not witness regular violence in their neighborhoods?

In summary, it is critical that the research questions for your study are answerable and any ambiguous terms are clearly defined. This is a necessary first step because the research questions will guide the rest of your study and the methodology (e.g., research design, setting, participants, measurement instruments, data collection, data analysis) that you use to answer the questions.

Creating a Realistic Timeline

Now that you have narrowed your topic and developed answerable research questions, it is time to create a timeline. A **timeline** is a schedule that is created by the researcher that outlines all the necessary steps and phases to complete the study within the allocated time. This is necessary because often students will be so excited about finding an interesting research problem that they plan a study that does not have a realistic timeline. For example, imagine that you have 1 academic year to complete your study, and it is due by the end of the spring semester (typically in May). Your intervention is going to take three months, and you cannot start the intervention until the beginning of January. This will leave you one month to score all the data, complete the data analysis, report the data, and write up the results (not to mention the multiple revisions you will have to make). This narrow timeline will not only put unnecessary stress on you (and your chairperson), but it may also deter you from completing the study. A better timeline would be to start the intervention earlier or, if that is not possible, shorten the intervention.

A realistic schedule or timeline is one that gives you some cushion and a reasonable amount of time to complete each section or chapter. Keep in mind that when developing a timeline, every part of the process will probably take longer than you expect, and there are sure to be surprises along the way. You should also expect to write multiple revisions of every chapter. In addition, there may be events or situations (personal or professional) that cause interruptions that you cannot predict or control. Thus, putting buffers into your timeline will give you the flexibility to stay on track (and not feel guilty about always being behind schedule).

Here are some possible tasks to include in your timeline and a sample schedule for 1 academic school year. Because every institution is different, it is best to check what the expected procedures are at your institution.

August–September

- Conduct preliminary research to find possible research topics
- Speak to colleagues about possible research topics

- Meet with chairperson to discuss how to narrow topic and refocus study
- Develop answerable research questions
- Obtain permission from research site to conduct study and access participants

September–October

- Meet with chairperson to discuss Chapter One
- Locate and finalize sample group of participants
- Submit application to university's Institutional Review Board
- Submit application to organization, school district, or other entity for permission to conduct research
- Submit first draft of Chapter One

October–November

- Make revisions and submit final draft of Chapter One
- Locate and finalize measurement instruments
- After receiving permission from all parties involved, start the pretest phase (if appropriate)
- Begin conducting interviews or classroom observations (if appropriate)
- Meet with chairperson to discuss Chapter Two
- Conduct literature review
- Submit first draft of Chapter Two

November–December

- Make revisions and finalize Chapter Two
- Begin the intervention phase of your study (if appropriate)
- Continue with the interviews and field observations (if appropriate)
- Meet with chairperson to discuss Chapter Three
- Gather information and demographic data of participants and research site
- Submit first draft of Chapter Three

December–January

- Meet with chairperson to discuss ongoing progress
- Begin the intervention phase of your study (if appropriate)
- Continue with the interviews and field observations (if appropriate)
- Make revisions and finalize Chapter Three

January–February

- Complete intervention or data collection
- Begin the posttest phase (if appropriate)
- Meet with chairperson to discuss data analysis

February–March

- Score measurement instructions and complete data analysis (if appropriate)
- Transcribe field notes and complete data analysis (if appropriate)
- Meet with chairperson to discuss Chapter Four
- Submit draft of Chapter Four

March–April

- Make revisions and finalize Chapter Four
- Meet with chairperson to discuss Chapter Five
- Submit draft of Chapter Five

April–May

- Make revisions and finalize Chapter Five
- Double-check all citations and references for appropriate format (e.g., APA)
- Create necessary tables and figures
- Locate all documents for appendices
- Create abstract and table of contents
- Conduct final formatting

- Meet with chairperson for final printout and review
- Bind and copy final thesis

May

- Submit final revisions and copies of the thesis to committee members for signatures
- Graduation celebrations

June

- Take a much-deserved vacation

Time Management

Realizing all the tasks that need to be done for the entire thesis can be a bit daunting. However, if you manage your time well, meet regularly with your chairperson, and try to stick as closely as possible to your timeline, it is very possible to complete the study in a reasonable amount of time and do a high-quality job. Because the thesis is different from traditional course assignments where there are hard-and-fast deadlines, it is easy to let the months go by without any real progress. Unfortunately, the thesis is not like those term papers that you wrote in college the night before (and got an A!). You will need to make consistent progress on the research and data collection aspects as well as the writing process. There are two strategies that will help you be successful in this process.

Reserving Time

The first strategy is to *reserve time* for the thesis. In this day and age, we are all busy, all the time. There never seems to be enough time to finish everything that needs to be done—who can possibly eat healthy food, exercise, and get enough sleep? Like other big projects (e.g., cleaning the garage), the thesis will fall to the bottom of the to-do pile unless you allocate and reserve time to work on it on a consistent basis. The reserved time can be 1 day a week, 1 hour every morning, or even 20 minutes every evening. You can pick whatever works best for you and your schedule; however, once you have made that reservation with yourself and the computer, you must treat it as sacred time. This means there are no excuses for not keeping the "appointment" or putting it off and saying, "I'll do double time tomorrow or next week." Let's face it, if you could not find 20 free minutes today, why would you be able to have 40 free minutes tomorrow? Of course, there will be emergencies and surprises that come up now and then, but it is really critical that you devote a consistent and regularly scheduled amount of time to work on the thesis and be self-disciplined. This means turning off the cell phone, e-mail, television, or anything that will disrupt you. You should also find a place to work where you will be most productive whether it is in a home office, library, or café. Meeting with a writing partner on a regular basis might also keep you from canceling thesis appointments, although make sure it does not become a social event! You can also set up reminders on your smart phone and computer calendars. Rather than just writing it on a to-do list (which can easily be forgotten), you can set the phone reminder with your alarm for a specific time, date, and location. In this way, you can at least be thinking about your thesis at regular intervals during the week. In Google Calendar, the reminders carry over the next day until you mark it as done. Kind of like having your own guilty conscience following you around!

Chunking Method

Another strategy that will help you be successful in the process is the chunking method. The **chunking method** refers to breaking up large tasks into smaller, more manageable chunks such as writing one section of a chapter rather than the entire chapter. If the task is to write an entire chapter or transcribe all the interviews, this will seem very intimidating, and the natural response is to do anything (e.g., clean out your desk, reorganize your closet) to avoid the required task. Believe me, I am the master of procrastination and have a very clean desk. However, if you set a goal to work on only one small chunk of the larger task (e.g., one section of the chapter, one transcription), this will feel less daunting, and you will be more likely to start the task. Writing the thesis is similar to sticking to an exercise plan (something I had to do after an ankle injury). When I set my goal to ride the exercise bike for 40 minutes every other day, it was almost impossible to find 40 minutes of "free time," and I just kept putting it off until the next day. Since my riding time was supposed to be every other day, this meant I never rode the bike. Meanwhile, the bike was a constant reminder of my "failure" and was being used as a very expensive clothes hanger. However, when I set the goal to ride the bike 15 to 20 minutes at the beginning of my day, I was able to stick to this schedule more regularly, and sometimes I even stayed on the bike for another 20 minutes! Once I got into the habit of getting on the bike, it became part of my daily routine. I can now proudly say that I ride the bike for 30 minutes almost every day and even look forward to it (that is a bit of an exaggeration). The point is, one of the hardest parts of writing the thesis will be to motivate yourself to sit down and just turn on the computer. However, once you start and begin to build momentum and form a routine, you will find that not only will it be easier to continue, but you also might actually enjoy yourself in the process. Building in small rewards after each completed chunk is another way to reinforce your productive behavior (eating a bag of chips as I did after the bike ride is not recommended). The next time that you are feeling overwhelmed and ready to quit, take some deep breaths and remember this quote by the ancient Chinese philosopher and writer Lao Tzu: Do the difficult things while they are easy and do the great things while they are small. A journey of a thousand miles must begin with a single step (https://www.brainyquote.com/quotes/lao_tzu_398196).

SUMMARY

Selecting your research topic/problem is perhaps the most important (and difficult) phase of the thesis process, so I hope this chapter has given you ideas on where to start and how to narrow the focus. In the next chapter, I discuss in detail how to research the existing literature related to your research topic/problem. Here is a summary of the most critical points from Chapter 2:

- The topic that you choose for your thesis should be related to your field or discipline and address a *research problem* and *questions.*

- The research problem that you select should have personal significance, could be a problem or issue that you or your colleagues are currently facing in the immediate environment, and should make a contribution to the research literature.

- In electronic databases such as ERIC, you can find citations and summaries to journal and newspaper articles, dissertations and theses, books and book chapters, technical and government reports, and tests and measures related to your field.

- An important factor to consider when selecting a research topic is ethics, because you should not jeopardize the participants' well-being in any way.

- Every institution of higher education requires that graduate students submit their master's thesis study proposals through the Institutional Review Board (IRB) for approval *prior* to conducting the study.

- Three important factors to consider when narrowing your study are feasibility, accessibility, and available time and resources.

- The most important consideration when developing a research question is whether or not you can *answer* the question (i.e., the question is researchable).

- There are three ways you can define terms related to your research question and study: by dictionary, by example, or operationally.

- There are at least three types of questions that would *not* be good research questions: philosophical/rhetorical, value/moral, and hypothetical.

- Once you have narrowed your topic and developed research questions, create a schedule and timeline (including reminders) so that you can complete the study within the allocated time period.

RESOURCES

Common Obstacles and Practical Solutions

1. A common problem that students face at this stage is feeling anxious about selecting a research topic. Words that come to mind are, "Everything sounds interesting—how do I choose just one topic?" At this point, do not put so much pressure on yourself to find the perfect research topic. Instead, select a few, do some scanning of the research, and then see which one seems the most interesting, feasible, and accessible. Remember that you can always change topics, and sometimes in doing the research, the topic will "find" you.

2. Another common obstacle that students face at this stage is thinking about the time issue. Words that come to mind are, "How will I ever have enough time to write?" If you are like me and your days are packed from the moment you open your eyes in the morning until you close them again in the wee hours of the morning, finding free time is like winning the lottery without buying a ticket—chances are pretty slim. That is why it is critical for you to *schedule* time to write—schedule writing time in your daily planner just as you would a doctor's appointment. Think of it as an appointment to benefit you (without copayments!).

Reflection/Discussion Questions

As you begin to think about possible research topics, it is important to frame them in the context of research questions. Having answerable research questions related to problems in your field or discipline will help narrow the focus of your study (and ensure that you have a feasible study). The following reflection/discussion questions will help guide the process of developing answerable research questions and defining the appropriate terms.

1. What makes a research question answerable versus nonanswerable? What are the different types of nonanswerable questions? Brainstorm critical problems in your field and develop three answerable questions and

three nonanswerable questions related to the problem. Discuss why the questions are answerable or not answerable.

2. What are the differences in the three methods for defining terms? Discuss the pros and cons of each type of method. Based on the answerable research questions you developed earlier, identify and define ambiguous terms using the most appropriate method.

Try It Exercises

The following exercises (Activities One and Two) will help you identify a potential topic for the thesis and ways to narrow the topic so that it is feasible to study. Activity Three is designed for you to create a timeline with the help of your chairperson. This timeline and personal writing schedule will help you stay on track and finish the thesis in a timely manner (remember the rewards from Chapter 1!).

1. Activity One: For this activity, focus on the knowledge and experience you have gained from your master's degree program that will help you throughout the thesis process.

    DREAM TOPIC: In the perfect world where I had limitless time, money, and energy, I would conduct a study with this topic:

    Now that you have that out of your system, follow the steps below to choose a topic for your master's thesis. Remember that you're saving the dream topic for your doctoral dissertation.

    - Make a list of the topics/problems (based on course work) that would be interesting to research further.
    - Make a list of the topics/problems (based on community, fieldwork, or clinical experience) that would be interesting for you to research further.
    - Based on the information above, answer the following prompts:
        1. A topic that has personal significance:
        2. A topic that is a critical issue in my field:
        3. A topic that I found in existing research:
        4. A topic that is ethical to research:
    - Now choose the BEST topic for *you* from 1 to 4 and write a one-paragraph description of the research topic/problem that you are interested in pursuing for your master's thesis study.

2. Activity Two: Based on the research problem that you selected for Activity One, discuss with a colleague or your chairperson how to narrow the focus of your study considering feasibility, accessibility, and time/resources.

3. Activity Three: Meet with your chairperson to create a realistic timeline for completion of the thesis. Use the sample list of tasks from this chapter and modify the tasks and timeline to match the chairperson's and university's expectations for submitting written work and the final thesis. Then create a personal contract where you schedule when and where you will focus on the writing tasks. Sign both the timeline and contract, give one copy to your chairperson, and tape one copy by your work space. Set up reminders on your phone and computer calendar.

Key Terms

accessibility 33

advanced search 27

answerable research question 35

chunking method 42

dictionary definition 36

electronic database 30

example definition 36

feasibility 32

Institutional Review Board (IRB) 31

nonresearchable question 37

operational definition 37

research question 35

resources 34

sample group 32

search engine 27

time 34

timeline 38

Suggested Readings

Bell, J., & Waters, S. (2014). *Doing your research project: A guide for first-time researchers* (6th ed). New York, NY: Open University Press.

Lei, S. A. (2009). Strategies for finding and selecting an ideal thesis or dissertation topic: A review of literature. *College Student Journal, 43*(4), 1324–1332.

Shon, P. C. H. (2015). *How to read journal articles in the social sciences: A very practical guide for students* (2nd ed.) (SAGE Study Skills Series). Thousand Oaks, CA: Sage.

Web Links

Academia

https://www.academia.edu/

Figshare

https://figshare.com/

Mendeley

https://www.mendeley.com/

MIT Libraries: Selecting a Research Topic

https://libguides.mit.edu/select-topic

ResearchGate

https://www.researchgate.net/

CHAPTER 3

Using the Literature to Research Your Problem

The greatest part of a writer's time is spent in reading, in order to write; a man will turn over half a library to make one book.

—Samuel Johnson

Now that you have finished selecting and refining your research problem, it is time to determine how important your research problem is to others and what is already known about the problem. The way to do this is to search the literature to identify prior research about the problem.

One of the questions that might occur to you is, "Why do I need to know about what others think of the problem when I already know what I want to do with my study? Isn't that just going backward?" Keep in mind the goal for your master's thesis is to do research that yields answers to problems that have not been fully answered. If you can find an answer to your research problem in the literature, then it is not necessary to do all the work that is involved. Through the literature review, you will read what is known about your research problem and also learn who else shares your interest. Later, you may find it helpful to correspond with them as you progress in your research.

Although the literature review can be a time-consuming and arduous process, it is also one of the most important aspects of completing the master's thesis. Once you become familiar with the tools and strategies available to you in conducting literature reviews, you will be knowledgeable and up-to-date with historical and current studies, learn new ideas, and have a better feeling about how your study fits into the existing research (Fraenkel, Wallen, & Hyun, 2015). How to actually write the literature review will be covered in Chapter 6 of this book.

Benefits of Conducting a Literature Review

There are several benefits of conducting a literature review. One major benefit is learning how important your research problem is and what is already known. This includes being familiar with the historical and seminal theories and research studies as well as the most recent cutting-edge studies. Once you are able to bridge the existing literature with your research topic, you enhance the credibility of your study and yourself as the researcher. The literature review shows that you are knowledgeable of the content related to your topic and can now apply it to new situations (McMillan, 2015). The knowledge base in disciplines such as social sciences and the humanities moves very quickly as researchers develop new theories and confirm or repudiate existing ones. Additionally, new interventions and processes are continually tested and supported through research studies. Thus, it is important for you to keep up with the research by subscribing to and reading professional journals and attending research conferences in your field so that your knowledge is not outdated.

Another benefit of conducting a literature review is to get new perspectives or ideas that you can incorporate into your study. This prevents you from having to reinvent the wheel. By reviewing the existing research related to your problem, you can learn from other researchers' successes and mistakes (and try not to repeat them). This will make the task of refining the research questions and methods much easier and should strengthen your study. This may also help you narrow further your research problem and focus or restate your research hypothesis (McMillan, 2015). For example, by examining a previous study's research questions, methodology, and results, you can determine what has worked and not worked with a particular sample group. If a particular intervention or process was successful with a sample group (e.g., adolescents) that is similar to yours, you may want to replicate part of or the entire study. Similarly, if a particular intervention or process was successful with a sample group (e.g., children) that is very different from yours, you may want to study whether or not the same results would be obtained with your sample group (e.g., adults). Sometimes you can find a validated measurement instrument or data analysis process in the *Methods* section that would be relevant to include in your study. A great place to look for the researcher's advice is in the *Limitations* section. In this section, the researcher usually discusses some of the problems that were encountered, mistakes that were made, and suggestions for how to improve the study.

Finally, conducting a literature review allows you to see how your study fits into the existing literature. Remember that one of the goals of your research will be to move the field forward and add to the current knowledge base. This means either adding to, extending, or building on previous research (McMillan, 2015). By reviewing the literature, you will be able to determine whether your study will fill a gap or need in the literature or will extend what is known about a specific topic. A great place to see how your study fits into the existing literature is to read the *Recommendations for Future Research* section in the studies. This section usually offers suggestions for how future studies can extend the current research and indicates the unanswered questions related to the topic. The citation reference section at the end of each article is also a treasure trove to find additional research that is relevant to your topic; you can follow an author's "arc" or line of research studies.

Meeting With a Reference Librarian

Before embarking on your literature review journey, the first thing you should do is make an appointment with a reference librarian at your institution's library. Besides your thesis chairperson, the reference librarian is the other most important person in helping complete your thesis! Plus all reference librarians must have a master's degree in library science, information studies, or library and information science, so they will be empathetic to your needs.

Because we live in the information age, meeting with a reference librarian is even more critical to cull through the vast amount of research that is not relevant to your topic. With easy access to Internet search engines, hundreds of electronic databases, and hundreds of thousands of research articles, it will be easy to become overwhelmed with information overload. The English-American poet Wystan Hugh Auden characterized it best with the following quote (which interestingly was written before the advent of the Internet).

> The greatest problem of today is how to teach people to ignore the irrelevant, how to refuse to know things, before they are suffocated. For too many facts are as bad as none at all. —W. H. Auden

Often there are reference librarians assigned to different discipline areas (e.g., business, education, psychology), so it will be important to find out who is the librarian in your area. The reference librarian will be able to customize your search and give you a tutorial on how to use and log in to the library services at your institution, use basic research skills, access and select specific databases, and find research articles and books. Having an individualized research consultation with your reference librarian will save you many, many hours of time and frustration later on. Also remember that it always better to log in to the university's online library (rather than open access) because the library has already paid the fees to subscribe to different databases; this will ensure that you have access to free resources (put your tuition dollars to work!).

Sources of Data: Primary Versus Secondary

Before you begin your literature review, it is important to distinguish between the different sources of data available in the literature. The two main sources of data are primary and secondary. Each serves a different purpose, but both are important to consider in your literature review. I discuss each type of data source briefly and how you might want to use each in your search.

Primary Sources

Primary sources are the actual or the original results of studies reported by researchers (i.e., firsthand information). These research articles are usually very detailed and include all the information about the study: research questions, sample, methodology and research design, data analysis and results, discussion, and conclusion. Primary sources are typically published in professional journals in the form of articles or monographs but can also be papers presented at conferences. Basically, to identify a primary source, ask yourself whether the information comes directly from the person(s) who developed and conducted the research, similar to someone writing an autobiography.

Secondary Sources

Secondary sources describe or summarize the work of others (i.e., secondhand information). These sources are typically not as descriptive or comprehensive as primary sources. Secondary sources are typically published in research journals in the form of meta-analyses, literature syntheses, research reviews, or textbooks. You can also find secondary sources in reference materials. **Reference materials** are collections of information such as encyclopedias, handbooks, indexes, and dictionaries. Listed below are sample reference materials found in academic libraries. Make sure to check what reference materials are available through your library (this varies depending on which reference package the library buys).

- Multidisciplinary:
  - *Gale Virtual Reference Library*
  - *Oxford Reference*
  - *SAGE Knowledge*
- Business and Management:
  - *Encyclopedia of Business in Today's World*
  - *GMID: Global Market Information Database (Euromonitor)*
- Communications:
  - *Communication Yearbook 40*
  - *Oxford Bibliographies Online Research Guide*
  - *The SAGE Encyclopedia of Intercultural Competence*
- Education:
  - *Encyclopedia of Educational Philosophy and Theory*
  - *Gender and Education: An Encyclopedia*
  - *International Handbook of Survey Methodology*
  - *The SAGE Handbook of Research on Teacher Education*
- Philosophy:
  - *Concise Routledge Encyclopedia of Philosophy*
  - *Internet Encyclopedia of Philosophy*

- Sociology:
  - *The Blackwell Encyclopedia of Sociology*
  - *The Encyclopedia of Criminology and Criminal Justice*
  - *International Encyclopedia of the Social and Behavioral Sciences*
  - *The Oxford Handbook of American Immigration and Ethnicity*

In addition, secondary sources may appear in articles published in newspapers and magazines. When identifying secondary sources, ask yourself whether the information comes from a source other than the work of the original researcher. If it comes from someone who is describing the research of others, then it is a secondary source (like a biography). Secondary sources help you identify primary sources and illustrate the value placed on the primary sources.

There are advantages of reviewing both types of data sources. Secondary sources are probably the best place to start your research because they give you a broad overview of the information related to your topic, and they offer a wide range of materials to explore. Searching through secondary sources may also help you refine your research problem and questions (Fraenkel, Wallen, & Hyun, 2015). Starting with secondary sources is also a good way to immerse yourself in the literature (without drowning) because the articles or summaries are typically short and easy to read, so you will not be bogged down with too much specific information. They will give you leads on some specific research articles related to your topic.

Keep in mind you will still need to locate primary sources to write Chapter Two, Literature Review of the thesis. The primary sources give you a full depiction of the research study, and you can synthesize the data as they relate to your specific research topic and questions. In addition, by making your own analysis, you can avoid the possibility of relying on someone else's erroneous interpretations of the results. Thus, you should use the secondary sources to help you identify critical primary sources or other secondary sources related to the research topic.

Selecting Keywords

A comprehensive review of secondary sources will also help you find primary sources through the use of keywords. **Keywords** are typically two to three words or short phrases that are fundamental to the research topic, problem, or questions and are used to refine the search process. Selecting appropriate keywords early in the search process will save you a lot of time and frustration later on. A good strategy is to use the words or phrases that are commonly used in the current literature related to the specific topic (Creswell & Poth, 2018).

For example, my research topic involves immigration and human trafficking, so I start my search in the reference *The Oxford Handbook of American Immigration and Ethnicity* (Bayor, 2016). Some of the listed keywords in *The Oxford Handbook of American Immigration and Ethnicity* are immigration, ethnicity, race, panethnicity, assimilation, transnationalism, and nativism. However, not all these would be good keywords for my research study because they are not all centrally related to the topic. Some keywords related to my topic are "human smuggling and human trafficking," which I type in the search box (see Figure 3.1 for a quick search for articles).

With this quick search, I retrieve 113 articles and 2 books. If I want to further refine my search for the specific group I am interested in, I can add "refugee minors" as keywords in the search (see Figure 3.2 for refined search). Now I retrieve 17 articles that will give me a general context and gist of my research topic and some background information that I will need to write Chapter One, Introduction of the thesis. These articles will be more closely related to my research topic, and at the end of each article, I have a list of citations for primary sources that I can use for my literature review.

Figure 3.1 Quick search in *The Oxford Handbook of American Immigration and Ethnicity.*

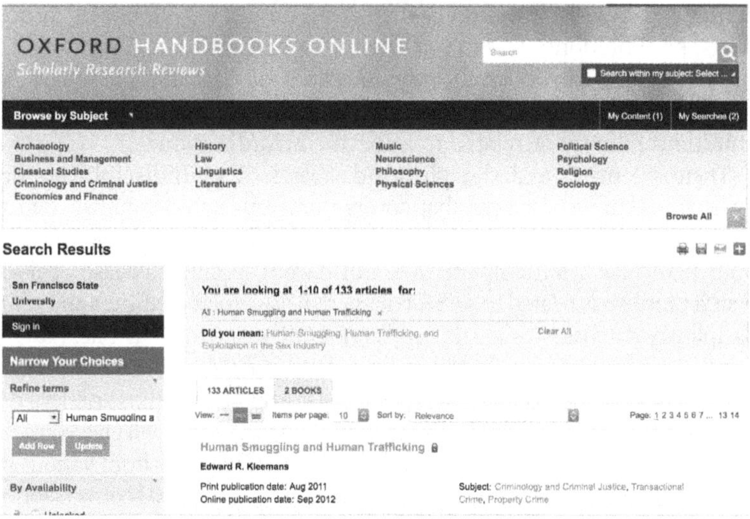

From Oxford University Press, *Oxford Handbooks Online.* © Oxford University Press. Reproduced by permission.

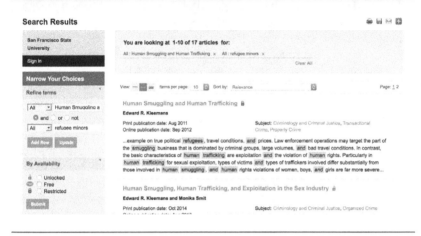

Figure 3.2   Refined search in *The Oxford Handbook of American Immigration and Ethnicity*.

From Oxford University Press, *Oxford Handbooks Online.* © Oxford University Press. Reproduced by permission.

Conducting Searches in Electronic Databases

One of the best places to research the literature is in electronic databases. Electronic databases are storage banks of thousands of books, articles, reports, presentations, and so on. The major benefits of an electronic database are that you can set limits on your search such as dates, language, and type of resource, and search using different descriptors. The database can be multidisciplinary or related to a specific field/discipline.

There are many multidisciplinary databases. A **multidisciplinary database** is an electronic database that covers numerous subjects rather than just one specific field/discipline. These are important databases to search through if your particular field/discipline does not have a specific database or if your research problem is related to several different fields. Some of the common multidisciplinary databases—Google Scholar, JSTOR, Academic OneFile, ProQuest Central, Academic Search Complete, and Academic Search Premier—include articles, citations, and abstracts across subjects. Another multidisciplinary database is the Dissertation Abstracts International database. This will give you access to doctoral dissertations and master's theses across disciplines from various universities and colleges. Although you can view the citations and abstracts for free, there is often a nominal fee to obtain a full copy of a dissertation or thesis.

One advantage of these multidisciplinary databases is they frequently offer the articles in full-text format. **Full-text** is when the entire resource is available either in a printable webpage format or a PDF format. The **PDF** format is a full-text electronic "picture" of a document and resembles how a research article actually looks in the journal. This often saves you time from searching other databases for the resource or taking a trip to the library to locate the hard copy. Here is an important tip for searching in full-text databases: If you have a choice between selecting the printable webpage format or PDF format, always select the PDF format because with the PDF format, you have the article's page numbers (e.g., 534–552) from the journal. Thus, you will be able to provide specific page numbers for APA style citations if you are selecting quotations from the article (see Chapter 10 for APA style). There are also many electronic databases available for specific fields or disciplines. Two very popular databases mentioned in Chapter Two were PsycINFO for psychology and ERIC for education. ERIC is one of the largest databases in education and is free to the public through the U.S. Department of Education. If you use the ERIC database through the U.S. Department of Education website (http://eric.ed.gov), the interface may be different from the one you will find at your institution's library because of the different commercial vendors that license databases to libraries.

Listed below are sample subject databases found in academic libraries (make sure you check to see what databases are available through your library).

- Business:
  - *ABI/Inform Collection*
  - *Business Source Complete*
  - *Key Business Ratios*
  - *Mergent Online*
  - *Standard and Poor's NetAdvantage*
- Communication:
  - *Communication and Mass Media Complete*
  - *GenderWatch*
  - *Linguistics and Language Behavior Abstracts*
  - *Sociological Abstracts*
- Education:
  - *Educational Administration Abstracts*
  - *Education Database*
  - *Education Full Text*
  - *Education Research Complete*
  - *ERIC*
  - *PsycINFO*

- Ethnic Studies:
  - *Bibliography of Native North Americans*
  - *Black Thought and Culture*
  - *Ethnic NewsWatch*
  - *HAPI Online*
  - *Humanities Full Text*
  - *International Index to Black Periodicals Full Text*
- History:
  - *America: History and Life*
  - *Historical Abstracts*
  - *International Medieval Bibliography*
  - *JSTOR*
  - *Middle Eastern and Central Asian Studies*
- Law/Political Science:
  - *CQ Researcher*
  - *Criminal Justice Database*
  - *Nexis Uni*
  - *Westlaw*
  - *Worldwide Political Science Abstracts*
- Nursing and Health Education:
  - *CINAHL Plus With Full Text*
  - *Cochrane Library*
  - *Human Nutrition*
  - *PubMed*
  - *Web of Science*
- Psychology:
  - *JSTOR*
  - *Mental Measurements Yearbook With Tests in Print*
  - *PILOTS: Published International Literature on Traumatic Stress*
  - *PsycARTICLES*
  - *PsycEXTRA*
  - *PsycINFO*
- Sociology:
  - *Family & Society Studies Worldwide*
  - *JSTOR*

- LGBT Life With Full Text
- Social Explorer
- Social Services Abstracts
- Social Work Abstracts
- Sociological Abstracts
- Urban Studies Abstracts
- Women and Social Movements in the United States

Although each database's search formats are slightly different, they all share common search tools and features that make it easy to navigate and switch from one database to another. In some cases, your institution's library may subscribe to a discovery service (e.g., OneSearch, EBSCOhost, ProQuest). A discovery service searches within the institution's entire library collection (e.g., books, journal articles, full-text) from a single find field. This makes library searches very fast and easy, because it is similar to using a search engine on the Internet (e.g., Google Scholar). To show you how to conduct a basic and advanced search on an electronic database, I use Academic Search Complete as an example since it is multidisciplinary and has a similar interface with other databases.

Basic Search

Electronic databases such as Academic Search Complete are large and hold thousands of records; the key to success is being able to narrow the search so that you find the resources most relevant to your research problem. With that in mind, it is critical for you to start with at least five to 10 keywords that are related to your research question or problem (other keywords will be generated during your search). For example, for my research topic above, some of the keywords could include refugees, refugee camps, unaccompanied minors, immigrants, immigration, human trafficking, human smuggling, and so on. These are the keywords that you would type into the "find field" box and then click the "search" button (see Figure 3.3 for the basic search screen). The basic search option also allows you to limit or expand your search. I will briefly explain each of these features.

Search Modes

In Academic Search Complete, there are four different ways to conduct your search.

Boolean operators are used in electronic databases and other search engines to define the relationships between keywords or phrases. Besides being a really cool word, Booleans allow you broaden or narrow your search.

Figure 3.3 Basic search screen in Academic Search Complete.

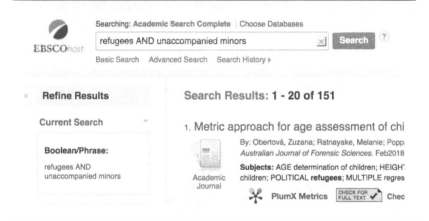

Figure 3.4 Basic search using AND Boolean operator in Academic Search Complete.

Three Boolean operators will be critical for your search: AND, NOT, and OR. The **AND** Boolean operator combines two or more terms so that each record contains all the terms. For example, I could search for the terms "refugees" AND "unaccompanied minors" (see Figure 3.4 for basic search using AND Boolean operator). This would provide me with records where both "refugees" and "unaccompanied minors" are present. In essence, using AND between keywords or phrases *narrows* my search because it does not include records that have only one or the other. The **NOT** Boolean operator searches terms so that records with certain terms are excluded from the results. This would be another way to narrow the search. For example, if I search using the terms "family-based immigration" NOT "immigration policy," my results would contain records where only "family-based immigration" is present but not "immigration policy" (see Figure 3.5 for basic search using NOT Boolean operator). The **OR** Boolean operator searches terms so that at least one of the terms is present in the record. For example, if I search using the terms "human smuggling" OR "human trafficking," my results would contain records where either "human smuggling" or "human trafficking" are present (see Figure 3.6 for basic search using OR Boolean operator). In essence, using OR between keywords or phrases *broadens* my search because it retrieves records containing any of the terms included. If you are using both terms AND and OR in a search, the AND will take precedent over the OR.

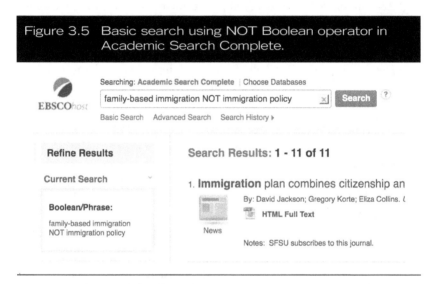

Figure 3.5   Basic search using NOT Boolean operator in Academic Search Complete.

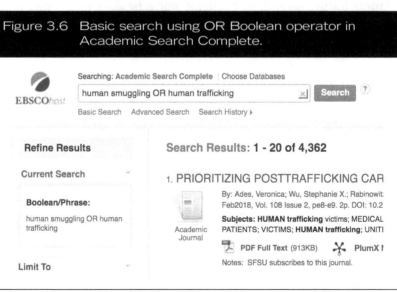

Figure 3.6   Basic search using OR Boolean operator in Academic Search Complete.

When using Boolean operators with a phrase, it is important to enclose the entire phrase within quotation marks; this will ensure the search includes all the terms and in that specific order rather than searching each word individually. In some databases, the Boolean operators have to be in capital letters, so to be on the safe side, make it a habit to type them in capital letters. If you want to be super fancy and have a decent understanding of algebra, you can also combine the Boolean operators using parentheses to nest terms within other terms. For example, you can search ((human smuggling OR human trafficking) AND immigrants) OR unaccompanied minors—in this case, the search engine will search the expression inside the parentheses first and then add on the terms outside of the parentheses and so on. If you did not understand order of operations when learning algebra, now isn't the best time to master it!

The search mode, "Find all of my search terms" is similar to using the AND Boolean, and the "Find any of my search terms" is like using the OR Boolean between the terms.

The fourth search mode in Academic Search Complete is SmartText Searching. In the SmartText searching mode, you can type in any amount of text or cut and paste from another source. The SmartText will magically summarize the text and match it with the most relevant search terms to find the results. I have to admit this one is pretty cool, but it's not available in all databases. You can combine any of these search modes with the limiters and expanders described below.

Limiters

If I want to narrow my search, I would use the limiters features. The **limiters feature** narrows an electronic search by allowing the user to set specific limits, so the search results will only contain research with the chosen specific criteria. For example, in Academic Search Complete, you can set the following limits:

- full-text: only retrieves records that have a link to the full-text copy of the article or document (be careful with this limit because you may miss important references that are not available through one database)
- scholarly (peer-reviewed) journals: only retrieve articles from journals that have a peer-review selection process
- publication: can specify the name of the publication (e.g., title of a book)
- number of pages: limits to the number of specified pages
- references available: only retrieves records that have a list of references from the publication

- published date: can specify the time period with beginning month and/or year to ending month and/or year

- publication type: can specify the type of publication (e.g., article, book chapter, report)

- image quick view or image quick view type: contains results with specific types of image quick view (e.g., chart, color photograph, graph map)

Because of the huge quantity of records, setting limits is a very critical step in narrowing your search. However, you have to be careful not to set too many limits at the beginning of the search because you may not get enough records or you may miss some critical records. A good strategy is to start with a few critical limits and then set more limits as needed. For example, in my search, I am going to set the limits for full-text, scholarly journal, references available, published dates from 2013 to 2018, and only periodicals (see 3.7 for limiters feature in basic search).

Expanders

If I wanted to expand or broaden my search, I would use the expanders feature. The **expanders feature** is the opposite of the limiters feature and broadens an electronic search by allowing the user to search using words related to the key words (see Figure 3.8 for expanders feature in basic search). Two common expanders are "apply related words" and "also search

Figure 3.7   Limiters feature in basic search for Academic Search Complete.

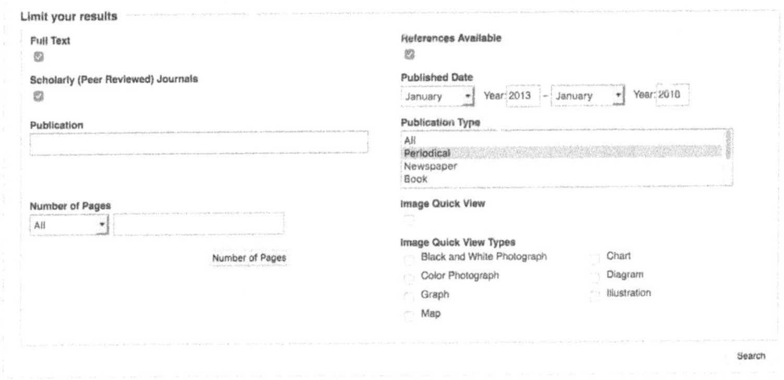

Figure 3.8 Expanders feature in basic search for Academic Search Complete.

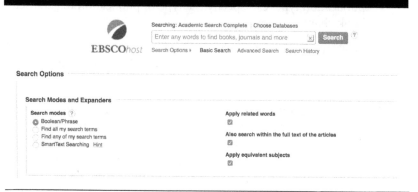

within the full text of the articles." For "apply related words," the results expand to include true synonyms and plurals of your keywords. For "also search within the full text of the articles," the results expand to include keywords that are found in the full text, abstract, and citations of the article."

Another expander feature in this database is "apply equivalent subjects." This is not to be confused with subjects (e.g., sample group) within a particular study. Instead, "apply equivalent subjects" refers to mapped vocabulary terms that are used to identify concepts used in subject indexing. Think about how subject indexes are organized at the back of most textbooks. By using this feature, it will increase the precision and relevance ranking of your keyword search. For example, let's say the user searches using keywords "workplace injury" because that's a popular term that is used in the industry. These keywords are related to the concept of "work-related injuries." However, as the user, you would not know how the concept of "work-related injuries" is mapped to subject-indexed concepts in different vocabularies. Different databases could map "work-related injuries" with "occupational injuries," or "occupational-related injuries." If you did not use the expander feature here, you would miss those records subject-indexed with this concept from other databases. Basically, when you turn this expander on, when your keywords match a known concept, the search will be expanded to include the exact terms for that concept in the mapped vocabularies. If I have only added to your confusion, my suggestion is that if your results seem too narrow or a bit "off" from the gist of what you are looking for, turn on this expander feature (it won't hurt and it may help!).

Advanced Search

Although a basic search is a good starting point, conducting an advanced search offers several features for a more refined and precise search. This is really helpful when you want to focus and narrow in on your specific research topic. For example, in the advanced search, you can set the following additional limits:

- document type: can specify the type of document (e.g., abstract, article, book chapter, report)
- language: can specify the written language (e.g., English, Chinese, Spanish)
- cover story: contains only articles that were featured as a cover story
- PDF full text: contains only articles that are available in full text

The advanced search also gives you the option to refine the search with the "select a field" from a drop-down menu. Some of the options are by "all text, author, title, subject terms" and so forth. By selecting the "subject terms" option, this will make my search more accurate than an "all text" search because the subject terms are assigned by the database and are included in its thesaurus (see below for a detailed explanation).

Using Subject Terms (Thesaurus)

Unfortunately, you can search electronic databases for hours typing in keywords and phrases that you think are most appropriate to your research question and come up with "no results were found" or hundreds of irrelevant records. That is when you want to pull out your hair or change your research topic! The problem is we tend to use our everyday language when conducting searches while the database uses its own language to catalog the resources. However, there is still hope by browsing through the database's thesaurus. The **thesaurus** contains alphabetized **descriptors** (i.e., subject terms) that are used in the electronic database to give every record a subject indexing term (i.e., controlled vocabulary). By finding out the exact two to three words used by the database to tag records for different concepts, you make your searches more efficient by taking out the guesswork of which keywords to use. The most well-known use of controlled vocabulary is the Library of Congress Subject Headings. A simpler example is how subjects were listed in the phone book yellow pages (you may be using one as a footrest right now). If I need to fix my car, should I look up car repair, auto repair, mechanic, automotive repair auto service, automobile restoration, motor rehabilitation . . . ; wouldn't it be nice to know the one term that the yellow pages used when they created the listings? That is exactly how the database thesaurus works! By using the correct subject term from the thesaurus, I increase the chance of retrieving relevant articles for my search.

For example, I use the phrase "unaccompanied minors" but when I searched the subject terms, the database uses "unaccompanied immigrant children" or "unaccompanied refugee children" to refer to the same population. By using the **relevancy ranked** option, the subject terms are displayed in hierarchical order from most to least relevant, which helps prioritize my search process (see Figure 3.9 for search subject term using relevancy ranked). Now I can use these subject terms for my searches that will give me more accurate records; I can spend those hours I would have spent pulling out my hair actually reading the articles!

Once I have a reasonable number of records, I usually do a cursory review of the titles and authors and either add them to my folder for a more detailed review later or click on the title to get more information about the record. The detailed record screen gives me very critical information

Figure 3.9   Subject term search using relevancy ranked in Academic Search Complete.

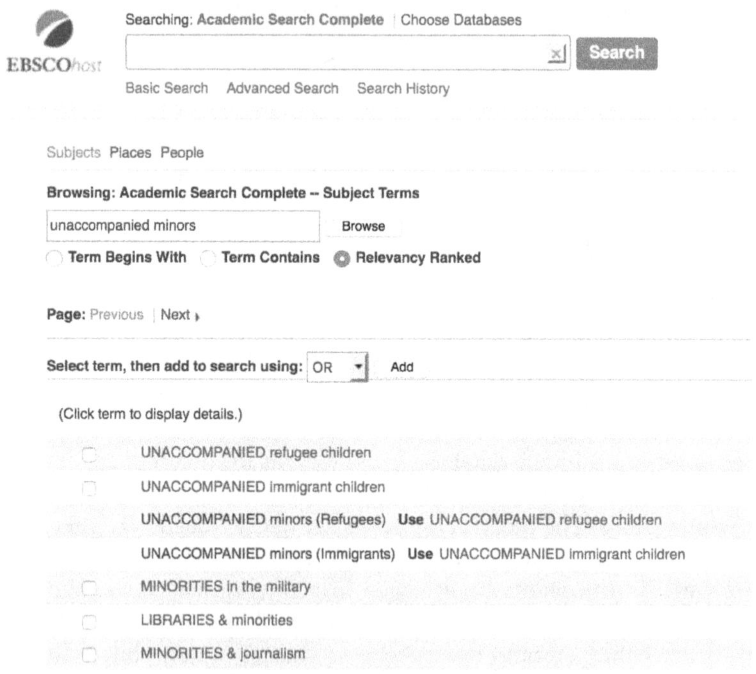

about the record: the title, authors, source (journal, volume, issue, and page numbers), subject terms, and abstract (see Figure 3.10 for sample record screen for a journal article). In addition, the record tells me whether or not the full-text article (PDF) is available. With the PDF full-text choice, I can download, view and/or print the article, save it to Google Drive, or e-mail it to another account. When doing searches, it is very easy to get lost in the process. Most library search interfaces allow you to keep a record of your search, save records to your computer, or e-mail searches and records to another computer; this keeps you from researching with the same key-words or losing precious findings. I highly recommend that you add rele-vant results to your folder as you find them. This way, you can have a record of your results and will be able to print, e-mail, or retrieve them later.

You can also get a full citation in the style that you need (e.g., APA, MLA) and export it to a citation management software. Citation manage-ment software is a tool that allows you to collect citations from various sources, organizes them, and then compiles them into a list of cited works or bibliography. Instead of going back at the end of your thesis to track down all the sources, the citation management software will help you man-age this bibliographical information while you are researching and writing. This is such a gift to students and will save you hours and hours of trying to put together a reference lists (by hand!) like we old-timers had to do when we wrote our master's thesis. There are many different software programs available (e.g. CITAVI, Easybib, EndNote, Mendeley, ReadCube, RefWorks, Reference Manager, Zotero) and you can select the style guide that is needed

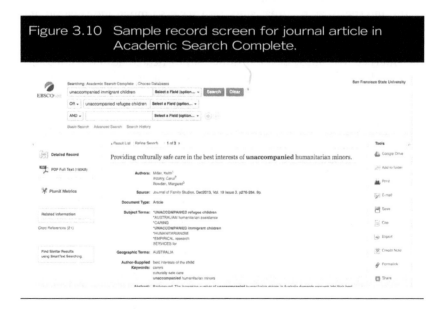

Figure 3.10   Sample record screen for journal article in Academic Search Complete.

(e.g., APA, MLA, Chicago). I list a website at the end of this chapter to help you decide which would be the most appropriate for your use, but four popular ones used by graduate students are EndNote, Mendeley, RefWorks, and Zotero. Check with your institution's library because they often have a license to citation management software, which would allow you to use the service for free.

As you are researching, it might also be a good idea to keep a notebook handy to note authors who have written a few articles related to your research problem (in case you want to contact them for more information) or articles that you may need to search for in other databases, on the Internet, in the library's catalog, or order through interlibrary loan. **Interlibrary loan** is a service provided by libraries whereby a user of one library can borrow books or acquire photocopies of articles in journals that are owned by another library (sometimes there is a fee involved).

Conducting Searches on the Internet

Conducting searches on the Internet offers advantages and disadvantages over conducting searches on electronic databases. The search process is similar to the electronic database in that once you type in a keyword the search engine will find websites and webpages that are related to your keyword. Some advantages of the Internet search are that it is fast, easy, and accessible anytime. In addition, the information is relatively current, and you will get a wide variety of resources. One disadvantage of the Internet search is that since you have so much information and it is not well organized, it may be more time-consuming and difficult to find relevant information. To be both effective and efficient in searching the Internet, you must develop rather sophisticated search techniques. An additional disadvantage is that the information may not be of high quality or reliable (Creswell & Poth, 2018; Fraenkel, Wallen, & Hyun, 2015; Mertler & Charles, 2010). For example, often there is no author listed on the website, so it is unclear whether or not the article was written by an expert in the field. Additionally, there is no way to check whether or not the article was externally reviewed. However, sometimes the Internet is the easiest or the only way to retrieve citations that are available through the library. Again, Google Scholar will probably be the most useful search engine to use for research. Typically, I use the Internet search engines only when I am looking for a specific reference. If you do retrieve information or documents from the Internet, keep a record of the website or webpage address and the date that you retrieved the information. You will need these for APA style citations and references (see Chapter 10 for APA style).

There are also several free websites that are easy to use, have a large collection of research documents (some charge a fee to access the articles), and are organized by subject areas. Some popular websites for research are IngentaConnect (http://www.ingentaconnect.com) and Directory of Open Access Journals (https://doaj.org/). These would be particularly helpful at the beginning of a search or if you do not have access to electronic databases. There is more information about open access databases in the *Resources* section. You may also find LibGuides on the Internet to help you with your research. LibGuides are compilations of recommended resources (e.g., databases, journals, webpages) in a particular area of study. To find a relevant LibGuide, type in "keyword + LibGuide" in the search engine's find field. These subject guides are created by librarians, so you know they will be amazing!

Different Types of Articles

As you continue your search in electronic databases or through the Internet, you will encounter different types of articles. This includes theoretical articles, empirical research studies, position papers, literature syntheses, and meta-analyses. **A literature synthesis** (also referred to as a research synthesis) is a type of article in which the results of several related studies are compared and summarized. **A meta-analysis** research study is one in which the results of several related studies are analyzed and reported with statistical measures (e.g., effect sizes). Each of the different types of articles serves a different purpose. For example, if I were looking for a theoretical rationale or basis for my research study, then I would want to search for articles that discuss an existing theory or suggest a new theory. If I want to review research that is based on systematic observation, I would search for empirical research studies (very critical for writing Chapter Two of your thesis). If I want an article that gives a broad overview or synthesis in a particular area such as "reading strategies," I would search for a meta-analysis or literature synthesis on that specific subject. Finally, if I want support for a particular position or to quote an expert's opinion on a particular topic, I would search for position and/or opinion papers.

Refereed Versus Non-Refereed

As a consumer (in this case of research), you always want to make sure that you get the best quality. Thus, when deciding on which research articles to include in your thesis and particularly the literature review, it is important to keep in mind that like most consumer products there is a hierarchy of quality involved. A natural tendency is to assume that if something has been printed in a journal or published on a website, the article is of high quality. Unfortunately, this is not always the case. In research, the main stamp of quality is refereed. A **refereed** (also referred to as peer-reviewed) article has been submitted for external review by a panel of reviewers before being accepted for publication. This means that when author(s) send in their manuscripts, the manuscripts are reviewed by the journal's editor as well as other experts in the field. Often, the reviewers are blind to the identity of the author(s) of the manuscript, which reduces the chance of bias. This panel then decides whether the manuscript should be accepted, accepted with revisions, or rejected for publication in the journal (Creswell & Poth, 2018; McMillan, 2015). Because the acceptance rate for most refereed journals is typically below 50%, this process ensures that only the most rigorous and high-quality research is accepted for publication. A **non-refereed** article is one that did not go through an external review process before being published. With that in mind, it is best for you to search in research journals that use a refereed review process (most databases will allow you to set this as a limit). Be wary of online journals where the author has to pay a publishing fee to have their article published on the site! These predatory journals typically do not have a rigorous peer-review process. This can be a real danger when searching for articles through the Internet because there are over 10,000 of these "pay to publish" online journals (they may also show up in Google Scholar results).

Staying Organized

One of the most important strategies during the literature search process is to stay organized. After all, you may end up with 40 or 50 articles, books, and documents by the time you are done searching. This means keeping track of your search records, saving, printing, or e-mailing relevant records, and also creating an organizational system. Some of you may want to have a physical organizational system while others will subscribe to a citation management software program. It really is a personal preference—as long you have a system to keep you organized! If you file alphabetically by the author's last name, this will be an easy way to retrieve the articles (as long as you can remember who wrote which article). You can also file the articles by date of publication if you are interested in a chronological or historical analysis. Finally, you can group the articles by themes and/or conceptual categories based on specific common attributes (e.g., topic, sample, intervention, methods). I prefer this method because it helps me conceptually organize the body of literature and will help facilitate the writing process later on. Remember that if the article or information comes from an electronic source (i.e., website), you need to record the website address and in some cases the date that you retrieved the information from the Internet (keep a log).

After you have selected your method for physical organization, it is time to organize the information within the articles. Rarely will you find an article that is completely relevant to your research problem or study. More often, you will use specific parts from different articles to support your ideas. Pulling together the studies in a literature review is very much like putting together a complex puzzle (with some missing pieces). Thus, how you organize the information within the studies is very important. You need to have a system that is not only efficient in terms of recording critical information but also easy to access for retrieval purposes. One method that I find helpful is using different color highlighters (old school, I know) as I read to code different types of information (e.g., yellow = problems, green = possible solutions, orange = background information, pink = definitions). There are also computer software and applications that have this capability if you are more comfortable reading documents and editing on a computer screen.

One method of organizing the information within the articles is abstracting. **Abstracting** is a method of organizing information about an article that includes a brief summary and selected critical information about the study (Creswell & Creswell, 2018). This is different from copying and pasting the author's abstract, which does not always include the most critical information about the study (from your perspective). The summary should be brief and does not have to be in complete narrative form. However, the abstract should contain the following components: the problem, the purpose of the study, the sample, and key results. Once you have abstracted the studies in your collection, it will be much easier to see the *relationships* between them. This is a critical step in the organization process because ultimately, in writing the literature review, you will need to make the explicit connections between the studies that you select and how they relate to your proposed study.

To help you find the relationships and connections between the studies, you can also create a literature review matrix. A **literature review matrix** is an organizational tool such as a table, chart, or flow chart to display the relationship or common attributes among multiple studies. The purpose is to show the relationships between the studies, so use the format that is best for you. For example, for a study dealing with "reading instruction," I may want to group all the studies related to reading instruction for bilingual learners together. Then, another group would be the studies of reading instruction for students with learning disabilities. Next, a third group would be studies of reading instruction for students who are bilingual learners and have learning difficulties, and so on. By grouping the studies together into subgroups, this will allow you to see if you have overlaps or gaps in your pool of studies (which may require you to conduct another search).

I realize that this may seem like a lot of hard work (and it is), but believe me, it will save you time later. This process will also make it easier for you to organize your thoughts about the research problem, conceptualize your research questions and study, and write the literature review in the thesis. There are websites with samples of a literature review matrix in the *Resources* section.

SUMMARY

Researching the literature related to your research problem is a giant step in the thesis process. As you immerse yourself in the literature, you will be inundated with resources, so be very critical and selective, keeping only those directly related to your research problem. In the next chapter, I discuss the ethics of conducting research and how to prepare a research study application for review by the Institutional Review Board (IRB). Here is a summary of the most critical points from Chapter 3:

- The major benefits of conducting a literature review are to know the research that has already been done that relates to your proposed study, learn from other researchers' successes and mistakes, and determine whether or not your study will fill a gap or need in the literature or extend what is known about a specific topic.

- Primary sources are the actual or the original results of studies reported by the researcher(s) (i.e., firsthand information).

- Secondary sources describe or summarize the work of others (i.e., secondhand information).

- Keywords are typically two to three words or short phrases that are fundamental to the research topic, problem, or questions.

- The major benefits of an electronic database are that you can search using multiple keywords and set limits on your search such as full-text, dates, peer-reviewed, and so on.

- Electronic databases and other search engines often use Boolean operators AND, NOT, and OR to define the relationships between words or groups of words.

- The thesaurus contains alphabetized descriptors (i.e., subject terms) that are used in the electronic database to give every record a subject indexing term (i.e., controlled vocabulary).

- Disadvantages of an Internet search include that it may be more time-consuming and difficult to find relevant information or the information may not be of high quality or reliable.

- The term *refereed* refers to a quality-control process that includes an external review of the research manuscript.

- One popular method of organizing the information within the articles is abstracting, that is, writing a brief summary about the article (usually a research study) that includes selected critical information.

RESOURCES

Common Obstacles and Practical Solutions

1. Since we live in a world of information overload, a common problem that students face at this stage is feeling overwhelmed and not knowing where to start looking for research. Words that come to mind are "Lost in cyberspace." If you have a general sense of your topic and are familiar with the Internet, Google Scholar would be a good place to start. If you have a focused sense of your research topic, I recommend searching within electronic databases that are multidisciplinary or specific to your field/discipline. If you feel completely lost in cyberspace, I recommend setting up an appointment with the reference librarian at your institution to help you get started. Remember that the search for research articles is like a treasure hunt; it is time-consuming and continual (finding one source usually leads to another).

2. Once you find the research articles, a common obstacle that students face is organizing them all. Words that come to mind are "My room is covered in research articles!" From the very beginning, it is really important to set up an organization system and stick to it (everything should have a home). Set up a filing system or subscribe to a citation management software program that you are comfortable with (not piles on the floor) and start categorizing your research articles either with hard copies or electronically (keep a backup). This will cut down the time later when you need to refer to a specific article or need to find missing references.

Reflection/Discussion Questions

As you begin to find research articles, it is important to consider how and why you are conducting the literature review and the types of sources that you will rely on. For example, the research literature can help identify existing gaps and weaknesses around a specific topic. In other cases, the research literature can be used to rationalize or justify using different components in an intervention.

The following reflection/discussion questions will help you determine how you want to approach the literature review and the advantages and disadvantages of different types of sources.

1. What is a literature review, and why is it an important part of the research process?

2. What are the major benefits of conducting a literature review before planning and implementing the study?

3. What are the differences between primary and secondary sources? What are the advantages and disadvantages of using each type of source? Brainstorm and list critical primary and secondary sources in your field or discipline.

Try It Exercises

The intent of the following exercises is to help you get started with your literature search. In Activity One, you will identify potential databases and websites where you can find research or information related to your field or discipline area. In Activity Two, you will use keywords and an advanced search to find empirically based research articles. In Activity Three, you will write a short abstract based on one of the research articles.

1. Activity One: For this activity, focus on the resources specific to your field or discipline area.

    • Through your institution's library, locate at least five electronic databases that have information related to your field or discipline area.

    • Through an Internet search engine, locate at least five organization-sponsored or open sources websites that have information related to your field or discipline area.

    • Through an Internet search engine, locate at least three national or state-sponsored (e.g., U.S. Department of Education) websites that have information related to your field or discipline area.

2. Activity Two: For this activity, focus on your chosen research problem as you conduct a literature search.

    • List 10 keywords that can be used for your literature search. You should use the thesaurus to help you find the subject terms.

    • Conduct an advanced search (using limits, expanders, and Boolean operators) in one of the electronic databases from

Activity One. Remember to keep track of the keywords and your search record.

- Select five empirically based research articles related to your research problem (make sure they come from refereed journals).

3. Activity Three: For this activity, focus on one of the selected research articles in Activity Two.

- Write an abstract for one of the research articles that includes the following information about the study: (a) research problem/question, (b) research design, (c) methods (e.g., sample group, intervention, measurement instruments, data collection, data analysis), and (d) results and/or findings.

Key Terms

abstracting 69
AND (Boolean operator) 58
Boolean operators 57
descriptors 63
expanders feature 61
full-text 54
interlibrary loan 66
keywords 52
limiters feature 60
literature review matrix 69
literature synthesis 67
meta-analysis 67

multidisciplinary database 54
non-refereed 68
NOT (Boolean operator) 58
OR (Boolean operator) 58
PDF 55
primary sources 50
refereed 68
reference materials 51
relevancy ranked 64
secondary sources 51
thesaurus 63

Suggested Readings

Kolata, G. (2017, March). A scholarly sting operation shines a light on "predatory" journals. *New York Times* online. https://www.nytimes.com/2017/03/22/science/open-access-journals.html?action=click&contentCollection=Science&module=RelatedCoverage&region=Marginalia&pgtype=article

Kolata, G. (2017, October). Many academics are eager to publish in worthless journals. *New York Times* online. https://www.nytimes.com/2017/10/30/science/predatory-journals-academics.html

Lomand, T. C. (2017). *Social science research: A cross section of journal articles for discussion and evaluation* (7th ed.). New York, NY: Routledge.

Subramanyam, R. (2013). Art of reading a journal article: Methodically and effectively. *Journal of Oral and Maxillofacial Pathology: JOMFP,* 17(1), 65–70. http://doi.org/10.4103/0973-029X.110733

Web Links

Duquesne University: Matrix Method for Literature Review
http://guides.library.duq.edu/matrix

EBSCO Free Databases
https://www.ebsco.com/who-we-serve/academic-libraries/subjects/free-databases

Education Resources Information Center (ERIC)
http://www.eric.ed.gov/

Google Scholar
http://scholar.google.com/

How to Choose a Citation Manager
http://guides.lib.uchicago.edu/c.php?g=297307&p=1984557

Ingenta Connect
https://www.ingentaconnect.com

UC Santa Barbara Library Free Publically Accessed Databases
https://www.library.ucsb.edu/search-research/free-databases

Walden University: Literature Review Matrix Template
https://academicguides.waldenu.edu/writingcenter/assignments/literaturereview/organization

Conducting Ethical Research

*I have learned two lessons in my life: first,
there are no sufficient literary, psychological,
or historical answers to human tragedy,
only moral ones. Second, just as despair can
come to one another only from other human
beings, hope, too, can be given to one
only by other human beings.*

—Elie Wiesel

You might be wondering why it is necessary to include a chapter on ethical practices in research in a book on writing a master's thesis. Isn't it obvious that when conducting a study involving human subjects, the researcher would have to disclose the purpose and procedures of the study to the participants and get their consent? Doesn't the researcher know that she must treat the participants with respect, minimize their risk of harm, and protect their rights for confidentiality? Unfortunately, history tells us that this has not always been the case. Past situations have indicated that researchers have intentionally deceived participants (at great personal cost) without their knowledge or consent. When conducting research of any kind, there is always the possibility that you will encounter ethical issues. Thus, it is especially important early in your research career that you understand the policies and standards governing research with human subjects and develop an ethical perspective that will guide your research. Central to doing research is ensuring that you take the necessary steps to protect the rights of the human subjects who consent to participate in your study. This chapter will provide you with an overview of the ethical standards related to the treatment of human subjects and prevailing policies that govern the research you will be conducting for your master's thesis.

Legal Regulations and Ethical Standards

Although the answers to the questions presented above were meant to be evident, it is important to recognize that until 1974, there were no legal regulations or ethical standards with regard to the treatment of human subjects in research studies. Three of the most well-known abuses of human experimentation were in the Nazi concentration camps during World War II, the use of the thalidomide drug by pregnant women, and the Tuskegee Syphilis Study on African American males. It was not until history revealed these research practices that placed subjects in very serious harm that the public and in turn policymakers addressed the need for laws and policies to govern all research conducted with human subjects. These policies are briefly discussed below.

In 1947, the Nuremberg Code was established as a result of the inhumane medical experiments on thousands of prisoners in concentration camps without their consent or knowledge during World War II. The **Nuremberg Code** is a set of standards of ethical medical behavior that all physicians should adhere to when involving human subjects in medical experiments (see *Resources* for a web link to the text of the Nuremberg Code). One of the main standards of the Nuremberg Code is **voluntary informed consent**. Voluntary informed consent exists when a person has the capacity to give consent and receives sufficient and accurate information about the study (e.g., purpose, methods, risks, benefits) to make an informed decision to participate. Although the Nuremberg Code was not a legal mandate, it was the first international document that supported voluntary participation and informed consent.

In the late 1950s and early 1960s, thalidomide, an unapproved drug, was sold and prescribed to pregnant women to abate symptoms of nausea and sleeplessness. Due to the unknown side effects of thalidomide, 10,000 babies were born with severe birth defects (stunted limbs or no limbs at all) (Kim & Scialli, 2011). As a result of this tragedy, in 1962, Congress passed the **Kefauver-Harris Drug Amendments**, which changed how drugs are tested, manufactured, and sold in the United States. The act increased the regulatory powers of the FDA so that drug manufacturers had to prove that their drugs were safe and effective before marketing and selling them to the public and also required that subjects from medical studies give their informed consent (Greene & Podolsky, 2012).

Finally, the Tuskegee Syphilis Study was another example of how abuse of experimentation with human subjects led to policy changes for research. In 1932, the U.S. Public Health Service and the Tuskegee Institute in Alabama began a study to monitor the effects of untreated syphilis on 600 low-income and mostly illiterate African American males. The study continued for 40 years, even after a cure for syphilis (penicillin) was made available in 1947. The men in the study were not offered the penicillin by the researchers, and many of them unnecessarily died of syphilis during the study (Kim, 2012).

Ultimately, the abuses in research from the Tuskegee Syphilis Study led Congress to pass the **National Research Act of 1974 (Public Law 93-348)**. The National Research Act created the **National Commission for the Protection of Human Subjects of Biomedical and Behavioral Research**, the first national public group whose responsibility it was to identify a set of basic ethical principles and guidelines for conducting biomedical and behavioral research involving human subjects. The commission fulfilled this responsibility by preparing and releasing the Belmont Report in 1979. The **Belmont Report** is a summary of the basic ethical principles and guidelines for conducting research with human subjects (see the *Resources* section for a web link to the full report). In the Belmont Report, the commission identified three fundamental ethical principles for conducting research with human subjects: (a) respect for persons, (b) beneficence, and (c) justice. These principles have implications for how researchers conduct ethical research today (USDHHS, 1979). I discuss each one briefly as it pertains to your thesis study.

The first principle in the Belmont Report, **respect for persons**, includes "two ethical convictions: first that individuals should be treated as autonomous agents, and second, that persons with diminished autonomy are entitled to protection" (USDHHS, 1979, Part B, para. 2). The first ethical conviction requires that participants (or their guardians if they are minors) must be provided with adequate information to give their informed consent. Participants must be fully aware of the purpose and procedures of the study, and the researcher cannot omit information about the study or give false information (i.e., **deception**).

Here are some basic information points that should be disclosed to your participants:

- Who is conducting the research, and how they can be contacted before, during, and after the study
- The purpose of the study
- The data collection procedures (e.g., tests, interviews)
- The potential risks involved
- The benefits of the study

If the information is incomprehensible to the participants or they are deceived about the purpose or procedures used in the study, even if they agree to participate, they are not giving their informed consent (Drew, Hardman, & Hosp, 2008). Once they are fully informed about the study, then individuals can voluntarily agree to participate (rather than be coerced). Informed consent also means that the participants can voluntarily withdraw from the study at any time, without penalty or negative repercussions (Orcher, 2014).

The second ethical conviction of respect for persons refers to protecting those individuals who are not fully autonomous because of age, illness, injury, disability, or restricted settings such as prison (i.e., vulnerable populations). **Vulnerable populations** are children, pregnant women, prisoners, or others who may need additional protection from harm, depending on the risks involved.

Beneficence. The second principle in the Belmont Report, beneficence, refers to two general rules: "(1) do not harm; and (2) maximize possible benefits, and minimize possible harms" (USDHHS, 1979, Part B, para. 7). The best time to examine the proposed research relative to potential risk to participants is when you are framing your research questions. By examining the potential risks early, you save time and also increase your feasibility to conduct the study. Here are some questions to ensure you are not proposing a study that may be harmful to participants:

- Is there potential for the participants to be harmed or be at risk for harm in any way (e.g., physically, psychologically, emotionally, socially, or academically)?
- If so, could I redesign my study so that I could protect the participants from harm but still get the information that I need to answer my research questions?
- Do I need to change my research questions to ensure my participants' well-being?

- Will this research require costly safeguards that require external support?

The second rule, "maximize possible benefits, and minimize possible harms," refers to the **cost-benefit analysis** where researchers must weigh the potential benefits against the anticipated risks. Here are some questions to analyze the cost-benefit ratio when designing your thesis study:

- Do the potential benefits outweigh the anticipated risks?

- Will the information that will be gathered as a result of the study be worth the potential risks placed on subjects?

- Have I designed the study in such a way that the risks have been minimized and the benefits maximized as much as possible?

- Have I explored all potential risks?

Justice. The third principle in the Belmont Report, justice, refers to fairness and equity in the selection of participants and the distribution of benefits. To meet this third principle, make sure you are selecting subjects because they are the group most directly related to your research questions and not because they are in a vulnerable position in society (e.g., low income, children). Also consider whether there are fair and equitable benefits for the participants in your study as well as the larger population that they represent.

In addition to the ethical principles laid out in the Belmont Report, researchers in different fields and disciplines have developed and adopted their own ethical standards specific to the type of research that is conducted with human subjects. For example, the American Educational Research Association (AERA) has a set of ethical standards that focuses on educational research that often involves children and other vulnerable populations (see the *Resources* for a web link to the AERA ethical standards). The American Psychological Association (APA) also has a set of general principles and ethical standards for psychologists referred to as the Ethical Principles of Psychologists and Code of Conduct (see the *Resources* for a web link to the APA ethical principles). As a professional, it is important for you to know the ethical standards and principles that guide your field or discipline, especially as it relates to research with human subjects.

The three ethical principles in the Belmont Report served as the foundation for the development of federal regulations in 1981 by the U.S. Department of Health and Human Services for the protection of human subjects in research studies. In 1991, the core regulations were formally adopted as the Federal Policy for the Protection of Human Subjects, known as the Common Rule. The **Common Rule** is a federal policy for the protection of human subjects followed by most of the federal departments and agencies that sponsor research with human subjects (e.g., Department of Education, Department of Justice, Environmental Protection Agency, National Science Foundation, Consumer Product Safety Commission) (USDHHS, 1991). Three of the central requirements in the Common Rule are (a) any research supported or conducted by any federal department or agency must ensure compliance with the policy, (b) researchers must obtain written informed consent, and (c) institutions must have an Institutional Review Board (IRB) in place to review and approve research studies. The Common Rule also includes three subparts, B through D, that have additional protections for research that involves pregnant women, fetuses, neonates, prisoners, and children as human subjects. On January 19, 2017, the U.S. Department of Health and Human Services issued a revision called the **Final Rule** to update the pre-2018 Common Rule. The revisions for the Final Rule are meant to strengthen the protections for human subjects while also reduce the administrative and regulatory burden on researchers. The effective and compliance date of the Final Rule was published in the *Federal Register* (FR) on January 19, 2017, and went into effect on January 21, 2019 (see the *Resources* section for a web link to the revised Final Rule). If you are completing your thesis after this date, you will likely follow under the new guidelines for the protection of human subjects. In the next section, I focus on the IRB protocol procedures since this may have implications for your thesis research. Before you go down this path, be sure to check with the IRB office at your institution to ensure that you are not already exempt from this process. That will save you a lot of time and energy (and you can skip the next section)!

Institutional Review Board (IRB)

As mentioned, all institutions of higher education that receive federal funds (for research or scholarships) must have in place an Institutional Review Board (IRB). In compliance with the Common Rule, the IRB committee is made up of at least five members, representing a diverse group of expertise and backgrounds (e.g., from different schools and colleges within the university). The major role of the IRB is to ensure that all research with human subjects conducted by persons affiliated with the institution (including administrators, faculty, staff, and students) is done ethically and in compliance with federal regulations. In doing so, the IRB adheres to the three principles of the Belmont Report: respect for persons, beneficence, and justice. To apply these principles, the IRB requires that researchers (including undergraduate and graduate students) submit an IRB protocol for IRB review. Some types of research (e.g., normal education practices) may not require IRB review, so make sure you check the requirements at your institution.

IRB Protocol Review Process

In this section, I describe the typical IRB protocol review process at a university. Although each IRB committee follows the Common Rule, the actual application process is university specific and will vary, so it is critical for you to find out the IRB procedures and guidelines at your institution (there should be an IRB website available with templates and forms that you can use). Typically, universities offering graduate degrees have a committee with responsibilities for assisting researchers in fulfilling their obligations in meeting the requirements related to conducting research involving human subjects. There is also usually a training program and short quiz that you can complete online (e.g., NIH, CITI certificate) to certify your knowledge of the IRB principles. If you have additional questions about the IRB procedures, you should discuss these with your chairperson or the IRB committee at your institution.

The IRB protocol review process begins with the initial completed application. This is to determine which category the protocol fits into: *exempt, expedited*, or *full committee*. If the protocol is determined to be *exempt*, no further review is needed and you can begin your research immediately (it's like winning the lottery!). The *exempt* process can take 1 to 2 weeks to receive the approval. If the protocol fits under the *expedited* category, then the protocol is reviewed by an IRB committee member to approve it or ask for additional revisions. If it is approved, you have 1 year to conduct the research (before you have to renew the protocol). The *expedited* process can take 2 to 4 weeks to receive the approval. If your protocol is categorized as *full committee* (i.e., nonexempt), then the protocol is sent to the IRB members to review and discuss at their committee meeting. The committee can fully approve or approve your protocol with contingencies that need to be met. They can also defer the protocol if substantive changes are needed. This process could take 4 to 8 weeks (depending on how often the IRB committee meets), so you need to plan for this possibility in your research timeline. See Figure 4.1 for a pictorial flow chart of a sample IRB review process. To prevent further delays, make sure that you have answered all the questions on the IRB protocol, use nontechnical language, and of course use proper grammar without spelling errors. Nothing irks the IRB committee more than grammatical and spelling errors!

Keep in mind that the IRB committee reviews applications from faculty, staff, and students from the entire university, so there will be times when they have a high volume of applications, especially at the beginning and end of the semester (this may cause longer process times). Thus, it is recommended that you start the IRB process well in advance of your anticipated research start date. The IRB approval must be granted *before* any recruitment procedures are enacted, contact with potential participants is made, or data are collected. Getting IRB approval before starting any

Figure 4.1 The Review Process at a Glance

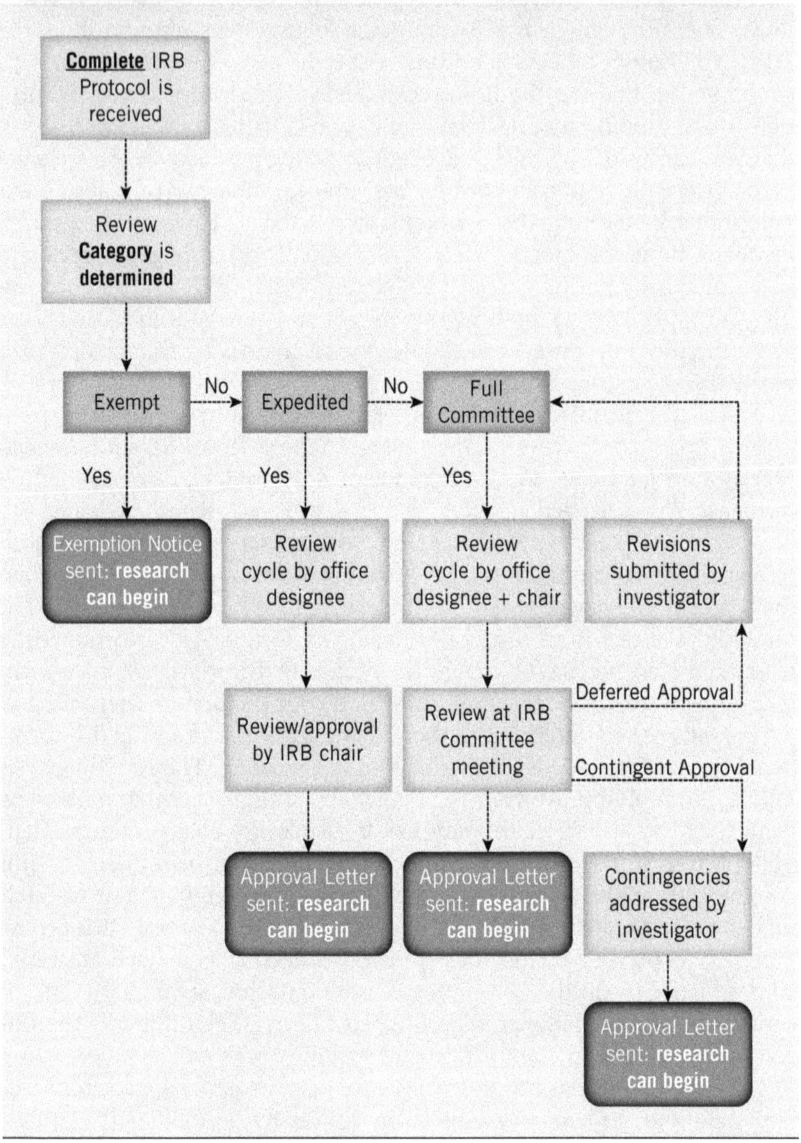

Complete IRB Protocol is received

Review **Category** is **determined**

Exempt —No→ Expedited —No→ Full Committee

Yes (Exempt)

Yes (Expedited)

Yes (Full Committee)

Exemption Notice sent: **research can begin**

Review cycle by office designee

Review cycle by office designee + chair

Revisions submitted by investigator

Review/approval by IRB chair

Review at IRB committee meeting

Deferred Approval

Contingent Approval

Approval Letter sent: **research can begin**

Approval Letter sent: **research can begin**

Contingencies addressed by investigator

Approval Letter sent: **research can begin**

component of your study is extremely important because the IRB does not retroactively approve applications, and if you start your study without IRB approval, you may not be able to use any of the data that were collected or complete your study, not to mention the ethical issues involved. Once you receive approval from the IRB committee, you typically have 12 months to complete your data collection involving human subjects. However, there are processes to renew the IRB application for additional time or to modify it for any changes to the study.

Once you have received approval from the IRB, make sure to obtain permission from any other necessary agency (e.g., school district, hospital, business). In some cases, you will need to go through a separate application process, and in other cases, outside agencies will require a copy of the IRB approval from your institution. Only when you have received approval from all parties can you access participants. If the participants are adults, have them sign a written consent form. Remember that you cannot simply ask the person to sign a consent form that he cannot read or comprehend (that would not be *informed* consent). Thus, if necessary, use an interpreter during a face-to-face meeting with the individual participant if she cannot read or hear. Translate the information about the study into the participant's native language if you are sending a written notice. If the participants are minors (under 18), you need to get informed consent from their parents or guardians. The IRB may also require you to give the participants a copy of their Research Subject Bill of Rights. The **Research Subject Bill of Rights** is a list of rights that is guaranteed for every participant in a study. Make sure the participants receive a copy of the informed consent form for their records and keep a copy for your files. After you have received the participants' informed consent, then you may begin your study!

Ethical Behavior

Completing the IRB approval process and adhering to the requirements when conducting your study is only one element of ethical behavior as a researcher. When conducting and reporting research, it is critical that you demonstrate ethical behavior and integrity at all times. Now is the time to learn as much as you can about ethics in research and internalize the information so it is a natural part of your professional behavior. This includes being honest in your interactions with participants as well as complying with ethical standards in your field for data collection, analysis, and reporting. As a beginning researcher, you will find that unanticipated situations will occur. When this happens, the appropriate solutions will be evident, but there may be less appropriate solutions in the form of shortcuts. These will be equally apparent and need to be avoided. Your master's thesis will be a public document that will be read by many researchers as they search the literature for similar problems. I do not go into all the situations that might occur, but following are some examples. During data collection, do not interfere with, influence, or modify the participants' responses to measurement instruments. This is critical when the participants do not answer in the way that you anticipate or want, which happens in the best of research studies. During data analysis, do not inflate, delete, or manipulate the data to obtain desirable results. This too is important. Remember it is not uncommon for your hypotheses to be unsupported by the results. You conduct the research to find that out. Keep in mind that in research the researcher is also taking risks, and the results may not always be what are expected or desired. Discovering that an intervention does not work for a particular sample is still making a contribution to the literature.

Plagiarism and Paraphrasing

Finally, in writing the thesis and reporting the results, it is important that you do not plagiarize, whether it is intentional or unintentional. Writing the thesis is a long, iterative process, and by the time you are done, you will have read and reread dozens of primary and secondary sources. It is not uncommon for students to unintentionally plagiarize along the way. However, plagiarism is a very serious offense, and you need to make every effort to avoid it. To **plagiarize** refers to using another person's ideas or words without giving them proper credit (Plagiarism.org 2017). Plagiarism can be any of the following:

> turning in someone else's work as your own; copying words or ideas from someone else without giving credit; failing to put a quotation in quotation marks; giving incorrect information about the source of a quotation; changing words but copying the sentence structure of a source without giving credit; or copying so many words or ideas from a source that it makes up the majority of your work, whether you give credit or not. (Plagiarism.org, 2017, para. 4)

You are not expected to know everything about the topic that you are researching, but you are expected to credit the individuals whose work you review and integrate into your study. Based on the definition above, there are several ways to prevent plagiarism: (a) do your own work, (b) use quotes and give credit to the original source or idea, and (c) paraphrase and give credit to the original source or idea. Quoting sources and paraphrasing are two very important skills that will help you be successful in writing the thesis. When you are quoting someone, you copy verbatim from the original source and use quotation marks to indicate that the text belongs to the original source. At the end of the quote, include a footnote or an in-text citation of the original source (often with a page number). Be careful not to overuse quotations in your thesis; quotes should be used sparingly and really only when you cannot paraphrase without losing the significance of the other person's words. **Paraphrasing** is rewriting the original text into *your own words* (with appropriate citations) while trying to maintain the idea or essence of the original work.

You would still need to include a footnote or an in-text citation of the original source to give credit to the original author. This is where students often get into trouble when they have paraphrased someone's work but forgot to give the appropriate credit. Another problem that students run into is changing only a few words from the original text. Paraphrasing is not using the thesaurus to find synonyms! Remember that paraphrasing involves using someone else's idea and then interpreting and rewriting it into your own words. Your paraphrased material should not look like the original source; it should be in your own words and have your own voice. Sometimes students are unsure if they should give credit to another source. If you are integrating someone else's ideas into your thesis, then that person deserves the credit for having that original idea in the first place. When in doubt, it is always better to be extra careful and give credit to the original author(s). It keeps you honest, and it makes the other person feel good to be cited by another researcher! Consider the following advice about how to paraphrase from the Purdue Online Writing Lab (copied and pasted verbatim from this website: https://owl.purdue.edu/owl/research_and_citation/using_research/quoting_paraphrasing_and_summarizing/paraphrasing.html)

6 Steps to Effective Paraphrasing

1. *Reread the original passage until you understand its full meaning.*

2. *Set the original aside, and write your paraphrase on a note card.*

3. *Jot down a few words below your paraphrase to remind you later how you envision using this material. At the top of the note card, write a key word or phrase to indicate the subject of your paraphrase.*

4. *Check your rendition with the original to make sure that your version accurately expresses all the essential information in a new form.*

5. *Use quotation marks to identify any unique term or phraseology you have borrowed exactly from the source.*

6. *Record the source (including the page) on your note card so that you can credit it easily if you decide to incorporate the material into your paper.*

Just as it has become easy for students to plagiarize because of easy access to the Internet, it has also become easier for instructors and universities to identify plagiarized material. Informed people are likely to identify content from other sources without a citation, and there are software programs (e.g., Plagiarism Checker X, Turnitin, Grammarly, Plagiarism Detector, Viper) that are designed to identify plagiarized material. If a student is caught plagiarizing, this can result in failing a class, expulsion from a program, or even withdrawal of a degree. If a member of a profession is caught plagiarizing, the consequences for her career cannot likely be overcome. Thus, it is not worth succumbing to the temptation of plagiarism (even if others around you are doing it), and it is easy to avoid by being professional in your behavior.

The purpose of a thesis is to demonstrate research skills and to do original work. Knowing and adhering to ethical practice is as important as knowing and adhering to sound research methodology. By maintaining your ethical behavior and integrity throughout the research process, you will have conducted an original study and written a master's thesis that you can be proud of.

SUMMARY

Understanding the ethical standards and principles related to conducting research with human subjects is a critical part of your formation as a researcher. As you plan and design your study, make sure that you take into consideration the main ethical principles and standards from the Nuremberg Code and the Belmont Report. This will ensure that you prepare an ethical and successful research study application for the Institutional Review Board (IRB). In the next chapter, I discuss how to write Chapter One, Introduction, for your thesis. Here is a summary of the most critical points from Chapter 4:

- The three main standards of the Nuremberg Code are (a) voluntary informed consent, (b) avoiding all unnecessary mental and physical pain and suffering, and (c) weighing the risks against the expected benefits.

- In 1962, Congress passed the Kefauver-Harris Drug Amendments, which increased the regulatory powers of the Food and Drug Administration.

- The National Research Act of 1974 created the National Commission for the Protection of Human Subjects of Biomedical and Behavioral Research.

- In the Belmont Report, the commission identified three fundamental ethical principles for conducting research with human subjects: (a) respect for persons, (b) beneficence, and (c) justice.

- Researchers in different fields and disciplines have developed and adopted their own ethical standards specific to the type of research that is conducted with human subjects.

- In 1991, the core regulations by the Department of Health and Human Services (USDHHS) for the protection of human subjects in research studies were formally adopted as the Federal Policy for the Protection of Human Subjects, known as the Common Rule.

- Three of the central requirements in the Common Rule are (a) any research supported or conducted by any federal department or agency must ensure compliance with the policy; (b) researchers must obtain written informed consent; and (c) institutions must have an Institutional Review Board (IRB) in place to review and approve research studies.

- The Final Rule legislation will replace the Common Rule, and it was implemented July 21, 2019.

- The major role of the IRB is to ensure that all research with human subjects conducted by persons affiliated with the institution (including administrators, faculty, staff, and students) is done ethically and in compliance with federal regulations.

- The IRB requires that researchers (including undergraduate and graduate students) submit an IRB application for approval *before* any recruitment procedures are enacted, contact with potential participants is made, or data are collected.

- When conducting and reporting research, it is critical that you demonstrate ethical behavior and integrity at all times.

RESOURCES

Common Obstacles and Practical Solutions

1. One of the common emotions that students face at this stage is anxiety about the IRB process. Words that come to mind are "What if I don't get approval?" Do not worry. Most student research puts participants at minimal risk of harm (unless you are doing something very bizarre or something you shouldn't). However, it is necessary for the IRB committee to review your protocol to make sure that your study is feasible and you have minimized potential harm with maximum benefit for the participants. Most likely you will be exempt from the full committee review. Think of the committee as a friendly guard dog.

2. Another common obstacle faced by students is getting approval to conduct research from other related organizations (e.g., school districts, hospitals, prisons). Most organizations have their own research approval process, and this tends to take longer than the university's IRB process. Therefore, it is critical that you find a main contact person, follow their guidelines exactly, and start the process early!

Reflection/Discussion Question

As you begin to design your study, it is important to consider the effects or consequences of your study on others, especially the participants. In doing so, reflect on the tragedies and unethical treatment of past research studies. The following reflection/discussion question will help identify the main standards and ethical principles that must be applied while conducting research with human participants. Remember the wise words of the great philosopher George Santayana who once said, "Those who cannot learn from history are doomed to repeat it."

1. What are the main standards and ethical principles from the Nuremberg Code and the Belmont Report? Give specific examples of how they relate or could be applied to your field or discipline area.

Try It Exercises

The following exercises are designed to help you successfully complete the Institutional Review Board (IRB) protocol for review at your institution. Doing this early in the process is critical, as you cannot begin data collection without IRB exemption or approval. In Activity One, you will research the IRB process at your specific institution. In Activity Two, you will develop the IRB protocol for your study (if applicable).

1. Activity One: For this activity, focus on the IRB website or campus office at your institution.
   - Search your institution's website to locate the IRB website or campus address.
   - Search the IRB website or visit the IRB office and list the name of the chairperson or contact person.
   - Search the IRB website or visit the IRB office and obtain a manual or guide to complete the protocol review process. Find out the process to apply for an exempt protocol.
   - Find out if you have to complete an online IRB certification training.

2. Activity Two: For this activity, focus on the IRB procedures and guidelines at your institution if you do not qualify for an exempt protocol.
   - Get copies of templates on the IRB website: protocol approval form, protocol template, informed consent, parental permission, permission to recruit, recruitment materials, photo and video release, and so on.

- Complete the protocol template (fill in all the required sections to describe your study in detail)
- Complete the protocol approval form (obtain signatures as required)

Key Terms

Belmont Report 77
beneficence 78
Common Rule 79
cost-benefit analysis 79
deception 77
Final Rule 80
justice 79
Kefauver-Harris Drug Amendments 77
National Commission for the Protection of Human Subjects
of Biomedical and Behavioral Research 77
National Research Act of 1974 (Public Law 93-348) 77
Nuremberg Code 76
paraphrasing 85
plagiarize 84
Research Subject Bill of Rights 83
respect for persons 77
voluntary informed consent 76
vulnerable populations 78

Suggested Readings

Cooper, H. (2016). *Ethical choices in research: Managing data, writing reports, and publishing results in the social sciences.* Washington, DC: American Psychology Association.

Greene, J. A., & Podolsky, S. H. (2012). Reform, regulation, and pharmaceuticals—The Kefauver–Harris Amendments at 50. *New England Journal of Medicine, 367*(16), 1481–1483. http://doi.org/10.1056/NEJMp1210007

Horner, J., & Minifie, F. D. (2011a). Research ethics I: Responsible conduct of research (RCR)—Historical and contemporary issues pertaining to human and animal experimentation. *Journal of Speech, Language, and Hearing Research, 54*(Suppl.), S303–S329.

Horner, J., & Minifie, F. D. (2011b). Research ethics II: Mentoring, collaboration, peer review, and data management and ownership. *Journal of Speech, Language, and Hearing Research, 54*(Suppl.), S330–S345.

Horner, J., & Minifie, F. D. (2011c). Research ethics III: Publication practices and authorship, conflicts of interest, and research misconduct. *Journal of Speech, Language, and Hearing Research, 54*(Suppl.), S346–S362.

Kim, W. O. (2012). Institutional review board (IRB) and ethical issues in clinical research. *Korean Journal of Anesthesiology, 62*(1), 3–12. http://doi.org/10.4097/kjae.2012.62.1.3

Nakray, K., Alston, M., & Whittenbury, K. (2015). *Social science research ethics for a globalizing world: Interdisciplinary and cross-cultural perspectives.* New York, NY: Routledge.

Shore, N. (2009). Student research projects and the Institutional Review Board. *Journal of Teaching in Social Work, 29*, 329–345.

Web Links

American Educational Research Association (AERA) Code of Ethics

http://www.aera.net/About-AERA/AERA-Rules-Policies/Professional-Ethics

American Psychological Association (APA) Ethical Principles of Psychologists and Code of Conduct

http://www.apa.org/ethics/code/

Federal Policy for the Protection of Human Subjects

https://www.federalregister.gov/documents/2018/01/22/2018-00997/federal-policy-for-the-protection-of-human-subjects-delay-of-the-revisions-to-the-federal-policy-for

Plagiarism.org

http://www.plagiarism.org/

Purdue Online Writing Lab

https://owl.english.purdue.edu/owl/resource/619/1/

Teaching the Responsible Conduct of Research in Humans (RCRH)

https://ori.hhs.gov/education/products/ucla/default.htm

The Belmont Report

https://www.hhs.gov/ohrp/regulations-and-policy/belmont-report/index.html

The Common Rule

https://www.hhs.gov/ohrp/regulations-and-policy/regulations/common-rule/index.html

The Nuremberg Code

https://www.hhs.gov/ohrp/international/ethical-codes-and-research-standards/index.html

U.S. Food & Drug Administration

https://www.fda.gov/ForConsumers/ConsumerUpdates/ucm322856.htm

How to Write Chapter One, Introduction

> *The beautiful part of writing is that you don't have to get it right the first time, unlike, say, a brain surgeon. You can always do it better, find the exact word, the apt phrase, the leaping simile.*
>
> **—Robert Cormier**

The rest of this book focuses on the writing process and formatting style for the master's thesis. You will write five separate chapters titled Introduction, Literature Review (i.e., Review of the Literature), Methods, Results or Findings, and Discussion (check if your institution has different chapter titles). Don't worry; I guide you through each chapter, offering writing tips, examples, and strategies that will help facilitate the process.

I purposely use the term *process* because for all the chapters in the thesis, you will need to write multiple drafts, edit, revise, and ultimately write more drafts. For each chapter of the thesis, I describe the sections and subsections that need to be included. After reading the description, I recommend that you read the examples in the appendixes from actual students' master's theses so that you can get a sense of the breadth, depth, and style of the writing. In this chapter, I first discuss the writing style for the thesis and then address each of the required sections for Chapter One.

Keep in mind that writing a master's thesis is an individualized experience, and each person or discipline may have a different way to approach it. Although this book is laid out in linear fashion (Chapter One, Chapter Two, etc.), your chairperson may suggest or you may wish to write the chapters in a different order. Some students may prefer to start writing the literature review and then go back to write the introduction. Others may want to write the introduction, literature review, and the methods section in tandem, going back and forth among the three chapters and revising as new information or ideas are presented. The key is to find what works best for you and your chairperson and to keep moving forward. At this beginning stage, it is also important to focus on the big picture and not get lost in the weeds. Do not get bogged down trying to write the perfect sentence or paragraph because more than likely you will have to revise and tweak everything a few times before the final draft. I have had students become quite upset when certain text that they were "attached" to (because it took hours to write) ultimately had to be cut out of the final version. Remember you're not directing a movie so each "scene" does not need to be perfect. I always advise my students to put the date on each document as you revise it even if you change only one sentence; when you compare the beginning draft to the final draft, they will look very different!

Writing Style

The writing style in a master's thesis is very different from that used in creative writing or narrative writing. The writing style is technical, formal, serious, and impersonal. This can be a very difficult transition for students who are used to writing poetry, reflections, or stories. For example, the tense should be in third person at all times (e.g., refer to yourself as "the researcher"), and you should not use an informal tone or colloquialisms (i.e., slang). In fact, the thesis should be free of personal biases, judgments, and opinions. As I often tell my students, "There is no room for *you* or *I* in a master's thesis." Thus any personal positions that you take throughout the thesis must be supported by the research literature.

For example, consider the sentence: "*I believe that college students spend a lot of class time on their cell phones instead of paying attention to the instructor.*" Some of the problems with this sentence are that it (1) is based on personal opinion, (2) is not cited by research evidence, and (3) has a vague description of the students' behaviors. A more scholarly sentence would be: "*According to a recent survey of college students, 89% of respondents reported that they were distracted by their digital device through texting, emailing, or social media for approximately 20% of class time (McCoy, 2016).*"

If you are having difficulty switching or you are unsure how to write in a technical style, refer to the APA publication manual (APA, 2010) or other style publication manuals in your field. I have also placed general writing tips in Appendix D.

Chapter One Sections

The goal of Chapter One is to introduce the research study to the reader. However, before you can start writing, you need to have a good feel for what will be included in the literature review and the methodology chapters. This level of planning prepares you to determine what to include in Chapter One. I have noticed that most of the students who struggle with writing Chapter One do so not because of the writing per se but because they have not read enough literature about the research problem. Only after you have "mastered" the necessary background information can you begin the actual writing process. Chances are if you get stuck in writing, it's because you need to go back to the literature and do more reading! There are risks in beginning to write too soon. The most serious risk is that you may invest energy and time going in the wrong direction. This can be frustrating and cause you to lose momentum and miss important deadlines. Although I know you are eager to start writing, make sure that you have read all the research and literature resources related to your research problem and have your organizational system in place. Writing a detailed outline of the chapter before you start writing can be very helpful. This will minimize your frustration and help you judge whether you have enough resources or need to do more researching and reading.

Chapter One communicates the major elements of the research study and sets the stage for subsequent chapters. Chapter One is the first page after the table of contents, and it starts on a new page. The major sections/headings within Chapter One are (a) *Introduction*, (b) *Statement of the Problem*, (c) *Background and Need*, (d) *Purpose of the Study*, (e) *Research Questions*, (f) *Significance to the Field*, (g) *Definitions*, (h) *Limitations*, and (i) *Ethical Considerations* (see Figure 5.1 for major sections in Chapter One). These sections are typical of a master's thesis, but there may be slight variations depending on your institution or the preferences of your chairperson. Make sure to check with your department and chairperson for the thesis requirements for your program. You should also keep in mind that these are general guidelines—you may need to write more or less, depending on your chairperson's and program's expectations. I discuss each section separately, but they should be considered as part of a whole with fluid transitions and segues between them.

Introduction

The *Introduction* section in Chapter One describes the general problem you will be addressing in your research study. Your goal is to present an overview of the study in a manner that allows the reader to understand the context of your research regarding the issues it addresses, the importance of the research to be done, and the specific research problem to be studied. Readers will expect the introduction to provide them with the context to understand the subsequent sections of the chapter describing the research. There should be at least four paragraphs in the *Introduction* section, and each paragraph has a different purpose. For this section, I have found it helpful to use a funnel writing strategy. In an actual funnel, the opening at the top is wide and then it slowly narrows to a small opening. A **funnel writing strategy** is analogous to a funnel where your first paragraph in the *Introduction* is broad and every subsequent paragraph narrows the topic toward the specific research problem (see Figure 5.2 for the funnel writing strategy for the *Introduction* section in Chapter One).

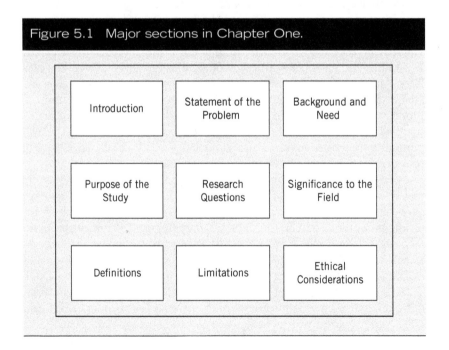

Figure 5.1   Major sections in Chapter One.

Introduction	Statement of the Problem	Background and Need
Purpose of the Study	Research Questions	Significance to the Field
Definitions	Limitations	Ethical Considerations

The first paragraph in the *Introduction* section should be a description of the broad issues related to your study. The purpose of this first paragraph is to give the reader background knowledge and a context for your study (without specifically mentioning your problem yet). Typically, in this paragraph, you discuss *broad* societal trends, or national or international phenomena that are *related* to your research problem. In other words, what is the big picture? A good type of article to help with this section is one that gives you a broad overview of your research problem such as a secondary source, meta-analysis, or literature synthesis. The introduction section of empirical research articles is also a good source to find broad issues.

One of the problems that students face in writing this paragraph is that they are so immersed in their immediate research problem that they cannot see beyond it. Thus, take three steps *back* from your specific research problem and ask, "What are the broad societal issues that have trickled down to cause or influence my specific problem?" For example, if you are focusing on broad issues in education, you might discuss federal mandates, common core standards, bullying, academic achievement data on large-scale assessments, demographic changes, the overrepresentation of students of color receiving special education services, teacher evaluation, and so on. If you are focusing on broad issues related to juvenile delinquency, you might discuss gang membership, crime rates, substance abuse, budget cuts in

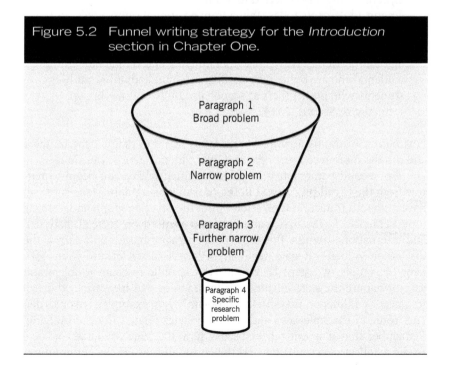

Figure 5.2   Funnel writing strategy for the *Introduction* section in Chapter One.

Paragraph 1
Broad problem

Paragraph 2
Narrow problem

Paragraph 3
Further narrow problem

Paragraph 4
Specific research problem

after-school programs, death penalty for juveniles, and so forth. If you are focusing on broad issues related to counseling, you might discuss mental illness, scarcity of mental health services, drug and alcohol abuse, family relationships, child and spousal abuse, posttraumatic stress disorder, and so on. If you are focusing on broad issues related to business and management, you might discuss the global economy, outsourcing, corporate social responsibility, debt crisis, and so forth.

No matter which societal, national, or international issue(s) you focus on, it is not enough to discuss the issue; you want to show how the issue manifests into actual problems and the consequences of the problems for society. You can do this by supporting your claims with citations from the research, especially from national and/or international reports with statistical data (e.g., percentages, average). One of the questions I often ask my students to answer is "So what? What are the implications of this issue?" By answering this question, you are making the problem(s) explicit for the reader and building a justification and rationale for your study. The key to writing this paragraph is to start broadly—if you are too narrow here, then you will not have any room to funnel in the next few paragraphs (see Figure 5.3 for a funnel for the *Introduction* section of Chapter One). Here is an example of a topic sentence for the first paragraph:

> Cyberbullying (also referred to as online bullying) is widespread among adolescents today. Taken from a national sample of 12–17 year old students, 34% reported that they had experienced cyberbullying during their lifetime. There is also a significant amount of overlap between school bullying and online bullying; students who are bullied at school are also bullied online and students who bully others at school also bully online. (Brown, Demaray, & Secord, 2014)

For the rest of the paragraph, I would describe and define cyberbullying and discuss more recent national and international trends over time.

The second paragraph is a one-step funnel where you begin to narrow from the broad problem(s) in the previous paragraph. Make sure you have a smooth transition (i.e., segue) from the first paragraph and a strong topic sentence. In the first paragraph, you focused on societal, national, and international trends. For the second paragraph, you will *narrow* the discussion to focus on state, regional, or local issues *related* to your problem. Thus, take two steps *back* from your specific research problem and ask, "What are the state, regional, or local issues that have trickled down to cause or influence my specific problem?" For example, I would discuss some of the state laws and school policies related to cyberbullying. Remember that it is critical to discuss how the state, regional, or local issues manifest into problems and the consequences for the communities

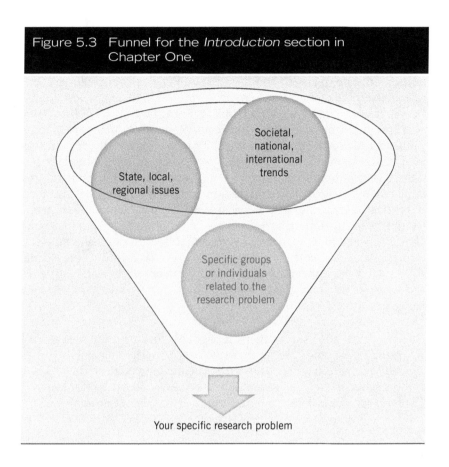

Figure 5.3   Funnel for the *Introduction* section in Chapter One.

State, local, regional issues

Societal, national, international trends

Specific groups or individuals related to the research problem

Your specific research problem

and neighborhoods. This adds to the justification and rationale for your study. In addition, support your claims with citations from the research, especially from state or regional reports with statistical data. Be careful not to focus too narrowly here; otherwise, you will not be able to funnel for the next two paragraphs. Here is an example of a topic sentence for the second paragraph:

> Since 2011, California legislators have passed multiple assembly and state bills related to cyberbullying noting its detrimental effects on students, including suicide and academic performance. Schools have the ability to suspend or recommend for expulsion students who bully by an electronic act (on or off the school site). (National Conference of State Legislatures, n.d.)

For the rest of the paragraph, I would describe California legislation and school policies that are in place to prevent cyberbullying and protect targets.

The third paragraph (with a smooth transition and topic sentence) is another one-step funnel where you begin to narrow from the local problem(s) in the previous paragraph. In the second paragraph, you focused on state, regional, and local issues. For this paragraph, you will narrow the discussion to focus on the *specific* group or subgroups of individuals *related* to your research problem. Thus, take one step *back* from your specific problem and ask, "How are the groups or subgroups of individuals related to my problem affected by the national, state, regional, or local issues?" For example, I would discuss gender differences between teenage girls and boys regarding rates of cyberbullying and its impact. This is the group(s) that will make up the sample group in the study. Remember, it is critical to discuss how the national, state, regional, or local issues manifest into problems and the consequences for the group or subgroup of individuals targeted in your study. This adds to the justification and rationale for the selection of your sample group. In addition, support your claims with citations from the research, especially from empirical research studies and reference materials. Here is an example of a topic sentence for the third paragraph:

> Based on a 2015 survey, more teenage girls than boys reported being cyberbullied (36% compared to 31%) in their lifetime while more teenage boys reported cyberbullying others (13% compared to 11%). Girls and boys may also experience different forms of online harassment including sexting and electronic forms of teen dating violence. (Hinduja & Patchin, 2015)

For the rest of the paragraph, I would discuss the statistics of cyberbullying based on gender differences and forms of cyberbullying (in my state or region if the data were available).

Finally, the last paragraph in this section focuses directly on the research problem. If you started with the broad problem and slowly narrowed the focus, this last paragraph should be a natural flow from the first three paragraphs. Avoid writing, "My research problem is about . . . ," which is the book report method you used in the 4th grade. Often this paragraph will start with words that cue the reader for some type of "disruption" term such as "however, unfortunately, alas, sadly, regrettably," and so on. For the rest of the paragraph, you will discuss how the specific problem affects the group or subgroups of individuals you have targeted. Then you want to expand on the consequences of the problem for this specific group. This is also where you would operationally define key terms that you will be using as part of your study. Remember to support your claims with citations from the research, especially from empirical research studies and reference materials. Here is an example of a topic sentence for the last paragraph:

> While most research on cyberbullying has identified the alarming prevalence of cyberbullying behaviors, few studies have explored the relationship between cyberbullying and self-esteem, especially for adolescent female targets.

For the rest of the paragraph, I would describe the existing research data on the impact of cyberbullying on female targets' levels of self-esteem (and related manifestations). Using statistical data strengthens my claim that this is a real problem that requires attention. This last paragraph is a great lead-in to the next section of the chapter, which focuses on the three areas related to your specific research problem. See Appendix E for a sample *Introduction* section for Chapter One.

Statement of the Problem

The next section of Chapter One, the *Statement of the Problem*, differs from the *Introduction* section where you discussed broad issues related to your problem. In the *Statement of the Problem*, you will delve deeper into the specific research problem by describing the problems in three areas that are related to your research problem. It will help to visualize your research problem as a ladder and each rung on the ladder as a related area (see Figure 5.4 for a ladder of the three areas related to the research problem). At this point, the ladder could be a rope ladder since you are still framing your research problem; it can turn into a more solid ladder as you begin fleshing out the research problem. Identifying the three areas related to the research problem can be the most difficult part in conceptualizing Chapter One. If you having difficulty with this process, now is a good time to make an appointment with your chairperson. You may also need to go back to read the existing research. Once you establish the three areas (and your chairperson approves), you will have the organizational framework that will guide you through writing Chapters One and Two.

The first step to identify the three areas is to read the research literature you collected for your research problem. This is where abstracting and a literature matrix really come in handy. Next identify three to four common themes or patterns that emerge from the literature. Then try to organize and group your literature resources along those themes (it helps to make actual piles or folders). Give each group a name that represents the essence of the theme (you can tweak this later if necessary). If you have too many groups, you may need to subsume smaller groups within a broader one. You may also need to create a "maybe" file for resources that are interesting but not closely related to your research problem. If you have too few groups, you may need to break one of the groups into two smaller ones or find more resources. Finally, select the three areas that are most relevant to your research problem. The areas may be a part of your research problem

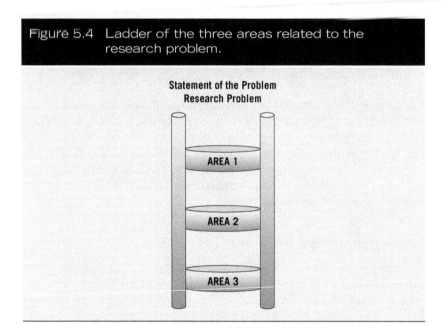

Figure 5.4 Ladder of the three areas related to the research problem.

Statement of the Problem
Research Problem

AREA 1

AREA 2

AREA 3

or a parallel area that is influenced by or affects your research problem. Keep in mind that the areas should not be too narrow because you will need to locate at least three empirical research articles related to each area for your literature review in Chapter Two.

For example, from my research problem of cyberbullying, three related areas that emerged from the literature are as follows: (a) psychological concerns; (b) physical health and somatic concerns; and (c) suicide ideation and behavior.

Once you have identified the three areas, you can write the *Statement of the Problem* section. This section has five subsections: (a) introduction, (b) area one, (c) area two, (d) area three, and (e) summary. The first subsection is a brief introduction to the three areas related to your research problem. This will serve as an outline for the rest of the section. Then write about each related area separately. Do not mix up the three areas because this will confuse your reader; you can use a heading to label each area to help you stay organized and on topic. A **heading** is the name of a section or subsection used to organize the paper. The headings are formatted depending on how many levels of heading there are in the paper (see Chapter 10 for APA style).

For each area, start with an introduction that briefly describes the area. Next, discuss the relationship between your research problem and the area (make sure you make this connection explicit for your reader). Then write about the *problems* within the area and how they affect your target group. Here is where you want to be very specific about the consequences and effects of the problem (i.e., answer the "so what?" question). For example, for my first area, I would discuss the problems that female adolescent targets of cyberbullying have with feelings of depression, loneliness, and isolation and other psychological issues. See Figure 5.5 for an example ladder of the problems within the three areas.

Figure 5.5 Example ladder of the problems within the three areas.

Statement of the Problem
Research Problem
Female adolescent targets of cyberbullying experience higher levels of psychological and physical health concerns and suicide ideation compared to their unaffected peers. These negative impacts have been correlated with lower levels of self-esteem, which can impact students' overall academic and behavioral performance.

Psychological Concerns
Adolescents who are targeted via cyberbullying experience many psychological concerns. They report increased levels of depressive affect, anxiety, and loneliness and also feelings of sadness, hopelessness, and powerlessness.

Physical Health and Somatic Concerns
Adolescent targets of cyberbullying experience severe forms of physical health concerns (e.g., stomachache, headache, poor appetite, skin problems). They are also more likely to experience sleeping problems than their unaffected peers.

Suicide Ideation and Behavior
Adolescents' involvement in cyberbullying is a strong predictor of suicide ideation and behavior. Targets of cyberbullying are almost two times as likely to have attempted suicide compared to their noninvolved peers.

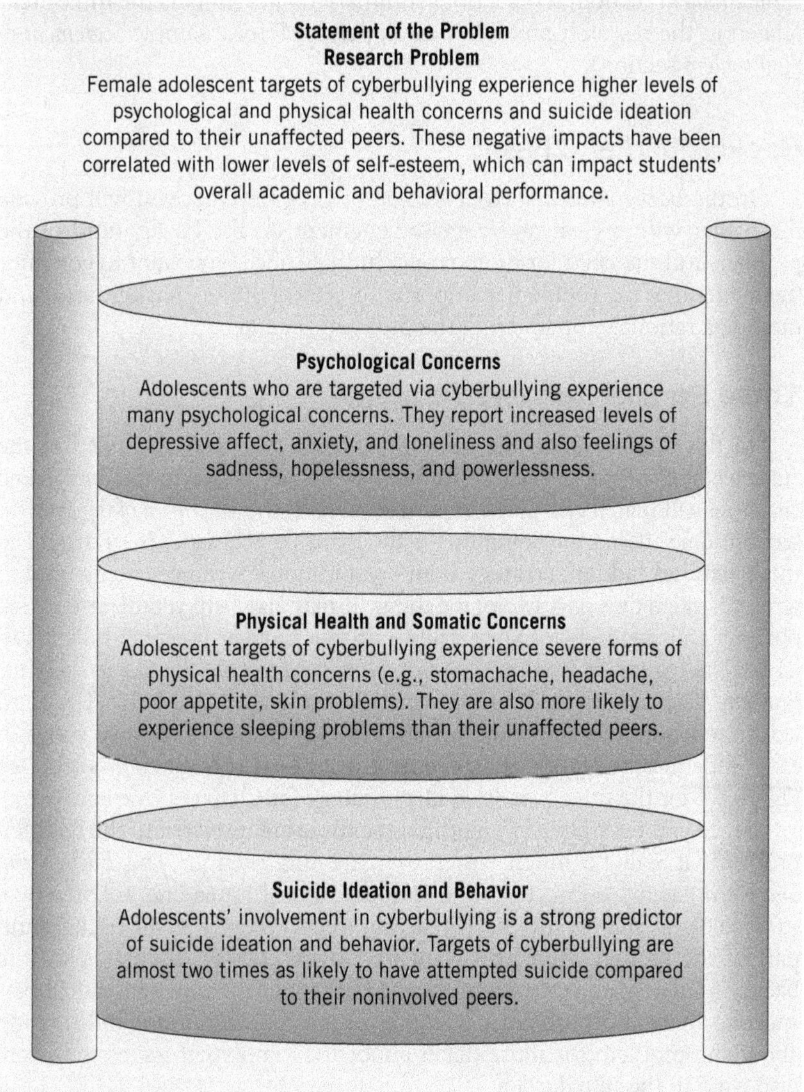

Remember to focus on the problems within the areas and do not mention any types of interventions or "solutions" to the problems yet—that will go into the next section (*Background and Need*). You should also define any ambiguous terms or phrases that are relevant to your study. Finally, support your writing by paraphrasing (not plagiarizing) information from the research literature and cite the sources using the appropriate editorial format. Include quotes sparingly and only if the author said something so brilliant that you could not paraphrase it without destroying the essence of the quote (see Chapter 10 for APA style). At the end of the entire *Statement of the Problem* section, write a brief summary that highlights the three areas related to the research problem (see Appendix F for a sample *Statement of the Problem* section).

Background and Need

In the *Background and Need* section of Chapter One, you will provide the reader with a clear and concise statement on the background of the problem and the need for more research. In essence, you want to convince the reader that the problem is important to research (i.e., background) and provide a rationale for studying the problem (i.e., need).

Three Parallel Ladders Strategy

In this section, I use the same three areas that were identified in the *Statement of the Problem* section. In other words, each area in the *Background and Need* will match one of the areas discussed in the *Statement of the Problem* section. One model for doing this is the three parallel ladders strategy. The **three parallel ladders strategy** is an organizational writing strategy used to write Chapters One and Two of the thesis. It may also help you determine the purpose and methods for your study. For this strategy, imagine three parallel ladders lying side by side. The first ladder represents the *Statement of the Problem*. The second ladder represents the *Background and Need*. The third ladder represents the literature review in Chapter Two. The three rungs in each ladder represent the same three areas related to the research problem (see Figure 5.6 for the three parallel ladders strategy for Chapters One and Two).

Since you have already identified the three areas related to the research problem, it will be much easier to write this section. The *Background and Need* has five subsections: (a) introduction, (b) area one, (c) area two, (d) area three, and (e) summary. The introduction serves as the background part of the section. Here you want to provide a brief discussion on the background of your research problem. This could include a historical perspective, how the problem developed over time, important information about the problem, or more detail about the contextual issues that were discussed in the *Introduction*.

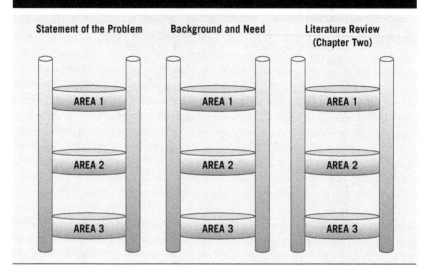

Figure 5.6   The three parallel ladders strategy for Chapters One and Two.

| Statement of the Problem | Background and Need | Literature Review (Chapter Two) |

AREA 1   AREA 1   AREA 1

AREA 2   AREA 2   AREA 2

AREA 3   AREA 3   AREA 3

The next three subsections revolve around the same three areas related to the research problem (don't forget to keep each area separate and use headings). However, in the *Statement of the Problem* section, you focused on the problems that emerged from the literature. In the *Background and Need* section, you will focus on the potential solutions to the problems from the literature (see Figure 5.7 for parallel ladders for the *Statement of the Problem* and the *Background and Need* sections).

First, include a brief introduction to the three solution areas related to your research problem. This will serve as an outline for the rest of the section. Next, start each subsection with an introduction that describes the area. Then write about the existing research that may help solve the problem within the area. This will serve as a preview of your literature review in Chapter Two. For example, for problem area one in my cyberbullying study, I would discuss different research-based prevention and intervention programs that have been effective in mediating the negative impacts on adolescents' psychological health such as enhancing adolescents' levels of empathy and self-esteem. Try to avoid telling the reader what should be done (i.e., do not preach). Instead, provide a brief description of what has been done and its effectiveness with a particular sample group. Whenever possible, report on practices that were effective for your targeted group or a similar group. This also serves as a justification to include these research-based practices in your study.

As you are discussing the solutions reported in the literature, point out the gaps that still remain in the literature related to this area. This is the

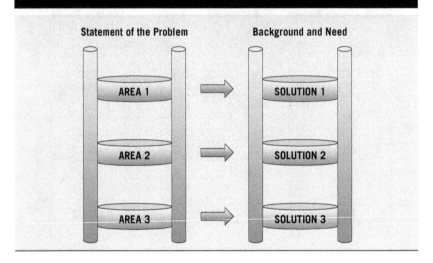

Figure 5.7 Parallel ladders for the *Statement of the Problem* and the *Background and Need* sections.

Statement of the Problem

AREA 1

AREA 2

AREA 3

Background and Need

SOLUTION 1

SOLUTION 2

SOLUTION 3

"need" part of the section. Identifying the gaps is very critical because it serves as a rationale to conduct your study and shows how your study will contribute to the existing research. If there were no gaps left in the literature, there would not be a need for your study! For example, a gap could be that the research-based practices were not conducted with your specific sample group. Another gap could be if your study proposes to adapt, enhance, or combine existing practices for your specific sample group. Another gap could be that your study is researching the problem from a different perspective or research methodology (e.g., qualitative, mixed methods). Make sure to support your writing by paraphrasing information from the research literature and cite the sources using the appropriate editorial format.

See Figure 5.8 for an example of parallel ladders for the *Statement of the Problem* and *Background and Need*. Notice how in this example the three solutions are linked to the three problems in each area.

At the end of the entire *Background and Need* section, write a brief summary that highlights the existing research that has been conducted and the gaps that still exist. Since I have given the reader a broad introduction, described my research problem in detail, and provided the background and need for my study, I am ready to connect these sections to the *Purpose of the Study*. By this time, my reader will be convinced that I have identified a significant problem that needs to be addressed, and I am aware of the most relevant research to influence the problem. This will serve as a smooth lead-in to the *Purpose of the Study*.

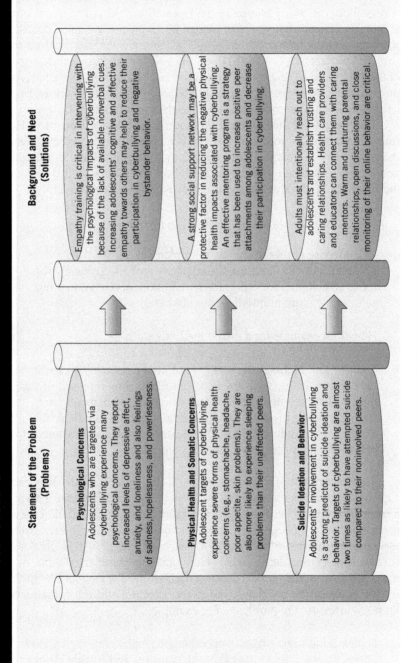

Figure 5.8 Example of parallel ladders for the Statement of the Problem and Background and Need Sections.

Statement of the Problem (Problems)

Psychological Concerns
Adolescents who are targeted via cyberbullying experience many psychological concerns. They report increased levels of depressive affect, anxiety, and loneliness and also feelings of sadness, hopelessness, and powerlessness.

Physical Health and Somatic Concerns
Adolescent targets of cyberbullying experience severe forms of physical health concerns (e.g., stomachache, headache, poor appetite, skin problems). They are also more likely to experience sleeping problems than their unaffected peers.

Suicide Ideation and Behavior
Adolescents' involvement in cyberbullying is a strong predictor of suicide ideation and behavior. Targets of cyberbullying are almost two times as likely to have attempted suicide compared to their noninvolved peers.

Background and Need (Solutions)

Empathy training is critical in intervening with the psychological impacts of cyberbullying because of the lack of available nonverbal cues. Increasing adolescents' cognitive and affective empathy towards others may help to reduce their participation in cyberbullying and negative bystander behavior.

A strong social support network may be a protective factor in reducing the negative physical health impacts associated with cyberbullying. An effective mentoring program is a strategy that has been used to increase positive peer attachments among adolescents and decrease their participation in cyberbullying.

Adults must intentionally reach out to adolescents and establish trusting and caring relationships. Health care providers and educators can connect them with caring mentors. Warm and nurturing parental relationships, open discussions, and close monitoring of their online behavior are critical.

Purpose of the Study

The *Purpose of the Study* section in Chapter One explains the purpose and goal of your study related to the research problem. The intent of this section is to refine what you have written into a precise statement describing what you propose to research and why. The *Purpose of the Study* has four main parts: (a) purpose statement, (b) need/rationale for the study, (c) description of the study, and (d) expected outcomes. I explain each part separately and provide some examples. Note that the *Purpose of the Study* is written in past tense because it is assumed that you have already completed the study.

The first part of the *Purpose of the Study* is the purpose statement. Here, state the purpose of your study in one sentence! Include in the statement the what, why, who, and where related to your study. Here is a template you can use: "The purpose of this study was to (what you did) (why you did this/issue) (who was your sample group) (where was the setting)."

Here is an example for an intervention quantitative study:

The purpose of this study was to implement the *We Care* program (what) to increase the cognitive and affective empathy levels (why/issue) for 6th-grade female students (who) in a high-achieving suburban middle school (where).

Here is an example for a mixed methods study:

The purpose of this study was to explore the perceptions about peer relationships (what) by female students who reported being targets of cyberbullying (who) and who were participating in a peer-mentoring program (why/issue) in an urban middle school (where). The students' levels of self-esteem were also measured before and after the peer-mentoring program.

The second part of the *Purpose of the Study* is the rationale. This briefly explains the need for focusing on this particular problem or issue. Providing a rationale is critical because it provides justification and validation for why it is important or necessary to conduct the study. In qualitative studies, the rationale may also be used to foreshadow the design of your study (Creswell & Plano Clark, 2018). Here you can summarize some of the main points from the *Introduction* and the *Statement of the Problem*. Include sentences about the problems (broad and specific) and the consequences for not addressing the problems. For example,

Female adolescent targets of cyberbullying experience higher levels of psychological and physical health concerns and suicide ideation compared to their unaffected peers. These negative impacts have been correlated with lower levels of self-esteem, which can impact students' overall academic and behavioral performance. Increasing adolescent students' cognitive and affective empathy levels for their peers have been reported to reduce overall participation in cyberbullying and negative bystander behaviors.

Here is another example:

Female adolescent targets of cyberbullying experience higher levels of psychological and physical health concerns and suicide ideation compared to their unaffected peers. These negative impacts have been correlated with lower levels of self-esteem, which can impact students' overall academic and behavioral performance. Developing social networks and strong peer relationships can act as mediating factors to prevent and intervene with the stressors from cyberbullying.

The third part of the *Purpose of the Study* is the description. This briefly explains the methods that you used to conduct the study. Include your sample group, description of your study or intervention (if you have one), and how you collected the data. For example,

The researcher implemented the *We Care* program to increase the cognitive and affective empathy levels of 6th-grade female students. The program teaches students to take another's perspective and experience someone else's feelings through acting and role-playing. Three classes of 20 6th-grade students (total 60) participated in the program three times a week during an elective dramatic arts class over a 6-week period. The students' cognitive and affective empathy levels were measured before and after the intervention program using a validated empathy assessment. The students' attitudes toward the *We Care* program were also measured with a student survey after the intervention was completed.

Here is another example:

To explore the students' perspectives about peer relationships, the researcher conducted focus groups with 20 female 7th-grade students who had reported being targets of cyberbullying. The students were participating in a peer-mentor program. The researcher also measured the students' levels of self-esteem before and after the program using the *DREAM* test, a validated assessment instrument.

The last part of the *Purpose of the Study* is the expected outcome or goal of the study. This briefly explains the benefits or impact that will result from your study. You can have several expected outcomes. For example,

The goal of the study was to measure the effects of the *We Care* program with 6th-grade female students. The 60 students were expected to increase their levels of cognitive and affective empathy after participating in the *We Care* program. While not directly measured, it was expected that the students would be less likely to participate in or support cyberbullying activities. Another goal of the study was to describe the students' attitudes about their experiences in the *We Care* program.

Here is another example:

The purpose of the study was to explore the perceptions around peer relationships from the perspective of 7th-grade female students who reported being targets of cyberbullying. This study also had implications for how peer mentoring and social supports can act as a mitigating factor for students' levels of self-esteem.

Once you have established the purpose of the study, you need to write research questions that are aligned with the purpose and the methods of the study.

Research Questions

The research question(s) is the question related to the problem that you are attempting to answer with your study. The key is to frame your research questions so that you are addressing the most critical elements of your study. This does not mean that you need to develop an exhaustive list of research questions. Instead, select those questions that are most important to you and can be studied within the available time and resources for doing a thesis. Remember that the more research questions you have, the more data you will have to collect and analyze (which require more time and resources). The research questions are aligned with the methods of the study and vice versa, so you should consider your research methods as you develop the research questions.

Make sure the research questions are written so that once you collect the data, you will be able to answer them. This might involve including the measured variables in the question. A good strategy is to convert the purpose statement into a question. For example, if I want to know the impact of the *We Care* program, I would convert the purpose statement into a question and ask,

What are the effects of the *We Care* program (independent variable) on the levels of cognitive and affective empathy (dependent variable) for 6th-grade female students (sample) in a high-achieving suburban middle school (setting)?

If I do not have an intervention but want to measure students' attitudes based on a survey, I would still include other measured variables in my research questions. For example,

What are the attitudes of 6th-grade female students toward the *We Care* program?

or

What is the relationship between the students' attitudes (measured variable) and their empathy levels (measured variable)?

Here is an example for a qualitative study (notice how the questions are more open-ended than for the quantitative studies above):

What are the female students' perceptions around peer relationships while participating in a peer-mentoring program?

or

What is the impact of the peer-mentoring program on the students' levels of self-esteem?

When developing research questions, try to avoid writing research questions that have a yes-no answer such as,

Can female adolescent students increase their levels of empathy?

or why questions such as,

Why do the female targets of cyberbullying struggle with peer relationships?

These questions are more rhetorical (or not answerable) and do not tell the reader or the researcher anything about the design of the study. In addition, a yes-no research question does not allow much room for discussion and interpretation. An open-ended question (with parameters) not only allows you to answer the research question but also discuss the implications of the findings.

Significance to the Field

The next section is the *Significance to the Field* (also referred to as *Significance of the Study*). In this section, describe the benefits (short and long term) for the participants in the study as well as the contribution that the study made to the research literature in your field. For example, if you conducted an intervention, you may have made a positive impact on the participants' academic, social, physical, or emotional well-being. If you conducted surveys, interviews, or observations for your study, you may have discovered important information about the participants' attitudes, perceptions, and behaviors. Although this section is typically included in Chapter One, you may want to write this section after you have completed the study.

Definitions

The next section in Chapter One is *Definitions*. This section is where you will define terms or phrases that need a more detailed explanation than the ones that were provided earlier in the chapter. Remember to use consistent terms to convey the same meaning as presented in the definitions. Thus, if you have labeled a concept or variable with a specific term, use this term consistently throughout the entire text. Once you formally define the term in this section, the reader will know exactly what you are referring to.

Perhaps the most difficult part of writing this section is determining which terms to define. There are three rules that I use in selecting terms to define. The first rule is to define all terms that a person outside of the field would not be familiar with (i.e., technical jargon). For example, *learning disability* is a very critical term in education today but might not be understood in other fields. Whenever possible, I would also use the legal, standard, or recognized definition from the literature and provide the appropriate citations. A second rule is to define all terms that have been "coined" by their users. This refers to familiar terms that may have new definitions because of changing cultural context. These terms would need to be operationally defined because the standard dictionary definition is not accurate for how the term is understood by the users. For example, the standard definition of *cyberbullying* or *bystander* might be different from how they are used in this area of research. Thus, I would have to define these two terms in this section. Finally, the third rule is to define all terms that may be ambiguous to the reader because the definition of the word is dependent on the context or the participant's interpretation. For example, *transition* has multiple meanings depending on the context. In counseling, *life transition* refers to moving from one life stage to another such as from work to retirement. In education, *transition* refers to moving between elementary, middle, high school, and postsecondary settings. In business, a *business transition* could refer to a change in ownership or management. Criminologists study how life-course transitions (e.g., marriage, employment, entering the military) are correlated with desistance from crime

(Warr, 1998). By defining the term (with a citation from the literature), this clarifies the concept for the reader and ensures that everyone is on the same page. After you have defined all the terms, list them with bullets and arrange them in alphabetical order so that it will be easy for the reader to find specific terms.

Limitations

The next section is *Limitations*. This section is where you will discuss all the limitations in the study. Limitations can be inherent to the research design, data analysis, time and resources, or a condition that was set by the researcher. Keep in mind that all studies have limitations, and it is not a personal reflection on you as a researcher. Thus, the best way to deal with limitations is to be upfront about them and explain how they affected the results or findings of the study; trying to hide or cover the limitations of a study will only further weaken the study. For example, lack of a control group is a common limitation in students' theses because of the limited access to participants. Another common limitation is small sample size (in a quantitative study).

A limitation is a flaw or weakness in the study that affects the internal validity and external validity of the results. **Internal validity** (within the study) refers to whether the changes in the dependent variable were due to the independent variable or some other variable. If there is no control group in an experimental study, this will reduce the internal validity because it is uncertain whether the changes in the dependent variable were due to the treatment or some other factors. **External validity** (outside the study) refers to whether the results of the study are applicable or can be generalized to other settings and groups (Mills & Gay, 2019). Having a small sample size would reduce a study's external validity because of the limited generalizability to other groups. However, depending on the research design, this would not necessarily be a limitation in a qualitative study. I discuss these in more detail in Chapter 9.

Ethical Considerations

The last section in Chapter One is *Ethical Considerations*. This section is where you will describe the procedures that you followed to ensure that the research was conducted in an ethical manner. This includes following the Institutional Review Board process for informed consent, obtaining permission from other agencies to access participants, and minimizing the potential risks to your participants. You may need to include a blank copy of the cover letter or informed consent form in the appendix of your thesis, so make sure you keep a copy.

SUMMARY

Chapter One is perhaps the most important chapter in the thesis because it provides a rationale for your study and establishes a structure for the rest of the chapters in the thesis. It is also typically the most difficult chapter to write, so try not to become frustrated if it takes a long time or if you have to write multiple drafts. Once you have described the research problem (and related areas), background literature, purpose of the study, and research questions, this will give you a structure for how to write Chapter Two, Literature Review, and plan for Chapter Three, Methods. In the next chapter, I discuss how to write Chapter Two, Literature Review, for your thesis. Here is a summary of the most critical points from Chapter 5:

- The *Introduction* section in Chapter One describes the general problem in the study.

- A funnel writing strategy is analogous to a funnel where your first paragraph about the problem is broad and every subsequent paragraph narrows the topic toward the specific problem.

- The *Statement of the Problem* section describes the three problem areas related to the research problem.

- The *Background and Need* section describes the background of the problem, solutions to the problems in the *Statement of the Problem*, and the gaps that still exist.

- The *Purpose of the Study* section has four main parts: (a) purpose statement, (b) need/rationale for the study, (c) description of the study, and (d) expected outcomes.

- The *Research Questions* section outlines the questions related to the problem that you are attempting to answer with your study and will determine the methods and data analysis that you use.

- The *Significance to the Field* (also referred to as *Significance of the Study*) section describes the benefits (short and long term) for the participants in the study as well as the contribution that the study made to the research literature in your field.

- The *Definitions* section is where you define terms or phrases that are ambiguous or need an operational definition.

- The *Limitations* section is where you discuss all the limitations in the study. A limitation is a flaw or weakness in the study that affects the internal validity and external validity of the results.

- The *Ethical Considerations* section is where you describe the procedures that you followed to ensure that the research was conducted in an ethical manner.

RESOURCES

Common Obstacles and Practical Solutions

1. A common obstacle that students face at this stage is starting the actual writing of Chapter One. Words that come to mind are "I have major writer's block." This is a very natural feeling because, up to this point, you have been focused on reading and conceptualizing your study. The best way to tackle writer's block is to sit down and write (or in most cases, type on the computer). Believe me—I have been there many times. Start your writing by opening a new Word document and putting in the major headers for the chapter. Next write an outline of the major topics that you will discuss in the Introduction—do not forget to use the funnel strategy! Once you begin to flesh out the outline and pull information from the research, the ideas will flow. If you do not have time to write it all out, make notes to yourself about what information needs to be included and where to find it.

2. Another common obstacle faced by students is formulating the *Statement of the Problem* and the *Background and Need* sections. Words that come to mind are "I don't know what my three areas are." If your three areas have not emerged yet, a good place to look for them is in your organizational filing system. Look to see how you organized your research articles and especially if you created a literature matrix. If neither is available, do a quick scan of the abstracts and try to put the articles into three piles and label each one with a broad heading. This will also inform you of whether you have enough articles or the most applicable research articles.

Reflection/Discussion Questions

Before you write Chapter One, it will save you much time and frustration if you discuss "the big picture" with your chairperson. Often, students get so focused on their own study that they lose sight of the broad context in which the study is situated (the rationale for why you are doing the study in the first place). The following reflection/discussion questions will help to identify the broader issues in your field or discipline related to your research topic and also how to narrow your research topic into the three related areas.

1. What are the foci of the first two paragraphs in the *Introduction* section? Brainstorm different types of problems and issues related to your field or

discipline area that would be relevant for these two paragraphs. Discuss how you could use the funnel strategy to transition between paragraphs in the *Introduction* section.

2. What are the similarities and differences between the *Statement of the Problem* and the *Background and Need* sections? What is the focus of each section? Give examples of how you could use the three parallel ladders strategy to organize the writing for these two sections.

Try It Exercises

The following exercises are designed to help you write Chapter One. In Activity One, you will begin to write the *Introduction* using the funnel method. In Activity Two, you will begin to identify the three problems in the *Statement of the Problem*. In Activity Three, you will begin to develop the *Purpose of the Study* and the *Research Questions*.

1. Activity One: For this activity, focus on the issues related to your research problem.

   - Make a list of the major *national* and *societal* issues related to your research problem. Describe the manifestations and consequences of these issues.

   - Funnel (narrow) one step and list the major *state, regional*, and *local* issues related to your research problem. Describe the manifestations and consequences of these issues.

   - Funnel (narrow) another step and list the *specific* group or subgroups of individuals *related* to your research problem. Describe the manifestations and consequences of the *national* and *state* issues for this group.

   - Funnel (narrow) one last step and list your research problem and the specific group related to your research problem. Describe the manifestations and consequences of the research problem for this group.

2. Activity Two: For this activity, focus on the specific areas related to your research problem.

   - Imagine that this ladder represents the *Statement of the Problem* section. Write an area that is related to your research problem inside each rung (total of three).

   - Then list the problem(s) within each area.

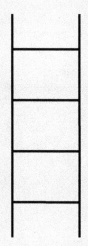

3. Activity Three: For this activity, focus on the purpose of your research study.

   - List the four parts that need to be included in the *Purpose of the Study* section.

   - Write your purpose statement using the model template from the chapter: "The purpose of this study is to (what do you want to do?) to (why do you want to do this?) for (who is your sample group?) in (where is the setting?)."

   - List three main points for the rationale of the study.

   - Write a brief description of the methods that will be used in the study.

   - List the expected goals and outcomes of the study.

   - Convert the purpose statement into a research question.

Key Terms

external validity 111
funnel writing strategy 94
heading 100

internal validity 111
three parallel ladders strategy 102

Suggested Readings

American Psychological Association. (2010). *Publication manual of the American Psychological Association* (6th ed.). Washington, DC: Author.

Badley, G. (2009). Academic writing as shaping and re-shaping. *Teaching in Higher Education, 14*(2), 209–219.

Miedijensky, S., & Lichtinger, E. (2016). Seminar for master's thesis projects: Promoting students' self-regulation. *International Journal of Higher Education, 5*(4), 13–26. doi:10.5430/ijhe.v5n4p13

Ondrusek, A. (2012). What the research reveals about graduate students' writing skills: A literature review. *Journal of Education for Library and Information Science, 53*(3), 176–188. Retrieved from http://www.jstor.org/stable/23249110

Schwartz, B. M., Landrum, R. E., & Gurung, R. A. R. (2017). *An easy guide to APA style* (3rd ed.). Thousand Oaks, CA: Sage.

Wallace, M., & Wray, A. (2016). *Critical reading and writing for postgraduates* (2nd ed.). London, UK: Sage.

Web Links

APA Formatting and Style Guide: The OWL at Purdue
http://owl.english.purdue.edu/owl/resource/560/01/

APA Style
http://www.apastyle.org/

Center for Writing Studies (University of Illinois, Urbana-Champaign)
http://www.cws.illinois.edu/

Graduate Writing Center (Teachers College, Columbia University)
http://www.tc.columbia.edu/graduate-writing-center/

Modern Language Association (MLA)
http://www.mla.org/

The Chicago Manual of Style Online
http://www.chicagomanualofstyle.org/home.html

The Elements of Style, William Strunk, Jr.
http://www.bartleby.com/141/

The Writing Center (University of North Carolina, Chapel Hill)
https://writingcenter.unc.edu/tips-and-tools/introductions/

The Writing Center (University of Wisconsin-Madison)
https://writing.wisc.edu/Handbook/

How to Write Chapter Two, Literature Review

*It does not matter how slowly you go
so long as you do not stop.*

—Confucius

Bravo on getting through Chapter One of the thesis! This chapter focuses on how to write Chapter Two, Literature Review (also referred to as the Review of the Literature). The literature review is an important component of a thesis. While it does not describe your research or the methodology that you employed, it provides the reader a context for understanding why and how you conducted your study. Additionally, it communicates your knowledge of related research and of the conditions surrounding the justification for your research.

By now, you are knowledgeable of the literature related to your study. You have translated your knowledge into a statement of your research problem. In addition, you have had the advantage of examining research conducted and reported by other researchers with interests similar to yours and are aware of the gaps that still remain in the literature. The purpose of writing Chapter Two is to provide the reader with an overview of the *significant* research related to your research problem. In doing so, Chapter Two provides contextual background information for your research problem as well as justification and rationale for your research design.

For some researchers, this chapter is difficult to write. There are several reasons for this. First, it may be difficult to determine what literature to report and what to exclude. A common misconception is that the literature review is a comprehensive or chronological summary of every research article that has been written about the topic. If this were the case, you would never finish reading all the articles or have time to write about them! This can be a serious problem because you will have read an extensive amount of material and may feel that it is all important. Yet judgments will need to be made on what is most relevant to convey the significance of how the prior research relates to your research problem and study. Most likely for every five articles you read, maybe one or two will actually be relevant to your study (if you're lucky!).

Consider the different ways that an article could be relevant to your study (Creswell, 2015, p. 92):

- *Topic relevance: Does the literature focus on the same topic as your proposed study?*

- *Individual and site relevance: Does the literature examine the same individuals or sites that you want to study?*

- *Problem and question relevance: Does the literature examine the same research problem that you propose to study? Does it address the same research question you plan to address?*

- *Accessibility relevance: Is the literature available in your library, or can you download it from a website? Can you obtain it easily from the library or a website?*

If you are still having difficulties finding relevant research studies, definitely make an appointment to spend time with a reference librarian. You should also look at the reference section from articles that you do think are relevant; researchers will often reference other studies and authors in the same topical area. There are also some Literature Review LibGuides created by different universities in the *Resources* section that have some helpful information and tips.

Another common misconception of the literature review is that it is simply a summary or description of research articles around a particular topic. Although you will need to write a summary of the selected research studies you reviewed, your task is to evaluate and critically analyze the research that has been conducted and connect it to your research study. I discuss this in more depth in the research synthesis section.

Unlike the term papers you wrote as an undergraduate, Chapter Two is not one of those assignments that you can do the night before it is due (and still get an A!). You can anticipate spending more time on this chapter than any of the others. The time required to review the literature will be extensive, as will be the time devoted to writing this chapter. You must research the literature, make decisions on which studies are most relevant, critique those studies, and describe how they relate to your research study and to each other. In other words, your writing is specific to individual or groups of studies reported in the literature and not a broad overview of what has been done. The tone and style of writing for the literature review will continue to be formal and scholarly. Remember you will need to include a proper citation for every source that you reference in the literature review, so this is where those reference management software programs really come in handy!

This chapter also tends to be the longest one in the thesis, so remember to pace yourself and use the chunking method (i.e., one step at a time). In addition, allow yourself the time to read the research before you start to write. This may be the only chance you get to delve into a specific research topic, and you might actually find yourself enjoying the process! Similar to Chapter One, you need to decide what is the best process for you in writing this chapter. Some students may want to do all their reading first and then write. Some may want to read one article at a time and write about each one separately and connect them at the end. Others still may want to skim, abstract, sort, create maps, and then write to clarify your ideas, and so on. In other words, the process can be individualized so it is best to understand what is most effective for you. Remember the key is to keep your momentum going forward, so create a timetable for the literature review with target dates, milestones, incentives, and rewards! In this chapter, I discuss how to organize your research articles, write each of the required sections, and synthesize a research article.

Preparation and Organization

In Chapter Two, you will retain the same three areas related to your research problem that were identified in Chapter One. Thus, you will use the same three parallel ladders strategy as before. For Chapter One, the first ladder represented the *Statement of the Problem* section where you wrote about the problems within the three areas. The second ladder represented the *Background and Need* section where you discussed the existing solutions and interventions for the problems. For Chapter Two, we are going to expand the third ladder, which represents the body of the literature review. The three rungs in the ladder represent the same three areas from Chapter One.

Each area will consist of at least three empirical research articles that are related to that area, some of which you may have introduced in Chapter One. Thus, you will need to have a total of nine empirical research articles to write Chapter Two (see Figure 6.1 for an expanded ladder of the three areas for the Literature Review). Check with your chairperson for the required amount of studies per section because it may be less or more. Remember that empirical research articles are those in which data are collected through quantitative, qualitative, or mixed methods. You want to stick with primary sources and will not use secondary sources, position papers, literature syntheses, and so on to write Chapter Two (although this may depend on the preferences of your chairperson). Keep in mind that it will be rare for you to find articles that fit your topic exactly. In fact, you may not find any (which adds to the rationale for your study!). The key will be for you to show how the research study (or parts of it) is related to or supports your research.

Thus, you will need to retrieve articles from research journals (preferably refereed or peer-reviewed journals). Depending on your field, the research literature changes very quickly, so you want to get the most recently published articles. I would not recommend using an article that

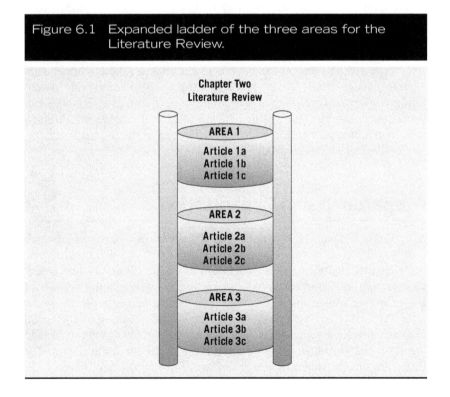

Figure 6.1   Expanded ladder of the three areas for the Literature Review.

is more than 5 years old unless it was a seminal article. A **seminal article** is one that was significant to the topic (e.g., classic) or created a change in the field. If you are having difficulty finding recent research articles, try the following quick search strategies in relevant search engines or electronic databases: (a) Set a limit on the dates, (b) set a limit to scholarly journals, (c) search the table of contents in high-quality journals in your field, (d) search the reference lists of relevant articles, and (e) search for authors who have written extensively on your research problem. Finally, make an appointment with the reference librarian and ask your chairperson for some recommendations to get you started.

The first step in preparing the literature review is to read and organize your empirical research articles according to the three areas. This will indicate whether or not you have the most significant and relevant research in each area or need to go back to do more research. A good strategy to use is **skimming** where you read the abstract, introduction, and conclusion, and skim through the rest of the article to get the main idea (Machi & McEvoy, 2016). Consider this like speed dating the research! As you skim you can also write a short summary of each article on a note card. Then you can sort the cards in a logical order that tells the "story" about the research. For example, you can sort by what they have in agreement (or disagreement), by research methodology, by the sample group, by the intervention, and so on. One thing to keep in mind through this organizing and sorting process is to keep asking yourself, "How does this research article relate to my research problem?" If you cannot answer that question, then perhaps this article is not a good fit for your literature review.

After you have selected the first round of articles, now it is time to go back and read them more thoroughly to find the relationships between the research literature and your study. A good strategy to use at this stage is mapping. There are many different types of maps (e.g., concept, mind, subject tree, content), so you can pick one that best suits your needs. There are also different types of software programs and applications that you can use to "draw" your thoughts into maps (see examples in *Resources* section). You can organize your research into maps around a core issue, theme, author, and so on with supporting elements (Machi & McEvoy, 2016). The advantage of using a **mapping** strategy is that it helps you visually organize the research literature and see meaningful connections. Ask yourself, "What is the relationship among the studies to the core issue and to each other?" Having a visual diagram also allows you to analyze the research to find gaps in your literature search. Sometimes the most relevant studies are those that diverge from the pattern or the findings are inconsistent with the others. Ideally you should have at least one map for each of your three areas of the literature review. This will prepare you to write the body of the literature review.

Chapter Two Sections

Once you have reviewed and organized the research articles, you can use your note cards and maps to write the literature review. Chapter Two starts on a new page in the thesis. Chapter Two has three main sections: (a) introduction, (b) body of the review with research syntheses, and (c) summary. I discuss what needs to be included and how to write each section. Keep in mind that there are different ways to organize a literature review, so it is a good idea to check with your chairperson for program guidelines. One way is to discuss the overall theme from a group of studies and make references to specific studies to support your claims and arguments (Creswell & Creswell, 2018; Machi & McEvoy, 2016). Some people choose to write the literature review in response to a "precisely stated question" (Fink, 2014, p. 3). If you are using this type of organizational format, be sure that you frame your research around a specific question rather than a broad, nonspecific one. For example, "What is the impact of cyberbullying?" is too broad. A more specific question would be, "What is the psychological impact of cyberbullying on female adolescent targets?" There are suggested readings at the end of the chapter if you would like to explore these other ways to organize and approach the literature review. In the example below I organized each area of the literature review around one core issue with a descriptive synthesis of each article. In each synthesis I describe how the research study relates to my current study. When using this type of organizational format, it is also important to connect the articles back to each other.

Introduction

The introduction in Chapter Two has two purposes. The first purpose is to remind the reader about your research problem, and the second purpose is to inform the reader of the three research areas that will be addressed in the chapter. The first paragraph in the introduction is the opening. In this paragraph, revisit the broad problem and research problem from Chapter One. Remember, you want to refer to these problems in general terms. Do not write, "My research problem is . . . ." Instead, briefly describe the broad problem (e.g., national) and then funnel to the research problem that your study is addressing. Your statement of the research problem should be concise and clearly identify the key issues from your study. This paragraph may seem a bit redundant because it is. As you continue writing, you will notice that there will be a respectable level of redundancy throughout the thesis, especially at the beginning of each chapter.

However, the redundancy is purposeful rather than random. In this context, **purposeful redundancy** refers to intentionally reiterating main points about the research problem and study throughout the thesis. This serves two purposes. First, purposeful redundancy allows each chapter to stand alone. This means that a reader can begin reading the thesis at any chapter and understand the gist of the research problem and your study. Second, purposeful redundancy links the chapters together so that there is a seamless connection between them. This gives the writing fluidity and unity, and the reader is not left trying to fill in gaps. Think of it as a silk thread that tells the narrative of your study throughout the thesis. However, you want to avoid simply repeating verbatim what has already been written unless it is serving a strategic purpose. In other words, you do not want the reader to have a déjà vu, I've-read-this-before moment.

Advance Organizer

The next paragraph in the introduction is the advance organizer. In this context, an advance organizer is an outline for the literature review and informs the reader of what will be addressed in the chapter. The advance organizer should be based on the three areas related to the research problem from Chapter One. In the advance organizer, explicitly state the areas that will be discussed in the body of the literature review. For example, here is an advance organizer for the three areas from Chapter One:

> The literature review addresses three areas of research related to the adverse impact of cyberbullying on female adolescents' psychological health, physical health, and suicide ideation and behaviors. In the first section, research studies related to the negative psychological effects experienced by cyberbullying targets and also promising interventions to counteract those effects are addressed. In the second section, there is a discussion on the physical health and somatic concerns that these adolescents experience and how supportive social networks have lessened the impact or decreased adolescents' participation in cyberbullying. Finally, the last section focuses on cyberbullying as a predictive factor in adolescents' suicide ideation and behavior and how close and nurturing relationships with parents and adults has been a positive mediating factor.

Here is an example template that you can use to write your advance organizer:

> The literature review addresses three areas related to (the research problem). The first section addresses research related to (the first area's problem/solution). The second section focuses on research studies about (the second area's problem/solution). Finally, the third section discusses research related to (the third area's problem/solution).

Once you have the advance organizer, follow this outline and organize the text for the body of the review around each of the sections.

Body of the Review

The body of the review is the heart of the literature review. This is where you will synthesize the research articles in each of the three areas related to your research problem. Remember to label each section with an appropriate level heading (see Chapter 10 for APA style). For example, my heading for the first section would be *Psychological Impact and Intervention for Adolescent Cyberbullying.* At the beginning of each section, write a brief description about the research area. Next provide a synthesis for each of the individual or group of research studies. Within each synthesis, inform the reader how the study is related to your research problem or study (i.e., supports what you are doing or how your study fills a gap). Although in the example below each article is synthesized separately, it is important to connect the research articles within each area as well as establish the connections between the three areas.

Research Synthesis

The synthesis of an empirical research article is part summary, part analysis, and part critique. In other words, your job is to summarize the study and apply your knowledge of research methods and quantitative or qualitative data analysis to critique the study. Providing a summary of the research article contributes to the body of information about your research problem. Providing a critical analysis of the research article strengthens the justification and rationale for your research study. Thus, you need to do both to synthesize the literature and relate it to your research problem. There are 10 basic components included in the research synthesis: (a) introduction, (b) purpose, (c) setting/sample, (d) intervention/issue, (e) procedures, (f) variables/measurement instruments, (g) data analysis, (h) results, (i) conclusions/implications, and (j) limitation/weaknesses (see Figure 6.2 for major components in a research synthesis). If you are not comfortable or familiar with these terms, it would be helpful to review a basic research methods text. Although there are 10 separate parts, some of them may be only one to two sentences while others may be one to two paragraphs, depending on the complexity of the study. I describe how to write each part with an example research synthesis adapted from a former student's master's thesis (Ho, 2006); there are additional sample research syntheses in Appendix G.

1. Introduction: Provide a brief introduction about the topic in the study. You should also define any new terms, if necessary. This

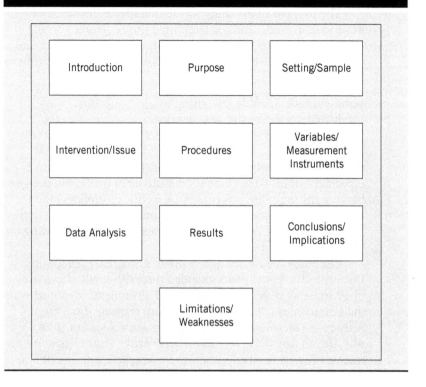

Figure 6.2   Major components of a research synthesis.

Introduction	Purpose	Setting/Sample
Intervention/Issue	Procedures	Variables/ Measurement Instruments
Data Analysis	Results	Conclusions/ Implications
	Limitations/ Weaknesses	

information is typically found in the first section of the article where the authors discuss the findings from their literature review. For example,

Teachers often have difficulty promoting students' knowledge and interpretation of historical events. This is especially true in diverse inclusive settings where students with and without disabilities are taught in the same classroom setting. One alternative method to teach history is through project-based learning. This type of teaching technique uses a project-based activity to help students comprehend and apply their understanding of subject matter content.

2. Purpose: Briefly state the purpose of the study and reference the authors in the text with the year of publication (the full citation belongs in the references section; see Chapter 10 for APA style). This information is typically found in the first section of the article right before the *Methods* section. If you are lucky, the authors will

explicitly state their purpose; other times, you will have to infer the purpose of the study from the given information. For example,

The purpose of the study was to investigate the effects of a curriculum model entitled supported project-based learning (SPBL) on students' historical knowledge, historical inquiry, and attitudes in inclusive 5th-grade classrooms (Ferretti, MacArthur, & Okolo, 2001).

3. Setting/sample: Identify the setting where the research was conducted, including the state or region. Then describe the participants of the study, including their demographic data (e.g., age, grade level, disability, and ethnicity). In some cases, you will need to explain how the participants were selected. This is especially critical if the study used a survey or qualitative design because the sampling procedures are a critical component of the data collection process. This information is typically found in the *Methods* section of the article (sometimes there is a subheading for "Participants"). For example,

The study took place in two urban elementary schools in Delaware. The participants included three 5th-grade classrooms of 59 students without disabilities and 28 students identified with mild disabilities (24 were identified with learning disabilities). Sixty-nine percent of the sample group was Caucasian, 28% was African American, and 3% was Hispanic. Four classroom teachers (two general education and two special education) also participated in the study.

4. Intervention/issue: Describe the intervention that was implemented in the study. This is a brief description of *what* treatment the participants experienced including the materials that were used, professional development or lessons/strategies that were taught, and so on. This information is typically found in the *Methods* section of the article (sometimes there is a subheading for "Materials"). If the study did not involve an intervention, such as in a survey or qualitative study, discuss the issue or phenomenon that was explored. Here is an example of an intervention:

The students were given a task to investigate the experiences of miners, farmers, or Mormons during the westward expansion period in U.S. history. As part of the intervention, the students were taught a strategy to help facilitate the analysis and interpret, and communicate the information they gathered. They were also given questions that they could ask each other and a narrative framework to organize their information.

5. Procedures: Describe the procedures that were used to conduct the study. This is a brief description of *how* the treatment was administered including the length of the intervention, how participants were put into groups, and under what conditions the intervention was implemented. If the study did not involve an intervention, describe other research procedures that may have been used. This information is typically found in the *Methods* section of the article (sometimes there is a subheading for "Procedures"). For example,

> The intervention lasted for 8 weeks over 25 to 29 class periods. The history unit consisted of 14 lessons. The students worked in heterogeneous mixed-ability cooperative groups. They were first shown a video of an emigrant group during westward expansion and then given primary sources (e.g., diaries, journals, photographs) to read and interpret; they were assigned to put together a multimedia technology presentation of the results of their investigation over eight class sessions.

6. Variables/measurement instruments: Describe the variables that were measured and how the data were collected. This is a brief description of the type of data the researcher collected and the types of measurement instruments used to collect the data. In a quantitative study, report the independent and dependent variables and describe the measurement instruments such as surveys, tests, and so on. In a qualitative study, report how the researcher collected data such as observations, field notes, interviews, and so forth. This information is typically found in the *Data Collection* or *Measurement Instruments* sections of the article. For example,

> There were four dependent variables that were measured in this study: content knowledge, historical knowledge, historical inquiry, and students' attitudes. The content knowledge of the unit was measured by a 16-item multiple-choice test on westward expansion (pretest and posttest). To measure historical knowledge and inquiry, 20 interview questions were administered before and after completion of the unit using scoring guidelines. The fourth measured variable was students' attitudes including self-efficacy, intrinsic motivation, and attitudes toward cooperative learning and collaborating with peers. This variable was measured through an attitude scale. No information was given about the structure, format, or scoring of the attitude scale.

7. Data analysis: Explain how the data were analyzed. For a quantitative study, this can include the type of statistics or statistical tests that were used. For a qualitative study, this can include the procedures for transcription (for interviews), organization of field notes (for observations), and the methods used for data coding. **Data coding** is a data analysis process used in qualitative research to categorize and label the major themes. This information is typically found in the *Methods* section of the article (sometimes there is a subheading for "Data Analysis") or in the *Results* section. For example,

> After the intervention was completed, several statistical tests were used to analyze the data. A 2 × 2 repeated measures analysis of variance (ANOVA) and a univariate ANOVA test were conducted to determine students' mean gains from pretest to posttest and if there were any statistically significant differences between students with disabilities and students without disabilities. Differences from pre- to posttest on the attitude scale were analyzed through a multivariate analysis of variance (MANOVA) test.

8. Results: Discuss the results of the study. For a quantitative study, this would include numerical data such as percentage scores, mean scores, or results from statistical tests (e.g., *t* tests). Remember to report the results for each of the variables from the measurement instruments that are relevant to your research problem or study. For qualitative data, report the major themes and significant quotes from the participants that support the major themes (remember to include page numbers for quotes). This information is typically found in the *Results* section of the article. For example,

> The results indicated that students in both groups improved their content scores. However, the students without disabilities scored significantly higher on the posttest than the students with disabilities. The results were similar for the historical content and historical inquiry questions. On the attitude scale, both groups improved slightly on the self-efficacy portion, but the students without disabilities made greater gains than the students with disabilities.

9. Conclusions/implications: Discuss the main conclusions and implications based on the results. This information is typically found in the *Discussion* section of the article. However, it is important that you make your own interpretations about the

conclusions based on the actual results because authors have a tendency to overstate their conclusions beyond the results. For the implications part, this is where you should make an explicit connection to your research study. Basically, answer the "So what?" question and discuss why these results are important for your research problem or study. For example,

Several conclusions can be made about the students' learning in response to the SPBL model. First, both students with and without disabilities improved significantly on the content test and interview questions based on historical knowledge and historical inquiry. After the intervention, students with disabilities were able to comprehend the concept of bias and why the interpretations of historians may differ. This provides support for both general and special education teachers to implement a project-based curriculum to improve their students' understanding of social studies content, especially in inclusive settings. However, some of the mean gains on the test and interview questions were relatively small, and the students with disabilities scored significantly below the students without disabilities on all measures. These results indicate that these students may need explicit instruction on the core content in addition to the project-based curriculum. Additionally, the researchers noted the challenges that general classroom teachers faced with the multimedia component, which questions the feasibility of this type of model in a classroom setting with limited resources and technological support. For future research in this area, providing an additional component using explicit instruction on the narrative framework with fewer technological demands might strengthen the intervention for teachers and students with disabilities.

10. Limitations/weaknesses: Address limitations or weaknesses of the study. This information is typically found in the *Discussion* section of the article (sometimes there is a subheading for "Limitations"). Similar to the *Conclusions* section, it is important for you to form your own criticisms of the study's design, methods, results, and so on rather than relying on the researcher's stated limitations. Just as researchers have a tendency to overstate their conclusions, they will also often understate the limitations and weaknesses of their study. The limitations and weaknesses section is another area where you should make an explicit connection to your research study. Basically, identify the limitations of the study and discuss how these weaknesses or gaps were addressed in your study. For example,

There were several limitations and weaknesses in the Ferretti et al. (2001) study that the current study addressed. First, there was an unequal level of participation from the students in the cooperative groups. The students with disabilities struggled to decode words while the students without disabilities quickly read through books on westward expansion. This could have been a decisive factor in their lower test scores and interview questions. Another limitation was the consistency of each of the instructional periods due to students with disabilities entering/exiting the class for supplemental services. Finally, some students lacked the background knowledge that was necessary to understand the content. In the current study, the students' participation levels were more equal because the text was read aloud. The instructional time and practice were also controlled to ensure that all students received comparable time. Further, the researcher incorporated activities that personalized the events for students and provided explicit instruction on necessary background knowledge.

The research synthesis process that was described is one model to summarize, analyze, and critique each of the research studies related to the three areas of your research problem. If you choose this format, be sure to include transition phrases (segues) between the research syntheses and the three areas so that they are seamlessly connected.

Section Summary

After you have synthesized the three articles in each area, provide a summary paragraph for the section. The purpose of this paragraph is to not only summarize and connect the main points and limitations from the three studies but also to show how they relate back to your study. For example,

> The research literature indicates that students with learning disabilities continue to struggle with instruction that is delivered in a traditional lecture format. The three research articles that were evaluated in this section provide support for using different types of instructional techniques, particularly project-based and authentic learning experiences that involve technology and cooperative groups. The students with disabilities in these studies who were taught history using these teaching techniques benefited from the instruction, as evidenced by their increase in test scores and attitudes. These findings provide rationale to integrate such instructional methods in the current study. However, there were several weaknesses to the previous studies

that limit their generalizability to other settings and populations. These limitations included small sample sizes and the limited age groups. Since all the studies were conducted with middle school students, it is unclear whether these results would be transferred to high school students, which is the sample group of this current study. Additionally, other limitations included the inconsistency of the instruction due to behavior or attendance of the students, which could have been a factor that affected the results. These weaknesses were controlled for in the current study.

Chapter Summary

The last section in Chapter Two is the *Summary*. The *Summary* should have its own level heading. In this section, summarize and connect the key points and limitations from the three areas of research as well as show how they relate to your study. For example,

To ensure that students with disabilities succeed, it is imperative that these students do not fall further behind in proficiency levels, especially in core content areas such as history. The current materials and traditional lecture methods of instruction in today's high schools seem to put students with disabilities at a disadvantage. Students with disabilities have a particularly difficult time comprehending expository texts, which is the dominant form used in history textbooks and curriculum. The research studies reviewed in this chapter indicated that students with disabilities benefit from direct and explicit instruction in different types of expository texts to assist in their comprehension of their textbooks. Additionally, researchers found that using and activating students' prior knowledge helped in their reading comprehension, memorization, and recall of information and text. Another area that has been studied and shown to be beneficial for students' comprehension was using different types of instructional techniques, particularly project-based and experiential learning strategies that involved technology and cooperative groups. Although these studies showed beneficial methods for the students involved, the studies used small sample sizes and a narrow range of student ages, particularly middle school ages, which made it difficult to generalize across the population. Additionally, some of the studies did not include students with disabilities in their sample groups. More research with a more diverse sample of students at different grade levels is needed to determine if these strategies would be successful across student populations. This current study contributed to the existing research literature by measuring the effects of a project-based experiential learning strategy on the comprehension of historical content for high school students with disabilities.

In essence, the *Summary* provides a picture of the most pertinent research in the literature related to your research problem as well as a rationale for how your study contributes to the literature. Thus, you should conclude the summary with a brief statement of how the literature supports what you are addressing in your study. Writing a strong summary at the end of the chapter is vital because you want to leave a lasting impression on the reader and convince her that your study is absolutely essential.

SUMMARY

Chapter Two is a critical chapter in the thesis because it provides an overview of the research literature related to your problem and study. In doing so, you show the reader that you are knowledgeable about the existing research and that your study fills a much-needed gap. In synthesizing the empirical research articles, you have provided both a summary of the studies as well as a critique (which provides a rationale for your study). In the next chapter, I discuss how to write Chapter Three, Methods, for your thesis. Here is a summary of the most critical points from Chapter 6:

- The purpose of writing Chapter Two is to provide the reader with an overview of the *significant* research and how they relate to your research problem.

- A common misconception is that the literature review is a comprehensive or chronological summary of every research article that has been written about the topic.

- A required skill to write Chapter Two is to be able to evaluate and critically analyze the research that has been conducted and connect it to your research study.

- In Chapter Two, you will retain the same three areas related to your research problem that were identified in Chapter One.

- You will need to have a total of at least nine empirical research articles to write Chapter Two.

- Chapter Two has three main sections: (a) introduction, (b) body of the review with research syntheses, and (c) summary.

- Skimming, note taking, and mapping are effective strategies to help organize your research and in preparation for writing.

- Purposeful redundancy allows each chapter to stand alone and links the chapters together so that there is a seamless connection between them.

- There are multiple ways to organize and write a literature review.

- To synthesize an empirical research article, you will need to summarize the study and apply your knowledge of research methods and quantitative/qualitative data analysis to critique it.

- Make your own interpretations about the conclusions based on the actual results because authors have a tendency to overstate their conclusions beyond the results.

- Form your own criticisms of the study's design, methods, results, and so on rather than relying on the researcher's comments.

RESOURCES

Common Obstacles and Practical Solutions

1. A common obstacle that students face at this stage is selecting the articles to include in Chapter Two. Words that come to mind are "I have over 30 articles!" Although it seemed like a good idea at the time to collect as many as possible, having 30 research articles for Chapter Two is about 20 too many. Remember that the purpose of the literature review is to synthesize the most critical and relevant articles for your research topic; the purpose is not to write the historical chronicle of your research topic. With that said, pick only the research articles that fit the three related areas and can support, justify, or reveal a gap related to your research study.

2. Another common obstacle faced by students is synthesizing all the research articles. Words that come to mind are, "I don't have time to read and critique all these articles!" If you took my advice in the first tip above, you should only have to synthesize between nine and 12 articles. This is where the chunking method is critical. Plan a schedule where you tackle one article per day (or one per thesis session). At the first session, read the article carefully and highlight the 10 main components (see Figure 6.2). Make notes on the article where you can critique the study's design, methods, results, and conclusions/implications, and also note how the article relates to your study. At the next session, use your notes to summarize and synthesize the article. Take a much-deserved break and start the next article.

Reflection/Discussion Questions

Before you write Chapter Two, it is important to identify the common thread that will be carried over from Chapter One so that the thesis appears to be seamless. Chapter Two also requires you to extract your prior knowledge of research methods as you synthesize the articles. The following reflection/discussion questions will help guide you through these two processes.

1. What is the goal of using purposeful redundancy in the thesis? Give examples of how and where you can use purposeful redundancy in Chapter Two. In other words, what is the narrative of your study from Chapters One and Two?

2. How does a research synthesis differ from a summary? Use an empirical research article to locate and describe the parts that should be included in the research synthesis.

Try It Exercises

The following exercises are designed to help you write Chapter Two. In Activity One, you will identify the empirically based articles that are related to your three areas. In Activity Two, you will write the introduction and advance organizer paragraphs for Chapter Two. In Activity Three, you will synthesize one of the research articles for Chapter Two.

1. Activity One: For this activity, focus on the research literature related to your research problem and study.

   • List the three areas from Chapter One that are related to your research problem or study.

   • For each area, write the full citation of three empirical research articles that can be included in Chapter Two (you should have a total of at least nine articles).

2. Activity Two: For this activity, focus on your research problem and study and the three related areas.

   • Write an introduction paragraph to Chapter Two, Literature Review. Remember to use purposeful redundancy (tell the story of your study) when you address the broad issues and then funnel to your specific research problem.

   • Write an advance organizer for Chapter Two, Literature Review. Remember to outline the three areas of research that will be discussed. You can use the following template:

The literature review addresses three areas related to (the research problem). The first section addresses research related to (the first area's problem/solution). The second section focuses on research studies about (the second area's problem/solution). Finally, the third section discusses research related to (the third area's problem/solution).

3. Activity Three: For this activity, focus on one of the empirical research articles from the three related areas.

- Write a research synthesis for one article for the literature review. Remember to include the following parts: (a) introduction, (b) purpose, (c) setting/sample, (d) intervention/issue, (e) procedures, (f) variables/measurement instruments, (g) data analysis, (h) results, (i) conclusions/implications, and (j) limitations/weaknesses. Then submit the synthesis to your chairperson for review to make sure you are on the right track!

Key Terms

data coding 128
mapping 121
purposeful redundancy 122

seminal article 121
skimming 121

Suggested Readings

Booth, A., Sutton, A., & Papaioannou, D. (2016). *Systematic approaches to a successful literature review* (2nd ed.). Thousand Oaks, CA: Sage.

Creswell, J. (2015). *Educational research: Planning, conducting, and evaluating quantitative and qualitative research* (5th ed.). Upper Saddle River, NJ: Pearson.

Fink, A. (2014). *Conducting research literature reviews: From the Internet to paper* (4th ed.). Thousand Oaks, CA: Sage.

Harris, M. J. (2006). Three steps to teaching abstract and critique writing. *International Journal of Teaching and Learning in Higher Education, 17*(2), 136–146.

Hart, C. (2018). *Doing literature review* (2nd ed.). Thousand Oaks, CA: Sage.

Machi, L. A., & McEvoy, B. T. (2016). *The literature review: Six steps to success* (3rd ed.). Thousand Oaks, CA: Sage.

Rhoades, E. A. (2011). Literature reviews. *Volta Review, 111*(1), 61–71.

Web Links

Literature Review LibGuides

Literature Review (California State University, Chico)
https://libguides.csuchico.edu/c.php?g=414315&p=2822745

Literature Review: Conducting & Writing (University of West Florida)
https://libguides.uwf.edu/litreview

Literature Review Basics: University of LaVerne
https://laverne.libguides.com/c.php?g=34942&p=222060

The Writing Center (University of North Carolina at Chapel Hill)
https://writingcenter.unc.edu/tips-and-tools/literature-reviews/

Writing the Literature Review (SUNY Empire State College)
https://www.esc.edu/online-writing-center/resources/academic-writing/types/
review-of-the-literature/

Mapping Software

Coggle
https://coggle.it

Mind42
https://mind42.com

MindMeister
https://www.mindmeister.com

MindMup
https://www.mindmup.com

Mindomo
https://www.mindomo.com

SimpleMind
https://simplemind.eu

Visual Understanding Environment
http://vue.tufts.edu

XMind
https://www.xmind.net

How to Write Chapter Three, Methods

*The discipline of the writer is to
learn to be still and listen to what
his subject has to tell him.*

—Rachel Louise Carson

If you have successfully completed Chapter Two, Literature Review, of your master's thesis—well done! Feel free to take a short break and reward yourself for the hard work up to this point. Then roll up your sleeves, grab the coffee mug, and wipe the dust off the computer! This chapter focuses on how to write Chapter Three, Methods (also referred to as Methodology), of the research study and thesis. Preparing for Chapter Three with your chairperson and committee members is very important because they will carefully determine if the research design and research methods are appropriate to fulfill the purpose of the study and allow you to answer the research questions. After sweating through Chapters One and Two, Chapter Three will probably be the most enjoyable to write because this is where you describe your research design and the methods implemented in your study. In doing so, you will apply what you have learned in your research preparation and in the literature review.

Research Designs and Research Methods

While they are related, there is a difference between research design and research methods. The research design can be considered as the overall logical plan or framework (including philosophy, worldview, and theoretical foundation) that is used to address the study's research problem and answer the research questions. If you have ever been involved in the headaches of a remodeling or construction project, consider the research design as the architect's and structural engineer's blueprint plans. It is critical to remember that the research problem and research questions will inform or drive which research design is used (and not the other way around). A researcher does not start out by saying, "For my study, I want to use a mixed methods research design." Instead, it is up to the researcher to provide a rationale (and justification) for which research design is best suited to address the research problem and answer the research questions.

There are many different types of research designs that can be used. They are divided into three broad categories: quantitative, qualitative, and mixed methods. Within each category, there are also specific research designs (also referred to as types or approaches). For example, quantitative research designs include descriptive, survey, correlational, and experimental designs (including quasi-experimental and single-subject). Qualitative research designs include narrative, case study, ethnography, grounded theory, and phenomenology. Mixed methods research designs include three core designs: convergent, explanatory sequential, and exploratory sequential (Creswell & Plano Clark, 2018). Mixed methods research designs have received a lot of attention within the past decade. While there are several opinions of what constitutes mixed methods research, there are some common core characteristics (Creswell & Creswell, 2018):

- *collects and analyzes both qualitative and quantitative data rigorously in response to research questions and hypotheses*

- *integrates (mixes or combines) the two forms of data and their results*

- *organizes these procedures into specific research designs that provide the logic and procedures for conducting the study*

- *frames these procedures within theory and philosophy* (Creswell & Plano Clark, 2018, p. 5)

The advantage of using a mixed methods research design is that it provides evidence to answer research questions that could not be answered by using either a quantitative or qualitative design alone. The challenge is that it requires more skill and resources (e.g., time, personnel) to collect and analyze the data. If you need a refresher on different research designs, check out the list of *Resources* at the end of the chapter.

Once you have selected the best research design to address the research problem and questions, then decisions need to be made about the research methods or the tools that will be used to implement the study. If the research design is the *logic*, then the research methods can be considered the *logistics* of the study. In other words, the research methods are how the researcher plans data collection, procedures, and analysis, in alignment with the research design. This includes where (site/setting), who (sampling plan/sample/participants), what (variables, measurement instruments), how (procedures), and why (data analysis, reliability, validity). Going back to the remodel and construction analogy, the research methods is the part where the contractors take the blueprint plans and decide what tools and materials they will use for the actual building process.

The Methods chapter needs to be written with sufficient detail to provide a context for the results in Chapter Four and for replicability purposes. **Replicability** refers to the ability to replicate (i.e., copy) the study to verify and interpret the results or adapt and expand the study. Do not worry, replicability does not mean you have to redo your study, but others may want to. If you have selected a research problem that has wide interest, it is likely that someone will want to conduct a study in hopes of confirming or expanding your results. For this reason, you want to be certain that the full details of your design and methods are sufficiently described so that someone can independently replicate your study as you conducted it. Since Chapter Three focuses on *your* study, it will be based on what you have already done. Now, it is just a matter of writing it in a systematic and comprehensive way.

Preparation and Organization

There are several items that need to be prepared and organized before you begin to write. First, if you have not already done so, it is critical that you prepare a draft or proposal of Chapter Three before you actually conduct the research. At a minimum, the proposal should include an outline of the type of research design and methods that were discussed in the previous section. This should be very similar to the research proposal that you submitted as part of your application for the Institutional Review Board (IRB). During the proposal stage, your chairperson and committee members will want and need to be very much involved. In many ways, this is an opportunity for them to teach and for you to learn. If the research design and methods are not appropriate for the study, then your work in carrying out the study may not meet the requirements for an acceptable thesis. Sometimes your chairperson may ask another colleague to assist you on some component of the research methods such as the data analysis. Just make sure that Chapter Three's proposal is approved by your chairperson and you have IRB approval (or exemption) before you actually begin to collect data!

Chapter Three Sections

Once you have received all the necessary approvals, you can start to write Chapter Three. Chapter Three starts on a new page in the thesis and is divided into eight main sections: (a) *Introduction*, (b) *Setting*, (c) *Participants*, (d) *Intervention*, (e) *Materials*, (f) *Measurement Instruments*, (g) *Procedure*, and (h) *Data Analysis* (see Figure 7.1 for major sections in Chapter Three). If you remember the research synthesis structure from the literature review, the sections in Chapter Three are very similar to a research article. Keep in mind that although they are written and discussed separately, the sections are intertwined and collectively they form the methods of the study.

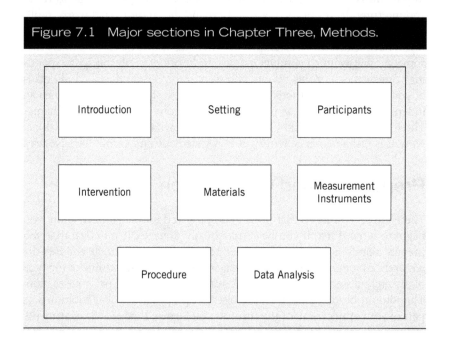

Figure 7.1 Major sections in Chapter Three, Methods.

Introduction   Setting   Participants

Intervention   Materials   Measurement Instruments

Procedure   Data Analysis

Depending on your research design, some of the sections listed above may have different titles or may not apply to your thesis. For example, *Intervention* would only be applicable if you conducted a quantitative study (i.e., experimental). Thus, before you start writing, check with your chairperson for which sections to include. Writing Chapter Three can be enjoyable because it is similar to storytelling. You want to tell the reader the "story" of how you conducted your research study, so it should include a setting, characters, and main events (the conclusion of the story is told in Chapters Four and Five). However, remember that the writing style must be technical in nature, and you must describe the critical elements of the research methods you employed. Consider that the broad audience (readers) may be experienced researchers and/or practitioners. Thus, they will expect to see the elements of your research described in a manner that is accurate but easily understood.

To guide you in writing Chapter Three, I first discuss how to write each section in general. Then I provide examples of written work adapted from former students' completed master's theses or other studies. I include examples from quantitative (including single subject design), qualitative, and mixed methods studies when a distinction among the approaches is helpful. You will notice that the examples are written in the past tense to indicate that the studies have already been completed. Most likely, you will write the Chapter Three proposal in future tense (to indicate what you plan to do) and then come back after the research has been completed to rewrite the chapter in the past tense. However, I recommend consulting with your chairperson to make sure that this is the advised approach.

Introduction

Chapter Three opens with an introduction that has several elements. The first part of the introduction is a brief reminder of the general research problem. This is where *purposeful redundancy* (see Chapter 6) is a good writing technique. Use purposeful redundancy to connect Chapter Three seamlessly to the previous chapter but also to enable it to stand alone. In the second part of the introduction, remind the reader of the research question(s) from Chapter One. By revisiting the research questions here, you are providing a justification and bridge to the specific research design that was used to answer the questions. Finally, the third part of the introduction is an overview of the research design and a brief explanation of the research methods that were used in the study.

Providing the reader with an overview of the research design is critical because it sets the tone (and layout of the sections) for the rest of the chapter. For example, if you used a quasi-experimental research design, the reader will expect to see large groups of participants, independent and dependent variables, and hypothesis testing. If you used a qualitative case study design, the reader will expect to see a small group of participants, description of observation forms or interview questions, and coding of narrative data. If you used a mixed methods research design, the reader will expect to see both elements of quantitative and qualitative research methods.

Here is an example of research questions and an overview of a quantitative research design adapted from a former student's master's thesis.

The following research questions were addressed in this study:

1. What are the effects of a self-directed learning program on the behavior of high school students with learning disabilities?

2. What are the effects of a self-directed learning program on the levels of self-determination for high school students with learning disabilities?

This study followed a quantitative research design, using a pre-experimental one-group pretest–posttest design. Self-directed learning strategies were embedded into the curriculum of the participating teacher's high school special education English classes. The effects of the self-directed learning program on students' behavior and self-determination levels were measured through a survey. The self-directed learning program included writing assignments designed to encourage self-reflection on the student's approach to his education, a weekly self-evaluation form that allowed students to self-monitor academic and behavioral performance, and goal development strategies that incorporated appropriate feedback and attributional perspective. Pre- and post-intervention data were collected and analyzed using descriptive and inferential statistics. (Williams, 2006)

Here is an example of research questions and an overview of a qualitative research design adapted from a previous student's master's thesis.

The research questions of this study included the following:

1. What are the factors of communication (verbal or nonverbal) that trigger behavioral outbursts or promote positive behavior and effective communication in a classroom serving students with emotional disturbances and learning disabilities?

2. What are the cultural differences in communication (verbal or nonverbal)?

3. What are the factors leading to positive student–teacher relationships?

4. What are the factors that promote a high degree of instructional efficacy?

This qualitative research design used a case study to describe the cultural views of high school teachers and staff and students with emotional disturbances and learning disabilities. Interviews and observations were used to collect data in teacher–student communication with the primary goal of revealing the relationship between positive and negative verbal or nonverbal communications and students' behavior. The narrative data were transcribed, coded, and categorized into four themes related to the research questions. (Kendall, 2006)

Here is an example of research questions and an overview of mixed methods research developed from our literature review sample from Chapter 6. The research questions of this study included the following:

1. What is the relationship between psychological health and physical health for adolescent male and female targets of cyberbullying?

2. How do adolescent males' and females' experiences of cyberbullying influence their self-perceptions of psychological and physical health?

3. To what extent do adolescent male and female targets of cyberbullying share common self-perceptions of psychological and physical health?

In this mixed methods convergent design research study, both quantitative and qualitative methods were used to explore the relationship between psychological health and physical health of 60 (30 male, 30 female) middle school students who self-identified as targets of cyberbullying. The Beck Youth Inventories (BYI-2) was used to measure the students' psychological health and the Child Health Questionnaire (CHQ-CF45) was used to measure their physical health. Follow-up interviews with 10 students (5 male, 5 female) were used to explore any commonalities between the two groups' self-perceptions of psychological and physical health. (Adapted from Way, Stauber, Nakkula, & London, 1994)

Here is an example of a research question and an overview of a quantitative single subject design study.

The research question of this study included the following:

1. What is the effect of a class-wide, peer-mediated social skills intervention on the social interactions (as measured by initiations and responses) of students with low-functioning autism and typically-developing peers?

This single-subject study examined the effects of a peer-mediated intervention on initiations and responses of four K–2 students with low-functioning autism and their 2nd-grade peers. Students were taught a shared reading intervention using visual support, role-play, discussion, and peer reinforcement. Three participants with low-functioning autism increased mean responses to peer initiations from baseline to intervention stages. (Adapted from Simpson & Bui, 2016)

Setting

The second section in Chapter Three is the *Setting* (this is the first section that requires a level heading). In this section, describe the research site(s) where the research was conducted. Similar to the setting in a story, the setting in the thesis is where the study took place (i.e., data were collected). The setting could be in a number of locations such as a school, hospital, church, prison, office, home, or even on a bus. In writing about the setting, first provide a description of the broad setting (e.g., school, hospital, juvenile detention center, community center). Remember to include any background or historical information about the setting so that the reader can situate your research site in the broader context. In addition to the broad setting, include a description of the specific area(s) where the data were collected (e.g., classroom, a person's home, office). Include any demographic data related to the setting as appropriate.

Here is an example of a research setting adapted from a former student's master's thesis:

This study took place in an urban elementary school located in Northern California. Fifty-nine percent of students at the school qualified for free lunch, and almost 16% were English learners. Thirty percent of students were Hispanic or Latino; 28% were African American, not Hispanic; 17% were White, not Hispanic; 9% were Asian; 3% were Filipino; 2% were American Indian; less than 1% were Pacific Islander; and 11% declined to state or claimed multiple ethnicities.

The intervention was conducted on a pullout, individual basis. Instruction was provided in the resource room at the participants' elementary school during the regular school day. The resource room is a small classroom containing a kidney table with a half-sized chalkboard posted at the front wall. There is also a long rectangular table in the back of the room, which is where students received the intervention. (Irey, 2008)

Participants

The third section is the *Participants*. There are two parts to this section. The first part describes the sampling plan that was used in the study. **Sampling** refers to the process of selecting participants for a study (Mills & Gay, 2019). In this part, explain how the participants were selected from the broader population.

The sampling plan will vary depending on the research question and design of the study. For example, if you are using a quantitative research design, select a large, representative sample group from the specified population. Again, depending on the research question and design, you may need to have a random sample. In a **random sample**, every individual in the population has an equal and independent chance of being selected (i.e., drawing names from a hat).

Be careful not to confuse random selection with random assignment. Random selection refers to selecting participants from the population. Random assignment refers to how the participants are put into groups. In **random assignment**, each participant in the sample has an equal and independent chance of being selected for the treatment group. If you are conducting a true experimental study, participants are randomly assigned into different treatment groups. This helps eliminate the potential bias of having one group (e.g., experimental group) be "stronger" than the other and helps level the playing field before the intervention begins.

Since it is not always possible or necessary to randomly select from the population, a nonrandom sample is more commonly used in a master's thesis. One example of a nonrandom sample is a convenience sample. In a **convenience sample**, the researcher selects the individuals who are available and accessible at the time. An example of a convenience sample is a teacher who includes all the students in her classroom. People with clipboards at the shopping mall (the ones you avoid eye contact with and run away from) are also using a convenience sample when they select shoppers at the mall.

Another type of nonrandom sample is a purposive sample. In a **purposive sample**, the researcher selects individuals who are considered representative because they meet certain criteria for the study. For example, some important criteria for selection are whether the participant is willing and able to contribute to the understanding of the research problem, issue, or phenomenon being explored. In some cases, a specific site might be selected for the sample (Creswell & Creswell, 2018). This is very common in qualitative studies. Here is an example of a nonrandom sample from a qualitative study:

> The sampling procedure used by the researcher was purposive sampling. The participants were restricted to those at the researcher's school site who attended or worked at the high school and the participant's willingness to partake in the study. Participants included 12 high-school students, one teacher, two paraeducators, and one therapist who worked at a public high school in Northern California. The participants were also selected because they were from diverse cultural backgrounds and part of the same classroom environment where they had multiple opportunities to display and observe communicative behaviors [the focus of the study]. (Kendall, 2006)

The next part of the *Participants* section is the description of the participants. In this section, include the participants' demographic data such as age, gender, grade level, race/ethnicity, language, disability, socioeconomic status, occupation, years of experience, and so on. There are several reasons why the reader needs to have demographic information about the individuals who were involved in the study. First, if a researcher wants to replicate the study with the same type of participants, he needs to select participants who are comparable to yours. Similarly, if a researcher wants to replicate the study with a slightly different type of participant (e.g., age group), she would also need to know exactly who was included in your study in order to make modifications. Another reason for describing the participants is for generalizability purposes. **Generalizability** refers to the extent to which the results about a sample group from a study are applicable to the larger population. This is especially important in quantitative studies. By having a greater understanding of the sample group, the reader can make interpretations about whether or not the results apply to the larger population (assuming that the sample group is representative of the larger population). In qualitative studies, having a detailed description of the participants lends credibility to the researcher (and the findings) and helps the reader understand the phenomenon or issue that was explored. Since there is typically a smaller sample size in a qualitative study, each individual's contribution is heavily weighted regarding shedding light on the research problem(s). Usually there is a table of participants' demographic data included as part of the thesis (see Chapter 10 for APA style). Here is an example of the description of participants:

> The participants in the study were from diverse ethnic backgrounds. There were 12 high school students. Eight students were African American; five were males, and three were females.

Of the five African American males, there was one ninth-grade student, two 10th-grade students, one 11th-grade student, and one 12th-grade student. Of the three African American females, one was a 10th-grade student, and two were 12th-grade students. The three Latino students were all males and in the 11th grade. The one Caucasian male student was in the 11th grade. All of the students were enrolled in the special day class and were previously diagnosed with emotional disturbance (ED) or learning disability (LD). The participating teacher and therapist were Caucasian; the teacher was from the United States, and the therapist was originally from England. They were both in their mid-fifties and had over 10 years of professional experience. The two male paraeducators were African American and Latino, respectively. (Kendall, 2006)

Intervention and Materials

The fourth and fifth sections are the *Intervention* and *Materials* (if appropriate). In these sections, describe the intervention and instructional materials that were used in the study and how they were developed. These sections are necessary only if you included some sort of intervention (i.e., experiment) in a quantitative study. In writing about the intervention, you should describe both the independent and dependent variables. Remember that the independent variable is the cause or treatment that is expected to influence the dependent variable (i.e., the outcome or effect). For example, pretend a researcher implemented an algebra intervention with middle school students to prepare them for a statewide assessment. In this study, the algebra intervention is the independent variable and the dependent variable is the students' scores on the statewide assessment.

In our cyberbullying example study with two groups, we could compare the effectiveness of peer mentoring versus adult mentoring on the depression levels of adolescent targets of cyberbullying. In this study, the independent variable is the type of mentoring treatment received, and the two levels (e.g., groups) of the independent variable are peer mentoring and adult mentoring. The dependent variable is the depression levels of the adolescent targets of cyberbullying. When describing the intervention, we would include a detailed description of *what* peer mentoring and adult mentoring consisted of (the components) and how the two treatments differed.

Here is an example of an intervention adapted from a former student's master's thesis:

The independent variable measured by this study consisted of the intervention program: self-awareness training, social skills training, and increased transition planning involvement. The component of self-awareness training was intended to increase students' understanding and awareness of their specific disabilities, including knowledge of their individual strengths and weaknesses, and ways in which they could compensate for their disabilities. Social skills training involved the examination of conflicts frequently encountered by students and the development of alternative, positive solutions to these conflicts through direct skill instruction. Lastly, interventions in the area of transition planning required students to participate in activities that would prepare them for a smooth transition into adult life after high school.

The dependent variable consisted of students' perception of their own levels of resiliency, as defined by the researcher. Within the dependent variable there were three categories of student perceptions: self-awareness, social skills, and transition planning. (Kornhauser, 2006)

Here is an example from the single-subject design study:

The independent variable was a peer-mediated shared reading intervention designed to enhance social interactions among the students with low-functioning autism (LFA) and their typical peers. The Reading Buddies intervention had a peer-reading component and a peer-reinforcement component. Centering the intervention on shared reading was important because it incorporated an activity that all of the students with LFA enjoyed, encouraged social interaction related to the story, and was an academic activity in which most children would regularly participate.

The dependent variable in the study was the students' with LFA and the typical peers' initiations and responses towards each other. Initiations and responses were chosen as a means to examine social interaction between participants. Initiations were defined as any appropriate motor or vocal behavior demonstrated by the students to gain attention or a response from another student, including verbalizing to another student, looking at another student's face, touching the other student (e.g., tapping shoulder, touching hand), presenting the book to another student, and pointing to a picture in the book while looking at the student. Responses were defined as any appropriate motor or vocal behavior demonstrated by the students that was preceded by an initiation and occurred within 10 seconds of the initiation including looking at the other student's face, verbalizing to the other student, smiling at the other student, touching the other student, and giving a motor response such as nodding head or touching a picture in the book. (Adapted from Simpson and Bui, 2016)

In the *Materials* section, describe the materials that were used as part of the intervention. Sometimes these materials are from a commercial program and sometimes they are developed by the researcher. Remember to describe the materials in enough detail so that the reader could replicate or adapt the intervention. A good idea is to include a sample of the materials in the appendix of the thesis, so be sure to keep records and clean copies of everything that you used (see Chapter 10 for APA style).

Here is an example of a description of materials:

Three main types of instructional materials were used during the intervention for self-awareness, social skills, and transition planning. Instructional materials to improve students' levels of self-awareness were developed by the researcher. These lessons focused on the study and understanding of students' disabilities, including strengths and weaknesses presented by the disabilities, and ways in which they could compensate for their weaknesses. In addition, students watched a video and used Internet resources to help them understand and gain insight into their disabilities.

Curriculum used in the social skill development lessons was taken from *Skillstreaming the Adolescent* (Goldstein & McGinnis, 1997). Lessons in this area consisted of activities in which students were required to examine their behaviors in situations involving conflict and discover positive ways in which they could approach these situations. Social skills instruction during these lessons involved components of modeling, discussion, role-play, and feedback.

The transition planning series of lessons was developed by the researcher and drawn from the transition planning curriculum mandated by the school district for all students receiving special education services. The curriculum involved direct instruction that focused on services available to individuals and use of the Internet as a tool to gather information. The curriculum also focused on career planning and independent living after graduation from high school (see Appendix B for sample lessons and materials). (Kornhauser, 2006)

Measurement Instruments

The sixth section is a description of the *Measurement Instruments*, tools that the researcher used to collect data. Examples of measurement instruments include: questionnaire/scale, behavioral checklist, interview, focus group, observation protocol, public documents or records, tests, survey, interest inventory, and so on. In this section, there should be a title and brief description of each measurement instrument and how the instrument was scored or interpreted. You can decide the order of presentation of the measurement instruments, although I typically discuss the instruments in the order they appear within the research questions. The presentation of the measurement instrument in Chapter Three represents a ladder, and each rung represents one measurement instrument (see Figure 7.2 for a depiction of the ladder for Chapter Three). Keep in mind that you will keep the same order for Chapters Four and Five. To represent this visually, I use the three parallel ladders strategy to represent the order of the measurement instruments across the three chapters (see Figure 7.3 for a depiction of the three parallel ladders strategy for Chapters Three, Four, and Five). The actual measurement instruments will be included in the appendix of the thesis, so be sure to keep clean copies of all the instruments that you use (see Chapter 10 for APA style).

As mentioned, there are many different kinds of measurement instruments that can be used, and the one(s) that you select depends on the research design and research question in your study. For example, in

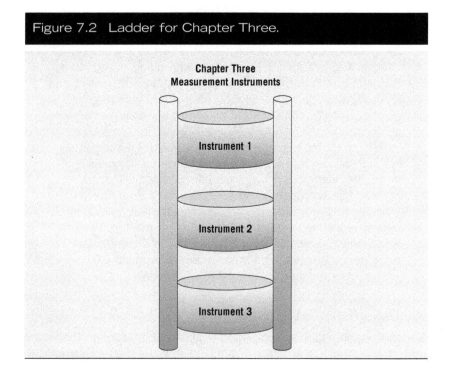

Figure 7.2 Ladder for Chapter Three.

Chapter Three
Measurement Instruments

Instrument 1

Instrument 2

Instrument 3

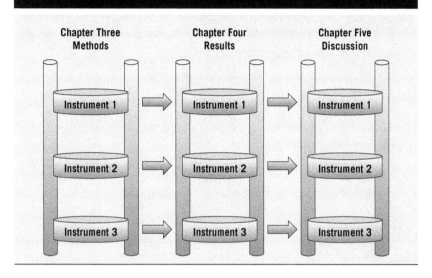

Figure 7.3 The three parallel ladders strategy for Chapters Three, Four, and Five.

Chapter Three Methods	Chapter Four Results	Chapter Five Discussion
Instrument 1	Instrument 1	Instrument 1
Instrument 2	Instrument 2	Instrument 2
Instrument 3	Instrument 3	Instrument 3

quantitative studies, researchers commonly use performance measures (e.g., tests), attitude scales (e.g., surveys), and structured behavior checklists (especially for studies that measure changes in behaviors). In qualitative studies, observations, interviews, and focus groups are commonly used.

There are at least three kinds of measurement instruments that can be used to collect data. The first kind is those tools that already exist and are available for public use (there will usually be a fee to use or score the instrument). An advantage of a standardized instrument is that it has been used widely in the field and validated for a particular purpose. For example, in education, the Woodcock Johnson III Tests of Achievement (Wendling, Schrank, & Schmitt, 2007) is a standardized battery of tests that measure academic achievement. A disadvantage of using existing measurement instruments is that they may not measure exactly what you want to study or need to answer your research questions. The second kind of measurement instrument is collecting data that are normally collected. This is helpful for students' master's theses because it saves time and resources since the data are already being collected for other purposes. For example, in business and management, companies often keep records of employee absences. A researcher might want to explore the relationship between the frequency of employee absences and their level of personal productivity. The third kind of measurement instrument is a researcher-made instrument. Oftentimes, researchers will modify an existing instrument or use parts of different instruments. This is very common in students' master's theses and sometimes preferable to standardized measures because it can be developed to be more "sensitive" to what is being studied. For example, a marriage and family therapist might want to develop her own survey to measure clients' satisfaction around a new communication technique she developed for family members. Keep in mind that if you are modifying an existing instrument, you need to receive permission to do so from the original author of the instrument. You will also have to pilot the modified instrument to make sure that it is valid and reliable (see more about this below).

In describing the measurement instruments, provide enough information so that the reader is able to replicate the study or interpret the results. For a quantitative measure such as a test or survey, this includes a title and a description of what the instrument measures, how it is administered, how many items and format of items, sample items, how it is scored, and any standardized benchmarks or norms. For a qualitative measure such as an observation or interview protocol, include a description of what it measures, how it is administered, type and number of questions asked, and sample items.

Here is an example description of one standardized test measure:

The Dynamic Indicators of Basic Early Literacy Skills Oral Reading Fluency (DORF; Good & Kaminski, 2002) assessment was used to measure students' fluency scores both before and after the intervention. The DORF is a standardized test that measures students' fluency and accuracy with leveled reading material. Students are given the test individually, and they read three passages aloud for one minute each. During this time, the administrator marks any omissions, substitutions, or hesitations (longer than three seconds) as errors. Self-corrections that are made within three seconds are not counted as errors. The median number of correct words per minute read on all three passages constitutes the student's oral reading fluency rate.

The DORF has benchmarks for each grade level. The benchmark goal for students in spring of first grade is 40 words per minute, the goal for students in spring of second grade is 90 words per minute, and the goal for students in spring of third grade is 110 words per minute. Students scoring below 10 in spring of first grade, below 50 in second grade, and below 70 in the spring of third grade are considered at-risk and require intensive instruction. (Irey, 2008)

Here is an example description of an observation checklist:

The researcher used an observation checklist to collect data. The purpose of the observation checklist was to describe the students', therapist's, teacher's, and paraeducators' communicative behaviors. The observations were conducted at five different times for an hour and a half for each observation, totaling 7.5 hours of observation. The behaviors observed for the school staff were yelling, frowning, smiling, laughter, physical contact, close proximity to student, medium proximity to student, long-range proximity, fat words, muscle words, negative comments, positive comments, rejection to requests, positive ultimatums, negative ultimatums, negative consequences, positive consequences, directives with no choice, and directives with a choice. The behaviors observed in the students were yelling, frowning, smiling, laughter, physical contact, close proximity to staff, medium proximity to staff, long-range proximity to staff, fat words (i.e., directives that are low in contextual cues), muscle words (i.e., directives that are high in contextual cues), negative comments, positive comments, posturing, horse play, or physical violence. Physical contact, rejection to requests, posturing, horse play, and physical violence all required a detailed description, including antecedent and subsequent behaviors, to describe the effect and nature of the behaviors (including verbal/nonverbal, voice tone, laughter, frowning, etc.). The communicative behaviors were tallied to produce a frequency count of each type of behavior. In addition, descriptive and reflective comments with regards to the communicative behaviors were noted on the observation checklist. (Kendall, 2006)

Validity and Reliability

The last part of this section is a description of the measurement instrument's validity and reliability. **Validity** refers to the extent to which the instrument measures what it was intended to measure. If a measurement instrument is not valid for the intended purpose, then it will be difficult to interpret the results in a meaningful way. A standardized achievement test such as the Woodcock Johnson III is a good example of a measure that has strong validity data. Just be sure to follow the standardized procedures for administration and scoring, as straying from these procedures will decrease the validity of the results. If you create your own measurement instrument, two ways to increase the validity is to pilot it with a small group and have content experts in the field review it and make any necessary adjustments.

Reliability refers to the extent to which an instrument *consistently* measures what it was intended to measure. If the measure (or individuals scoring the measure) has strong reliability, then you should get similar results every time it is administered. Reliability is very important when using two alternate forms of a test or when the scoring or interpretation of the measure is subjective (e.g., coding observations or open-ended questions). If you have two or more people scoring or coding the measures, it is especially critical to have a rubric and do some **interrater reliability** training beforehand to increase reliability. When conducting interrater reliability, two or more individuals independently score the same observation and then compare their scores with each other to see how similar or different they are. Keep in mind that a valid measure is always reliable but a reliable measure is not always valid. In other words, you could consistently be measuring the wrong thing over and over! In writing about the validity and reliability of a measurement instrument, be sure to describe how you considered these two issues and amended the instruments if necessary.

Here is an example description of the validity and reliability of some measurement instruments:

> The validity and reliability of the DORF and the McLeod Assessment of Reading Comprehension assessments have previously been established (Good & Kaminski, 2002; McLeod & McLeod, 1999), and each measure has been tested to ensure that the passages are correctly leveled to each grade level. To establish validity with the prosody checklist, it was used prior to the intervention with students at different reading levels to ensure that it measured all of the aspects it was intended to measure and was appropriate for all reading levels. To check its reliability, it was administered multiple times with the same students during a short period of time (so their skill level did not change) and modified as needed until it yielded similar scores on multiple trials. The same procedures were completed with the attitude survey. (Irey, 2008)

Here is an example description of interrater reliability procedures adapted from a former student's master's thesis:

> Another teacher from the researcher's school was enlisted to grade 25% of the reading comprehension tests to ensure

interrater reliability. The teacher was chosen because he had read all of the graphic novels used in the study, had taught each of the students, and had a good relationship with the researcher. The teacher was given one test from each group for each phase, totaling eight tests, which were chosen at random by the researcher. He was blind to the conditions of the study. The teacher was instructed by the researcher to use the rubric to grade each test. The researcher trained him to use the rubric by providing him with a sample test and guiding him in using the rubric to answer each question. He was also instructed to mark items as correct when the participants' answers contained synonyms to the rubric answers. Moreover, he was shown by the researcher where and how to mark the scores of each test. Interrater reliability was established using a point-by-point analysis. The teacher scored eight reading comprehension assessments using a rubric given to him by the researcher. The researcher compared her scores of the same eight assessments to the scores of the teacher. For each question the researcher and the teacher matched, a percentage point was awarded. A percentage of agreement was assigned to each assessment. (Gomes, 2008)

Procedure

The seventh section is the *Procedure*. In this section, describe the data collection and procedures used to conduct the study. In other words, explain *how* the data were collected and the procedures that were followed throughout the study. This includes procedures for administering measurement instruments, details of implementation for any intervention (e.g., length of treatment, time of day), and difference of conditions in treatment groups (if there were multiple groups). As mentioned, there are many different ways to collect data depending on the research design and research questions. However, detailed descriptions in this section are extremely important for both credibility and replicability purposes.

For a qualitative study, data collection could involve conducting observations, interviews, focus groups, or researching documents, artifacts, and audiovisual materials (Creswell, 2013). In writing this section, you need to explain exactly *how* these data collection activities were conducted. For example, if you conducted observations, describe the conditions in which you conducted the observations (e.g., time, place, frequency), your role as the observer (e.g., participant or nonparticipant observer), and how field notes were recorded.

Here is a description of data collection from a qualitative study:

The data were collected through observations and interviews. The observations were collected under natural, non-manipulative settings using an observation checklist (see Appendix B). The observations of the participants were conducted in their classroom which was the natural setting. The researcher was a nonparticipant observer and sat in the back of the room to avoid any interference to the setting. The data collection process took place over a five-week time period. Observations took place once per week for a one and a half hour time period, totaling five observations (7.5 hours of observation time). The interviews were conducted at the school site, and the procedure did not disrupt the participants' normal, daily, classroom activities. The interviews were conducted with the participants individually during their lunch or preparation period in a different classroom, using the interview protocol (see Appendix B). Each interview was tape-recorded for accuracy and lasted between 30 and 45 minutes. (Kendall, 2006)

To describe the data collection procedures in a quantitative study, it is easiest to describe each phase of the study. For example, in an experimental study, you could divide the procedures into phases using the following subheadings: pretest, intervention, and posttest; baseline and intervention. In the pretest phase, describe any procedures that were implemented prior to the intervention. This includes any measurement instruments that were administered as a pretest or pre-intervention actions such as meeting with the participants or training service providers.

Here is an example of the pretest phase adapted from a former student's master's thesis:

Each of the measurement instruments was administered to students two weeks prior to the intervention. The two reading comprehension measures were administered individually. The student was given a story to read silently (see Appendix B). Before the student read, the researcher prompted, "Please read this story carefully to yourself. As you read try to remember as much as you can. When you are done, I will ask you to retell the story back to me in your own words. I will also ask you some questions about the story." After the student read the story silently, he was prompted, "Now, please tell the story back to me in your own words." The student's retelling was tape-recorded, then transcribed, and used to score the story retelling checklist. At the conclusion of the retelling, the student was then prompted, "Now I am going to ask you some questions about the story." The researcher completed the story grammar checklist as the student responded to the questions. All responses were also tape-recorded in case they needed to be reviewed by the researcher later.

The motivation survey was administered to the students as a whole group. Before each administration, the students were prompted, "This is a survey about reading. Each question will tell you the way some people feel about reading. Under each question are five statements: a lot like me, a little like me, not sure, a little different from me, and very different from me. Fill in the bubble that shows how you feel about the question. Stop and think about each question before you answer. You will have as much time as you need to finish all the questions. This is not a test and does not count toward your grade. Please take each question seriously and answer it as honestly as you can." At the completion of the administration, surveys were collected and scored by the researcher. (Nixon, 2004)

In the posttest phase, describe any procedures that were implemented after the intervention. This includes any measurement instruments that were administered as a posttest or post-intervention actions such as a follow-up meeting with the participants. These procedures can be similar to the pretest phase, although sometimes researchers may implement additional measures that were not given during the pretest phase.

Here is an example of the description of the posttest phase:

Each of the measurement instruments was administered two weeks after the completion of the intervention. On the reading comprehension measures, students were asked to independently read a different story than the one used on the pretest but at the same reading level (see Appendix C). Posttest administration procedures for all these measurements were the same as those used for the pretest. (Nixon, 2004)

In a single subject design study, you would describe the procedures during the baseline and intervention phases. This includes the frequency and duration of the sessions of the intervention and any measurement instruments that were administered.

Here is an example of a description from the single-subject design study:

To introduce the two classes to each other at the first baseline session, the teachers and researcher again facilitated a short discussion about how everyone was both alike and different. Then the students were told who was in their reading buddy group, and instructed to find their buddies, choose a book and go to their assigned place (e.g., small table, floor, desk area) to read. Students were not given any directions about how to interact with each other. Classroom teachers and staff intervened only if students needed to be redirected for inappropriate behavior. Groups read with each other for 15 minutes over four baseline sessions.

The intervention one phase occurred over six sessions. During the first intervention session, the researcher and teachers taught all of the students the three steps of the Reading Buddies intervention using a picture chart, modeling, role-play, and discussion. Individual students were called upon to explain the steps of the intervention to other students, and to roleplay what it meant to be a good reading buddy. Students were shown how to use the happy face card to let their peers know they were doing a good job, and were reminded that they could earn a sticker for their own appropriate participation. Students then chose any desired book and read with the other members of their buddy group for 15 minutes, following a semi-structured format of 5 minutes for each book. Each subsequent session of the intervention phase began with a review of the three steps by the teachers and researcher using modeling, role-play and discussion. Students were also reminded to use the reinforcement system (e.g., "Remember to tell your buddy when they are doing a good job."). (Adapted from Simpson and Bui, 2016)

Data Analysis

The eighth section is the *Data Analysis*. In this section, describe the procedures that were used to analyze the data from the study. The methods used to analyze the data depend on the research design, research questions, measurement instruments, and the type of data that were collected. Just as there are numerous ways to collect data, there are also many different ways to analyze data. One suggestion that I give students is to analyze the data so that they can answer the research questions! For example, if one of the research questions asks whether the participants changed their behavior before and after the study, then one of the procedures for data analysis needs to be a comparison of the pre- and post-data. If the research question asks about the participants' understanding of a situation, then the data analysis should involve descriptions from interviews or observations.

In qualitative studies where the data are mostly narrative, data analysis typically involves a categorizing strategy through coding (Maxwell, 2013). Coding allows you to label and group the data into meaningful chunks. "Coding categories are a means of sorting the descriptive data you have collected . . . so that the material bearing on a given topic can be physically separated from other data" (Bogdan & Biklen, 2003, p. 161). This is necessary to interpret the data and draw out the major themes. A simple analogy would be sorting a pile of clothing to launder by color (lights or darks) or by temperature (hot or cold water). Throughout the data analysis process, qualitative researchers also write memos to themselves, keep reflective journals, and audio record their thoughts on an ongoing basis. I discuss this in more detail in Chapter 8.

Here is an example of data analysis adapted from a former student's master's thesis:

> The collected data were transcribed and categorized in terms of research questions and emergent themes. Specific interview questions were matched to answer the five research questions. A coding method was used to organize interview data into a limited number of themes and issues around these questions. Quotations were then selected from the interviews that illuminated the themes and concepts. Specific survey questions were also matched to specific research study questions. Data from the survey were also compared with the data from the interview to see if they were in corroboration. (Stephens, 2006)

In quantitative studies where the data are numerical, data analysis typically involves either descriptive or inferential statistics. This includes identifying the indices that will be used to describe the data (e.g., mean, standard deviation) or any statistical tests (e.g., t test). In single subject design studies, the data can be analyzed by visually inspecting the graphed data. I discuss quantitative data analysis in more detail in Chapter 8.

Here is an example of quantitative data analysis:

> Two methods of quantitative data analysis were used in this study. The results of the reading comprehension tests were analyzed using descriptive statistics and inferential statistics. The participants' reading comprehension tests were divided into two subgroups for data analysis purposes: Group 1 was the students' mean test score after having read a graphic novel with illustrations, and Group 2 was the students' mean test score after having read a text-version of the stories. Statistical analysis using

Statistical Package for the Social Sciences (SPSS) software was conducted on these two subgroups to identify the range, mean, and standard deviation for each group. An independent samples *t* test was then conducted to compare the mean scores and to identify if there was a significant difference between the two subgroups' mean scores.

The results from the reading motivation survey were analyzed descriptively. The use of zoomerang.com enabled the researcher to immediately view compiled results from the reading motivation survey. The results were reported in three ways: actual number of respondents, the percentages, and as bar graphs. The results were reviewed item-by-item by the researcher. The results could not be looked at by individual participants since zoomerang.com compiled all the responses together as a group. Therefore, the researcher had to analyze the results by looking at the total number of responses to each individual question on the presurvey and comparing them to the total number of responses to each individual question on the postsurvey. (Gomes, 2008)

Here is an example of single-subject data analysis:

Single-subject data analysis was used to compare the students' initiations and responses across baseline and intervention phases, including visual inspection of the data for nonoverlapping data points and a comparison of means across conditions. (Adapted from Simpson & Bui, 2016)

Here is an example of mixed methods data analysis:

In this study, the quantitative and qualitative data were analyzed separately and then merged into one database for discussion purposes. Correlation analyses (Pearson's *r*) were used to determine the relationship between the students' psychological and physical health (as measured by scores on the Beck Youth Inventory and the Child Health Questionnaire). A correlation analyses was conducted for the entire sample group and also for separate gender groups. A qualitative content analysis was conducted on the transcribed interview data to explore how the students' perceptions of their cyberbullying experiences had impacted their psychological and physical health. Finally, the quantitative and qualitative data were integrated to determine if there were any common themes and provide possible explanations for differences across the two gender groups. (Adapted from Way et al., 1994)

Although you are reporting the results in Chapter Four, it is important to describe the data analysis procedures in enough detail in Chapter Three so that the reported results will be meaningful. This means ensuring that for every data set collected, there is a description of how the data were analyzed. Many students struggle with this section because of their lack of familiarity with statistics or qualitative data analysis. If this is the case, your chairperson and committee members may offer recommendations; referring to a research methods textbook can also be extremely helpful. There are some textbooks listed in the *Resources*.

SUMMARY

Chapter Three is a critical chapter in the thesis because it explains the research design and research methods that were used in conducting your study. Chapter Three is also one of the more enjoyable chapters to write because you are telling the story of how you conducted your research. However, the essential aspect of writing this chapter is to be as detailed and comprehensive in your descriptions as possible. In doing so, you build credibility for your study by giving the reader the opportunity to verify, interpret, or replicate the study. In addition, you lay the groundwork for the focus of the next two chapters in which you will report and interpret your findings. In the next chapter, I discuss how to write Chapter Four, Results, for your thesis. Here is a summary of the most critical points from Chapter 7:

- Three broad categories of research designs are quantitative, qualitative, and mixed methods.

- Quantitative research designs include descriptive, survey, correlational, and experimental designs (including quasi-experimental and single-subject).

- Qualitative research designs include narrative, case study, ethnography, grounded theory, and phenomenology.

- Mixed methods research designs include three core designs: convergent, explanatory sequential, and exploratory sequential.

- The Methods chapter describes and explains the research design and research methods such as the setting, participants, measurement instruments, procedures, and data analysis that were used to complete the study.

- The Methods chapter needs to be written with sufficient detail to provide a context for the results and for replicability purposes.

- While conducting the study, keep a log or journal of the dates and times that you collected data, materials or lessons that were used, individuals that you met with, and any problems, surprises, or changes that occurred throughout the study

- The main sections are (a) Introduction, (b) Setting, (c) Participants, (d) Intervention, (e) Materials, (f) Measurement Instruments, (g) Procedure, and (h) Data Analysis.

- You can have a random or nonrandom sample depending on the research design, questions, and accessibility of participants.

- In writing about the intervention, you should describe the independent and dependent variables.

- There are at least three kinds of measurement instruments that can be used to collect data: (a) existing instrument available for public use, (b), data that are normally collected, and (c) researcher-made instrument.

- Examples of measurement instruments include: questionnaire/scale, behavioral checklist, interview, focus group, observation protocol, public documents or records, tests, survey, interest inventory, and so on.

- The measurement instruments should be valid and reliable.

- Data collection/procedures include how the measurement instruments were administered, details of implementation for any intervention (e.g., length of treatment, time of day), and difference of conditions in treatment groups (if any).

- One way to analyze data is to organize the analysis around the research questions.

RESOURCES

Common Obstacles and Practical Solutions

1. A common obstacle that students face in writing Chapter Three is failing to keep adequate records about their study. Words that come to mind are "I can't remember everything I did!" Since it is very likely that you will need to go back to update and revise Chapter Three after the research has been conducted, it is important to keep track of all the research activities. When conducting the study, keep a log or journal of the research activities throughout the study. There is

no set structure or format for the log, but you should write down information about the actual procedures that you used (especially details that you might forget about later). For example, write down the dates and times that you collected data, materials or lessons that were used, individuals with whom you met, and any problems, surprises, or changes that occurred. This will help ensure that you are implementing the research design and methods as you described in Chapter Three. Put dates and times on all field notes, observations, and transcripts. This will make the process of data analysis and writing Chapter Three more efficient and less frustrating. In addition to keeping a log, make sure to collect detailed information about the research site and the participants (e.g., demographic data). This will keep you from having to go back to the research site to retrieve this information. Remember to keep all collected data in labeled folders and in a safe place away from the research site (e.g., locked file cabinet in your home). You have confidential and personal information related to your participants, so you need to protect the data as much as possible. Finally, keep *printed* copies of any instructional materials, lessons, measurement instruments, audiovisual materials, field notes, and transcripts since you will need to refer back to them. In other words, do not throw any data away, ever, and always BACK UP YOUR WORK. In this day and age where computers are prone to viruses and hard drives crash on a whim, you do not want your master's thesis to be the victim of a "fatal system error" (also known as the "Blue Screen of Death").

2. Another common obstacle faced by students is data overload. Often students will enjoy the data collection process (especially when interacting with participants), but when the study is over, they end up with piles and piles of data. Words that come to mind are "What am I going to do with all these data?" When conducting research, more data are not always better. What is most important is that you collect enough accurate data to answer the research questions. In fact, having an overabundance of data may diffuse your research, especially when the data are not related to the research problem or questions. One way to reduce this problem is to align the measurement instruments with the research questions from the very beginning. For example, if you are using an interview protocol, try to identify which items for the interview will help you answer specific research questions (of course, you will always have initial buffer questions to build rapport that may not be related to the research questions). If you are using tests or surveys, make sure the items capture the essence of what is being asked in the research question.

Reflection/Discussion Questions

Before you conduct your study, it is important to identify the measurement instruments for data collection. Then, to write Chapter Three, you need to be able to "report" how the data were collected for replicability purposes. The following reflection/discussion questions will help guide you through these two processes.

1. What are the different kinds of measurement instruments that can be used to collect data? Give examples of measurement instruments that would be appropriate for your type of research design. Then pick a specific measurement instrument and discuss how you could use it in your study to collect data and how to make it valid and reliable.

2. Why is replicability important in research? Give examples of what information is critical to include in Chapter Three so that another researcher could replicate your study.

Try It Exercises

The following exercises are designed to help you write Chapter Three. In Activity One, you will outline the major sections of Chapter Three and begin to flesh out the components. In Activity Two, you will develop or find a measurement instrument that you could use for data collection.

1. Activity One: For this activity, focus on your research proposal.
   - Based on your research design, create an outline of the major sections that you will include in Chapter Three (e.g., setting, sample).
   - For each section, write at least three bullet points (they do not have to be complete sentences) about what you will include in the section (or information that you need to retrieve). For example, what is your sampling plan? Who will be the participants in your study? What measurement instruments will you use? How will you collect data?

2. Activity Two: For this activity, focus on one measurement instrument that you will use to collect data.
   - Find an existing measurement instrument or modify one that you will use to collect data for your study.
   - If you want to use a survey, develop or find a self-administered instrument that you can give or send to a group of people to measure attitudes, perceptions, behavior, and so on.
   - If you want to conduct an interview, create a list of questions to ask the research participant.

- If you want to do structured observations, create an observation checklist that you would use to observe, assess, tally, or otherwise document an event in a natural setting (e.g., behavior).

- If you want to use a cognitive test, create or find a written test that you would use to assess knowledge or skills in a subject area related to your research problem.

- Discuss the issues related to the measurement instrument's validity and reliability with your chairperson.

Key Terms

convenience sample 145
generalizability 146
interrater reliability 154
purposive sample 145
random assignment 145

random sample 145
reliability 153
replicability 139
sampling 145
validity 153

Suggested Readings

Babbie, E. (2016). *The practice of social research* (14th ed.). Belmont, CA: Thomson Wadsworth.

Creswell, J. W. (2013). *Qualitative inquiry and research design* (3rd ed.). Thousand Oaks, CA: Sage.

Creswell, J. W. (2015). *Educational research: Planning, conducting, and evaluating quantitative and qualitative research* (5th ed.). Boston, MA: Pearson Education.

Creswell, J. W., & Creswell, J. D. (2018). *Research design: Qualitative, quantitative, and mixed methods approaches* (5th ed.). Thousand Oaks, CA: Sage.

Creswell, J. W., & Plano Clark, V. L. (2018). *Designing and conducting mixed methods research* (3rd ed.). Thousand Oaks, CA: Sage.

Decuir-Gunby, J. T., & Schutz, P. A. (2017). *Developing a mixed methods proposal: A practical guide for beginning researchers*. Thousand Oaks, CA: Sage.

Maxwell, J. A. (2013). *Qualitative research design: An interactive approach* (3rd ed.). Thousand Oaks, CA: Sage.

Plano Clark, V. L., & Creswell, J. W. (2008). *The mixed methods reader*. Thousand Oaks, CA: Sage.

Simpson, L. A., & Bui, Y. N. (2016). Effects of a peer-mediated intervention on social interactions of students with low-functioning autism and perceptions of typical peers. *Education and Training in Autism and Developmental Disabilities, 51*(2), 162–178.

Web Links

Basic Business Research Methods
https://managementhelp.org/businessresearch/index.htm

Organization Your Social Sciences Research Paper (University of Southern California Research Guide)
http://libguides.usc.edu/writingguide

SAGE Research Methods
http://methods.sagepub.com/

Web Center for Social Research Methods
http://www.socialresearchmethods.net

CHAPTER 6

How to Write Chapter Four, Results and Findings

*However beautiful the strategy, you should
occasionally look at the results.*

—Sir Winston Churchill

I f you have completed Chapter Three and are ready to write Chapter Four, this means that you have finished collecting all your research data— bravo! You are more than halfway finished with the thesis, so keep the momentum going (and the coffee brewing). This chapter will focus on how to write Chapter Four, Results and Findings, of the thesis. In Chapter Four, you will report the study's results (for quantitative studies) or findings (for qualitative studies) or a combination of both (for mixed methods); in doing so, you will apply what you have learned from your data collection and analysis. In essence, this is the meat of your thesis. After all the blood, sweat, tears, eye strain, and hair pulling, what did you find out?

Chapter Four, Results, is an essential component of the master's thesis because you will report the outcomes of the study. This means reporting the results of the data analysis for each variable, data collection method, or measurement instrument that was used in the study (always keeping in mind the research questions). Therefore, you should have already consulted with your chairperson for the data analysis methodology. On occasion, you may need to make adjustments to the analysis or do additional analysis due to participants dropping out, and so on, before reporting the results. Depending on the research design and questions, the presentation of the results can be in narrative, numerical, tabular/graphic format, or a mixture of them all. For example, if you collected quantitative (i.e., numerical) data, the results will be reported in statistical or tabular/graphic format. These results are reported in a straightforward manner, the writing style is technical, and they can be monotonous. If you collected qualitative (i.e., nonnumerical) data, the findings will be reported in narrative and sometimes tabular and/or graphic format. You will provide thick descriptions of the data to paint a narrative "picture" for the reader. Chapter Four needs to be written with sufficient detail for replicability purposes in case someone wants to verify the results. In addition, how you report and organize the results here will determine how you interpret and discuss them in Chapter Five.

Preparation and Organization

There are several tasks that need to be completed before you begin to write. First, Chapter Four will be organized parallel to Chapter Three. Thus, I highly recommend that you make any final revisions to Chapter Three before writing Chapter Four. Second, make sure that all the data have been organized and analyzed according to the research questions. This will make the writing process go much faster. Typically, I advise students to analyze data collected from every measurement instrument (e.g., survey, test, interview, observation) to ensure nothing is overlooked. Depending on the data collected, this can involve simple scoring procedures and applying statistical tests or coding data and finding emerging themes. Third, if you are still struggling with data analysis, seek help from your chairperson. She can show you the best way to analyze the data or refer you to someone else. Your program or institution may also offer help with data analysis using a statistical software program for quantitative data (e.g., SPSS, SAS, R) or software computer programs to help code and analyze qualitative data (e.g., NVivo, Altas.ti, QDA Miner Lite). There are often free trial periods and tutorials available; definitely check with your library first before you purchase anything.

Chapter Four Sections

Once you have analyzed all the data, you can start to write Chapter Four. Chapter Four starts on a new page in the thesis. Remember that writing a master's thesis is like telling the "story" of your research study. In Chapter Four, you are telling the main events (in this case, main findings) of the research study. However, unlike the first three chapters, there are no predetermined sections except for a brief introduction. This is because the sections in Chapter Four are dependent on the research design, research questions, and the specific data that were collected. These will vary from study to study. Although there are no predetermined sections, there are common organizational strategies that are used to report the results. Keep in mind that although the sections are written and discussed separately, they are intertwined, and collectively they form the results or findings of the study. Check with your chairperson for how he or she wants you to organize the sections in Chapter Four.

To guide you in writing Chapter Four, I discuss how to report results for quantitative and qualitative data separately. The rationale for discussing them separately is that the data analysis and reporting procedures are very distinct. However, for mixed methods studies, your data analysis and reporting may actually be integrated together. I also provide examples from different types of studies adapted from former students' completed master's theses. You will notice that the examples are written in the past tense to indicate that the data have already been collected and analyzed.

Quantitative Data

If you collected quantitative data, I recommend that you organize Chapter Four by reporting the results from each research question or measurement instrument into separate sections. For example, if you had three research questions that used three measurement instruments, such as a test, survey, and an observation checklist, you would report the results in three separate sections with a subheading for each. You also want to report the results in the same order that the research question or measurement instruments appeared in Chapter Three. Remember to use the three parallel ladders strategy from Chapter 7 (see Figure 8.1 for a depiction of the three parallel

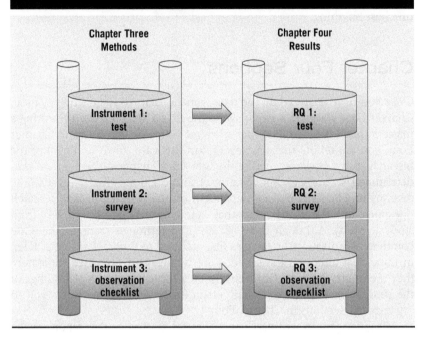

Figure 8.1   The three parallel ladders strategy for Chapters Three and Four.

Chapter Three
Methods

Chapter Four
Results

Instrument 1:
test

RQ 1:
test

Instrument 2:
survey

RQ 2:
survey

Instrument 3:
observation
checklist

RQ 3:
observation
checklist

ladders strategy for Chapters Three and Four). This will make it easier for you to write and less confusing for the reader.

When faced with a quantitative data set, researchers need a way to organize the data and display the results to others. Otherwise, the process of reporting the raw data would be overwhelming. There are two main ways to analyze and report quantitative data collected from a sample group—using descriptive or inferential statistics. The type of data collected and the research questions will determine how you should analyze and report the data from each measurement instrument. For example, if the data were collected from a survey, you would likely report the data using descriptive statistics. If the data were collected from an experimental study, you would likely report the data using descriptive and inferential statistics. As part of your master's program, I assume that you have already taken a research methods course with an introduction to statistics. Now is a good time to review those class notes! This discussion is a review to focus on the statistical procedures that are commonly used in a master's thesis. I discuss each type of statistical analysis and reporting separately and share some examples from students' completed theses.

Descriptive Statistics

Descriptive statistics refers to "a set of concepts and methods used in organizing, summarizing, tabulating, depicting, and describing collections of data" (Shavelson, 1996, p. 8). As the definition implies, researchers use this type of statistical analysis to *describe* the data set that was collected from the sample. Think of descriptive statistics as describing a picture of the quantitative results in a way that is comprehensible and meaningful for the reader.

Measures of Central Tendency

One major type of descriptive statistics is the measure of central tendency. The **measure of central tendency** is the "typical" or "average" score in a distribution. This is important because when you are looking at a large set of scores, there is too much information to digest. Knowing the typical or average score gives you a general sense of how the sample group fared. Usually, when someone says "average," I tend to think of the arithmetic mean. The mean is one type of measure of central tendency. The mode and the median are also measures of central tendency.

To help clarify and apply these concepts, I use a basketball example (I'm sure football would work, too). I select my favorite team, the Golden State Warriors, and my all-time favorite point guard, Stephen Curry (when it is your turn, you can pick your own team and player). From the 2009–2010 season through the 2017–2018 season (and hopefully for 10 more years), Curry was the starting point guard for the Warriors. Knowing his total career points gives an overall picture of him as a Hall of Fame point guard, but they do not show the pattern or trends of his nine seasons with the Warriors. It also doesn't show his wizardry as a three-point shooter. Using Curry's basketball statistics (rounded to the nearest whole number) on the chart as a sample group, I apply some basic descriptive statistical measures, explain how to calculate them, and discuss what these measures tell us about the data set.

Season	Games Played	Total Points per Game	3-Point Field Goals per Game
2009–2010	80	18	5
2010–2011	74	19	5
2011–2012	26 (injury)	15	5
2012–2013	78	23	8
2013–2014	78	24	8

(Continued)

Season	Games Played	Total Points per Game	3-Point Field Goals per Game
2014–2015	80	24	8
2015–2016	79	30 (Wow!)	11 (Yowsers!)
2016–2017	79	25	10
2017–2018	51 (injury)	26	10

The first measure of central tendency I address is the mode. The **mode** is the most common or most frequently occurring score in the distribution. To obtain the mode, simply go through the column and see which number appeared most frequently. For example, if I look at the total points per game from 2009 to 2018, 24 is the mode because it appeared two times, whereas all the other numbers appeared only once. Keep in mind that you can have more than one mode (bimodal), and the mode is not always the largest value.

Another measure of central tendency is the median. The **median** is the middle score in the distribution or the score that divides the distribution in half (50% above and 50% below). To obtain the median, I put the scores in order of magnitude from least to greatest. If there is an even number of scores, the median is the score value in the middle of the group. If there is an odd number of scores, the median is the score value halfway between the two middle scores. For example, to find the median number of Curry's 3-point field goals per game, I first need to put the numbers in order from least to greatest:

$$5 \quad 5 \quad 5 \quad 8 \quad 8 \quad 8 \quad 10 \quad 10 \quad 11$$

Since there is an odd number of scores, I can simply find the number in the middle, which is 8. This means that 50% of the numbers of 3-point shots are above and below 8. If there was an even number of scores, I would use the "magic finger trick," where I point two fingers at the outer ends and go in toward the center. Then I would find the value that is halfway by adding the two middle numbers and dividing by two.

Finally, the most commonly used measure of central tendency is the mean. The **mean** is the arithmetic average and calculated by the sum of the scores divided by the number of scores in the distribution. For example, to find the mean number of games that Curry played, I add up all the games and then divide the sum by the number of seasons.

$$(80 + 74 + 26 + 78 + 78 + 80 + 79 + 79 + 51)/9 = 69.4$$

This tells me that throughout his career with the Golden State Warriors, Stephen Curry had a mean of 69.4 games played per season. Now that you know how to calculate measures of central tendency to confirm what a spectacular basketball player guard Curry is, how would you apply them to data from your master's thesis? Basically, when you have a set of scores, you should report a measure of central tendency as part of your results to inform the reader about the average score. The scores can be for any variable (e.g., height, weight, achievement level, self-esteem, heart rates) and from a variety of sources such as tests, surveys, observation checklists, and so on. Typically, for the master's thesis, I recommend that students report the mean score because it is the most commonly used and takes into account every score in the data set. However, the mode and the median can also be appropriate (depending on the type of data that were collected) if the distribution is positively or negatively skewed.

Measures of Variability

Knowing the measure of central tendency is important, but it does not give enough information about the data. For example, calculate the mean for each of the two groups of students' math test scores below.

Group A: 5   8   7   10   5

Group B: 8   1   5   14   7

The mean score for each group is 7. Based on this information, I could assume that the two groups of students did similarly well on the math test since they have the same mean score. Now, put the scores in order of magnitude:

Group A: 5   5   7   8   10

Group B: 1   5   7   8   14

If the maximum test score is 15, notice how the scores in Group A are closer together while the scores in Group B are more spread apart. There is not a huge difference in performance between the students in Group A, and they cluster closer to the mean; however, for Group B, there was one student who received a score of 1 and one student who received almost a perfect test score. These scores are farther from the mean. With this information, I can see that the two groups are not very similar even though they have the same mean. Thus, knowing only the measure of central tendency (e.g., mean) is only part of the picture and can be misleading.

If you are describing a set of scores, you also need to report the measure of variability. A **measure of variability** indicates how close or spread apart (i.e., dispersed) the scores are in a distribution. In other words, how much do the scores differ from themselves and/or the mean of the distribution? If they differ quite a bit (scores are scattered), then there is a lot of variability. If they are pretty similar (scores are clustered), then there is less variability. There are many different kinds of measures of variability, but for the purpose of the thesis, I discuss only the range and standard deviation since they are the most relevant.

The range is one measure of variability that you are probably already familiar with. The **range** is the difference between the largest and smallest scores in a distribution. You can calculate the range by subtracting the smallest score from the largest score. For Group A, the range is $10 - 5 = 5$. What is the range for Group B? That's right. The range for Group B is $14 - 1 = 13$. In comparing the two groups, Group B has a larger range, and the scores are more spread apart than Group A's scores. However, the range is of limited use because it only looks at two scores, the largest and smallest scores, and does not take into consideration the other scores in the distribution.

A more commonly used measure of variability is the elusive standard deviation. The **standard deviation** indicates how much the scores vary from the mean in a distribution. The formula for the standard deviation is the square root of the variance, which is the average squared deviation of each number from its mean. Huh? Don't worry—it is not critical for you to calculate the standard deviation by hand because most computer programs or calculators will do it for you (although I think you would enjoy it). However, it is important to understand what it means in interpreting the results. Basically, if the standard deviation is small, then the scores are closer to the mean. If the standard deviation is large, then the scores are more spread apart from the mean. For example, look at the two normal distributions on the graph in Figure 8.2. They both have a mean of 50, but Distribution A is tall and skinny with a standard deviation of 5 whereas Distribution B is short and wide with a standard deviation of 10. This means that the scores in the Distribution A are closer to the mean, and the scores in the Distribution B are more spread apart from the mean. If I had graphed the two earlier datasets of Groups A and B, it would be a similar picture with Group A as Distribution A and Group B as Distribution B.

Since the standard deviation is in relation to the mean, it is critical to report them together (you should also include the sample size). Within APA format, this can be done in several ways (Kahn, n.d.). If you want to use abbreviations, they would be italicized, within parentheses, or at the end of the sentence. Here are the appropriate abbreviations to use: mean = M and standard deviation = SD. For example, "The 10 students in Group A had a higher mean score at the end of the intervention, $M = 18$, $SD = 2.3$."

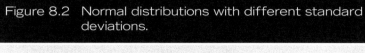

Figure 8.2 Normal distributions with different standard deviations.

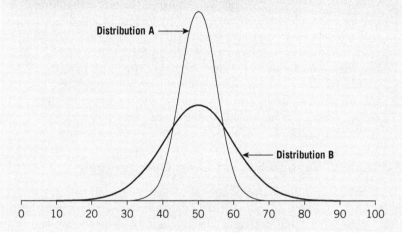

If there are two groups, then you can write, "The 10 students in Group A had a higher mean score (M = 18, SD = 2.3) than the 10 students in Group B (M = 14, SD = 1.7)." You can also write statistics spelled out as the subject of a sentence. For example, "The mean score on the math test for the 10 students in Group A was 18, and the standard deviation was 2.3." No matter which format you choose, remember to always report the sample size, mean score, and the standard deviation whenever possible.

Here is an example of results using descriptive statistics adapted from a former student's master's thesis:

The two measurement tools for social skill levels assessed students on their ability to perform 23 social skill tasks. These tasks ranged from making eye contact when speaking to someone to asking appropriately for help from an adult when needed. The first measurement tool was the teacher ranking survey in which the students' two teachers ranked the students individually on how well they were able to perform on each of the 23 social skill tasks. The only score generated from this survey was a total score. The range of scores for the teacher ranking survey was 36 (minimum 33, maximum 69). The mean total score of the teacher ranking survey was 52.29 points with a standard deviation of 10.13.

The second measurement tool for social skill levels was the student self-rating questionnaire. Similar to the teacher ranking survey, the student self-rating questionnaire also assessed how well students could perform social skill tasks. However, the student self-rating questionnaire relied on the 14 students to rate their own ability to perform the tasks. The range of scores for the student self-rating questionnaire was 50 (minimum 64, maximum 114). The mean total score of the student self-rating questionnaire was 88.50 with a standard deviation of 13.24. (Henderson, 2007)

Additional Ways to Report Data Descriptively

In addition to measures of central tendency and variability, there are other ways to report quantitative data descriptively. This depends on the research questions and design as well as the intended message you want to convey to the reader. For example, you could report individual scores, percentages, frequency counts, and so on. I recommend that you include tables, charts, and figures as a graphical representation of the results to supplement the narrative explanation (see Chapter 10 for APA style).

If you have a study in which the sample group has only one participant, you would report the individual's scores. Here is an example of results for one participant adapted from a former student's master's thesis:

Throughout the fluency intervention, Amber steadily increased the number of correct words per minute (CWPM) from baseline to phase III. During the baseline phase, Amber read 55, 60, 65, 63, and 58 CWPM, respectively ($M = 60$) (see Figure 1). During phase I, Repeated Reading, she read 64, 84, 73, 89, 89, and 84 CWPM, respectively ($M = 81$) (see Figure 2). During phase II, Error Correction, she read 85, 82, 74, 85, 78, 84, and 83 CWPM, respectively ($M = 82$) (see Figure 3). During phase III, Corrective Feedback, she read 76, 82, 83, 90, 87, 88, and 85 CWPM, respectively ($M = 84$) (see Figure 4). As indicated by the CWPM, Amber's mean reading rate greatly increased when she began Repeated Reading and increased slightly with the introduction of Error Correction and Corrective Feedback. (Irey, 2008)

If you utilized a survey as a measurement instrument, you could report the frequency of responses in percentages across participants or for specific items. Here is an example of survey results adapted from a former student's master's thesis. In this study, the student administered the survey before and after the intervention. Therefore, she also reported the change in responses from her participants.

> The first survey item asked students about primary language instruction, "Being taught in Spanish at school makes me feel good about myself." On the preintervention survey, the mean was 4.09 (SD = 1.37). The frequency of the responses from the preintervention survey was: 9.1% chose "(4) A little like me," and 63.6% chose "(5) Totally like me." The postintervention survey results had a mean of 4.81 (SD = 0.40). The frequency of the responses from the postintervention survey included: 18.2% of the students chose "(4) A little like me," and 81.8% of the students chose "(5) Totally like me." The mean difference from pre- to postintervention survey was 0.72 and the response of "(5) Totally like me" increased by 18.2 percentage points. (Iniguez, 2007)

If you observed participants' behaviors across multiple phases, you could report the individual or group data for each phase separately. Here is an example of frequency counts from a behavior intervention study adapted from a former student's master's thesis. In this study, the student had a baseline, treatment, and withdrawal phase. Therefore, he was able to compare the behaviors among the different phases and report changes in behaviors.

> Each type of off-task behavior was observed and recorded for the treatment phase. This information was used to determine whether there was an increase or decrease in behaviors from the baseline phase after the introduction of the Student Choice treatment.
>
> Incidents of *cross-talking* were observed and recorded for the treatment phase. Data indicated that there was a decrease in the range, total, and mean of cross-talking incidents from the baseline phase to the treatment phase. The range was eight, which was a decrease from 15. The total was 90, which was a decrease of 54 incidents. The mean number of incidents was 15, which was a decrease of nine incidents.
>
> *Total number of off-task behaviors* was observed and recorded for the *independent work time* of the treatment phase. Data indicated a decrease in the range, total, and mean number of total off-task behaviors observed during independent work time between the baseline phase and the treatment phase. The

range of observed off-task behaviors during independent work time decreased from 21 in the baseline phase to seven in the treatment phase. The total number of incidents decreased from 204 to 117. The mean number of incidents decreased from 34 to 19.5. (Rau, 2006)

Descriptive statistics are very useful to summarize, simplify, and describe the data in a study. However, they are also limiting because you cannot make any conclusions beyond the present data. For that I need to journey into inferential statistics. This would be a good time for that coffee and donut break.

Inferential Statistics

Inferential statistics refers to "a set of methods to draw inferences about a large group of people from data available on only a representative subset of the group" (Shavelson, 1996, p. 8). In other words, researchers use sample group data to make assumptions or conclusions about the general population. This is very useful because most of the time researchers do not have access or the resources to collect data from the population. For example, consider how statistics are reported on presidential elections—how do they know that 46% will vote for Candidate A, 44% will vote for Candidate B, and 10% are undecided? Obviously, pollsters cannot ask every single person whom he will vote for in the next election. Instead, they ask a representative sample, apply statistical tests, and then make inferences about the rest of the country (remember, there is always a margin of error). Keep in mind that the sample must be representative (best done through random sampling); otherwise, the conclusions may be skewed toward one segment of the population or another. Basically, it is more realistic and efficient to collect data from a representative sample of the population to make inferences about the population rather than include the entire population in the study.

Tests of Significance

Inferential statistics are also used in experimental studies. In these studies, tests of significance are conducted to determine if observed mean differences between groups or conditions represent a real difference or are due to chance. There are many different kinds of tests of significance, but for the purposes of the master's thesis, you would most likely not be required to go beyond applying a *t* test. A *t* **test** is a statistical test that is used to determine whether the observed difference between *two* mean scores represents a true difference or is due to chance. There are two different types of *t* tests: (a) independent-samples *t* test, and (b) nonindependent-samples *t* test (also referred to as dependent-samples *t* test or paired-samples *t* test). I discuss each one separately.

Independent-Samples *t* Test

In a basic experimental study where one independent variable (cause) is manipulated to see its effect on one dependent variable (effect), the **independent-samples *t* test** is used to determine whether the difference in mean scores on the dependent variable between two independent groups is a real difference or one that is due to chance. In other words, is the mean score difference for the dependent variable due to the independent variable (treatment) or the result of some other chance factor such as sampling error? To use the independent-samples *t* test, the participants and their scores from the two groups must be completely independent and separate from each other.

For example, a researcher wants to determine if a math intervention (independent variable) will improve students' performance on the state-wide math assessment (dependent variable). If the new math intervention results in significantly higher scores on the statewide math assessment, she will make a recommendation to the state education board to adopt the new math curriculum, so there is a lot at stake. The researcher randomly assigns 60 students into two groups: Group A gets the new math curriculum, and Group B gets the traditional math curriculum. The students are exposed to the two treatments daily for 8 weeks. At the end of the 8 weeks, they all take the statewide assessment. The mean score on the statewide assessment for Group A was 90, and the mean score for Group B was 85. Since there is a five-point difference in favor of Group A, can the researcher make the recommendation to the state education board to adopt the new math curriculum? Not so fast. Unfortunately, researchers cannot simply eyeball the test scores and say, "Yes, five points seems like a big enough difference so let's adopt that new curriculum." You see, in statistics (and life in general), there is always room for error. Therefore, the researcher does not know whether the five-point difference represents a real difference (due to the new math treatment) or one that is due to chance. This is where the independent-samples *t* test comes in handy.

With this test, the researcher can determine the *probability* of whether the observed five-point mean difference between the two groups is statistically significant (i.e., represents a real difference). First, she needs to set up a null hypothesis (sorry, I was hoping to avoid this). The **null hypothesis**, H_0, represents the "chance" theory, meaning any observed differences are due to chance, and the treatment has no significant effect on the dependent variable. For example, the null hypothesis for the study would be as follows:

H_0: There is no significant difference on the statewide math assessment scores between students who received the new math curriculum and the students who received the traditional math curriculum.

She can either reject or retain the H_0; typically, researchers want to reject the H_0 to "support" their new intervention. However, retaining the H_0 may be as valuable to the research literature as rejecting it (you may have discovered what treatment is not effective!). Remember that as the researcher, you are committed to reporting the findings objectively and accurately whether or not the data support your hypothesis.

Next, to determine whether or not to reject or retain the H_0, the researcher needs to set the probability or significance level (referred to as alpha, or α). The setting of the probability level is a bit like gambling, where the researcher gets to decide how much risk of making an error she is willing to accept. In social science studies, most researchers set the significance level at .05 ($\alpha = .05$), which means they are willing to take a 5% chance of making a Type I error. A **Type I** error is when you reject the H_0 when it is true. In other words, there is a 5% probability that the researcher concludes that the mean difference was due to the treatment when it was really due to chance. The good news is that she has a 95% of being correct (rejecting the H_0 when it is false)! After setting the significance level, the researcher conducts the independent-samples t test and compares the probability value (p value) with the preset significance level. If the probability value is less than or equal to the significance level ($p \leq$ .05, then she can reject the H_0. By rejecting the H_0, she can conclude that the treatment *did* have a significant effect on the dependent variable. In other words, the mean score difference was statistically significant and not due to chance.

In the math example, this means that the five-point difference between the two groups was due to the treatment of the new math curriculum. The researcher could then make the recommendation to the state education board to adopt the new math curriculum. If the probability value is greater than the significance level ($p \geq$ .05), then she retains the H_0. By retaining the H_0, she concludes that the new math curriculum treatment did not have a significant effect on the statewide assessment scores, and the five-point mean difference was due to chance. The researcher should not recommend the new math curriculum to the state education board.

While it is not important for you to be able to conduct the independent-samples t test by hand (and this is not a statistics book), it is critical for you to understand its importance in determining cause-effect relationships in research studies and how to report these results. If you would like more information about the independent-samples t test or other significance tests, I highly recommend taking an introductory statistics course or perusing a statistics textbook.

There are several variations of how you can report the results of an independent-samples t test in APA format. Be sure to include the two mean scores with standard deviations, t value with degrees of freedom, and the probability value. You also have to report an effect size (usually in the form of Cohen's d), which represents the magnitude of the mean difference. If you have a small effect size, the two group's mean scores are not that different. If you have a large effect size, then the mean scores are very different from each other. Here is one example:

> To test the efficacy of the new math curriculum, an independent samples t test was conducted. This test was found to be statistically significant, $t(58) = 4.15$, $p < .001$, $d = .4$. The results indicated that on average, the students in the new math curriculum group ($M = 90$, $SD = 4.92$) performed better than the traditional math curriculum group ($M = 85$, $SD = 4.41$) on the statewide math assessment.

The independent-samples t test is the most common and simplest test to use when comparing mean differences between two independent groups. However, for a master's-level research study, it may be difficult to have access to a large sample with two separate and independent groups. More commonly, you may have access to only one group. For this type of research design, you need to utilize the nonindependent-samples t test. I refer to this as the paired-samples t test since this is what is used in the SPSS computer software program.

Paired-Samples t Test

In a basic experimental study where one independent variable (cause) is manipulated to see its effect on one dependent variable (effect), the **paired-samples t test** is used to determine whether the difference in mean scores on the dependent variable between *two sets of related scores* is a real difference or one that is due to chance. This analysis is similar to the independent-samples t test except that with the paired-samples t test, there is no control group, and the scores are systematically related to each other. There are different ways for scores to be related, but typically the two sets of scores are from one group of participants. For example, a researcher wants to determine if a new reading intervention that uses bilingual high school students' primary language will enhance their vocabulary performance in English. He randomly selects one class of 30 high school students who are bilingual. The students are given a pretest to measure their vocabulary level before the intervention begins. Then they receive the new reading intervention daily for 10 weeks. At the end of the 10 weeks, he administers the same test to measure their vocabulary level as a posttest. The pretest mean score on the vocabulary measure was 86 (SD = 3.86), and the posttest mean score on the vocabulary measure was 88 (SD = 3.04). Since the two sets of scores (pretest and posttest) are from the same set of students, they are in fact related.

In this scenario, the researcher needs to determine whether the two-point mean score difference between the pretest and posttest indicates a statistically significant difference (related to the vocabulary intervention) or one that is due to chance. The null hypothesis for the study would be as follows:

H_0: There is no significant difference between the bilingual high school students' pretest and posttest English vocabulary mean scores.

To determine whether to reject or retain the H_0, he must set the significance level (α = .05) and conduct a paired-samples t test. If the probability is equal to or less than α = .05 ($p \leq .05$), I can reject the H_0 and conclude that there is a significant difference between the pretest and posttest mean scores, and it was not due to chance. If the probability is greater than .05 ($p > .05$), then I retain the H_0 and conclude that there is not a significant difference.

To report this in APA format, be sure to include the two mean scores with standard deviations, t value with degrees of freedom, the probability value, and an effect size. Here is one example:

To test the efficacy of the vocabulary intervention for bilingual high school students, a paired samples t test was conducted. This test was found to be statistically significant, $t(29)$ = −3.846, p = .001, d = .5. The results indicated that on average, the bilingual high school students scored significantly greater on the posttest English vocabulary test (M = 88.23, SD = 3.03) than on the pretest vocabulary test (M = 86.07, SD = 3.86).

Here is an example of the results of a paired-samples t test adapted from a former student's master's thesis:

To analyze the results of the Arc's Self-Determination Scale (ASDS), first descriptive statistics were calculated for the pretest and posttest scores for each subgroup of the ASDS domains. The pretest mean scores and standard deviations for each subgroup of the ASDS domains were as follows: Autonomy (M = .51, SD = .20), Psychological Empowerment (M = .73, SD = .15), Self-Realization (M = .75, SD = .16), and Self-Determination Total (M = .57, SD = .15). The posttest means and standard deviations for each subgroup of the ASDS domains were as follows: Autonomy (M = .63, SD = .18), Psychological Empowerment (M = .88, SD = .10), Self-Realization (M = .81, SD = .18), and Self-Determination Total (M = .68, SD = .14). There were mean gains of .12 in Autonomy, .15 in Psychological Empowerment, .06 in Self-Realization, and .11 in the Self-Determination Total from pretest to posttest results.

Next, a paired-samples t test was conducted to determine if there was a significant difference between the pretest and posttest mean scores for each domain. There was a significant difference between the Psychological Empowerment pretest mean of .73 (SD = .15) and posttest mean of .88 (SD = .10), $t(10)$ = −3.16, p = .01, d = .3, in favor of the posttest. There were no significant differences between the pretest and posttest mean scores for the other domains or total score. (Williams, 2006)

In summary, the t tests for independent-samples and paired-samples are essential statistical tests to conduct when trying to determine whether the difference between two mean scores is statistically significant. They are easy to conduct using a statistical software program (or even by hand), and the output is straightforward for interpreting and reporting the results in APA format. In addition to the narrative explanation, it is also helpful to include tables or figures as part of the results. Now that I have discussed how to report the results of quantitative data, for you adventurous types, I trek into our discussion on how to report the findings from qualitative data.

Qualitative Data

There is often a misconception among graduate students that interpreting and reporting data from qualitative studies is easier or faster than quantitative studies since there are no scary statistics involved. However, this is typically not the case. At the end of a qualitative study, a researcher may be faced with piles of data in the form of field notes from observations, transcripts from interviews, documents, memos, audio or video files, and so on. Therefore, there needs to be a way to organize and analyze the raw data to answer the research questions and provide a deeper understanding of the phenomenon being studied that is meaningful to the reader. This process often includes countless hours to read, organize, and prepare field notes, transcribe data, code data, categorize data, and identify supporting data. As mentioned, there are many different types of qualitative research designs and ways to analyze and report the narrative data. For more detailed information on qualitative data analysis and reporting, I strongly recommend taking a course in qualitative research or examining textbooks on this topic. However, from my experience advising graduate students, the three most commonly used data collection methods are interviews, focus groups, and observations. Therefore, I focus my discussion on how to report these types of narrative data according to (a) major themes and patterns and (b) research questions. I also discuss how to enhance the validity of the findings.

Major Themes and Patterns

One of the common ways to report findings from narrative data is to organize them around the major themes and patterns. Where do these major themes and patterns come from? Unlike quantitative studies where the researcher has a preset hypothesis that he tests, in qualitative research, you do not start with preset themes and patterns. Instead, the major themes and patterns *emerge* during the data analysis process. For you chefs out there, think of this process as reducing sauces, where you are producing a thicker, more flavorful, and concentrated sauce. Let us use the example of a case study where a researcher wants to examine business managers' communication styles. She spends 6 weeks audio recording and taking field notes as a nonparticipant observing the communication interactions between managers and their employees during weekly 1-hour staff meetings. At the end of the data collection period, she is ready to start analyzing her data. Like a true chef, she must first prepare the ingredients! This requires organizing and transcribing all the field notes and audio recordings, which can be very time consuming, so allow yourself an appropriate amount of time. At this point you also need to decide whether to use a qualitative computer software program (e.g., Nvivo, Atlas.ti) to help analyze the data or do it manually by hand. Whatever you decide, make sure you have multiple back-up copies of your files!

In our example, the researcher decides to analyze her data by hand. She rereads all the transcribed data and codes the data by labeling different topics that seemed important. She puts a code for "interaction" every time there was a communicative interaction between the manager and the employee and noted it in her codebook with a number and definition. Next, she analyzed all the interaction codes to see how they were related across participants and meeting times. She categorized or grouped the similar interaction codes into larger meaningful chunks with a new label.

For example, perhaps there was a clear distinction in managers who used verbal versus nonverbal interactions or collaborative versus coercive interactions. These larger chunks indicate a potential theme or pattern in the findings. Thus, by coding and recoding the data, the research identified the major themes or patterns that emerged from the data. An average of five to six major themes is reasonable. However, be sure the major themes and patterns are related to the research questions and purpose of the study. Remember that it is critical to leave your desires, judgments, and expectations of what you want the data to look like outside of the analysis and reporting process. Although it is inevitable that some personal bias will slip through, you want to minimize this as much as possible.

After the major themes or patterns are identified, each one represents a separate heading and section in the results chapter. Then for each theme, it is critical to paint a picture of the findings for the reader by providing a rich and thick description. A **thick description** is an explanation that includes both the behavior and the context in which the behavior was displayed. The concept of thick description was originally derived from the writings of British philosopher Gilbert Ryle and anthropologist Clifford Geertz (Ponterotto & Grieger, 2007). Then sociologist Norman Denzin expanded the definition of thick description in his work:

> Thick description evokes emotionality and self-feelings. It inserts history into experience. It establishes the significance of an experience, or the sequence of events, for the person or persons in question. In thick description, the voices, feelings, actions, and meanings of interacting individuals are heard. (Denzin, 1989, p. 83, as cited in Ponterotto & Grieger, 2007)

As part of the thick description, key pieces of evidence from multiple sources that support the major theme should be included. One major piece of support is in the form of the participants' quotations. This brings the participants' perspective into the study (Creswell, 2013). Keep in mind that you do not want to include everything that was said; instead, quotations should be selected carefully to represent the major theme. This will require you to interpret or infer the participants' true meaning while trying to stay as unbiased as possible. The descriptions could also involve the setting and participants, and the use of visuals in the form of tables or figures should be used to supplement the narrative description.

Here is an example of findings reported around major themes adapted from a former student's master's thesis:

> The informal group discussion provided a wealth of knowledge to the researcher with regards to the elementary students'

perceptions around their disabilities. During the discussion, the researcher read from the preselected text. At the end of each subtopic, the following questions were addressed: Can you relate to anything in the passage or can you make a personal connection? The discussions were then left purposely unstructured to allow the students to speak freely and openly but with the guarantee of confidentiality. Four patterns of responses emerged from the discussion group: *feelings about learning, disappointing others, how learning disabilities make you feel*, and *types of learning problems*.

Feelings about learning. The students were asked if they could relate to the statement: For some kids, school is not fun because they have trouble succeeding, and they just do not feel good about learning. All six students were able to verbalize that they do not always feel good about learning. Some students gave concrete examples such as Cesar saying, "I don't feel good when I can't do my work in class."

Disappointing others. The students were asked to make a personal connection to the provided statement: Some kids feel like they let down their loved ones. All six students stated that they could relate to disappointing their parents, teachers, or themselves. Cesar stated, "I disappoint my parents and teachers every day when I don't do my work and I act out in class." At first Jessica and Charlie were both reluctant to state that they disappointed anyone. Then Jessica said, "I know that my parents don't get mad when I do things wrong. But I know that I disappoint myself because there are things that I can't do. I try and try but I can't. Someone always tells me that I am wrong. This is why I sometimes don't want to come to school." Charlie stated that he knows he disappoints his teachers because, "I just don't get things, especially math. Even when things are explained over and over, I still have trouble."

How learning disabilities make you feel. This section provided a lot of opportunity for discussion. When the students heard the word "dumb" in the text, some students verbalized that they felt dumb at times. However, Jessica was also able to express that having a type of learning disability does not mean that you are dumb. She made the personal connection that her father also had a learning disability, and he too had difficulty in school.

Types of learning problems. In this section, the students had the opportunity to relate to the difficulties faced by students with learning disabilities. The text discussed difficulties such as memory, concentration, and the ability to make friends, and so on. Kenny, Cesar, and Jessica could all relate to the difficulty with concentration. In response to memory problems, Sam stated, "I just get so frustrated because I don't know my multiplication facts. I try and I try but I just don't know. I am never going to learn them so I just have to add." There were not many students who reported difficulty making friends or maintaining friendships, which appeared to be a sensitive topic. (Mireles, 2004)

Research Questions

Another way to organize the narrative findings is around the research questions. Here, the researcher is also reporting the major themes and patterns that emerge from the data. However, in this type of organizational format, the data collection methods (e.g., interview questions, observational strategies) should help you gain an understanding to answer the research question(s) (Maxwell, 2013). For example, a researcher wants to explore the leadership styles of school administrators at high-performing schools. The research questions are,

1. What are the leadership characteristics of administrators at high-performing schools?
2. How do these administrators overcome barriers to success?

She conducts 1-hour interviews with four administrators from high-performing schools. There are four main questions that she asks at each interview:

1. What is your leadership style?
2. What makes you an effective leader?
3. What are the barriers that you face as a school administrator?
4. How do you get faculty and staff to support your leadership style?

In this study, the four interview questions are designed to help answer the research questions; Interview Questions 1 and 2 help answer the first research question, and Interview Questions 3 and 4 help answer the second research question. These four questions are just a start; other questions or follow-up questions may be necessary as the interview proceeds. If possible, you should always pilot test your data collection methods with a similar sample group and setting to see if any revisions are necessary.

After conducting the interviews, the researcher must still follow a process for data analysis. First, she reads through and transcribes all the interview data. Next, she codes the data from the transcripts by labeling different topics. Then, she categorizes or groups the codes into larger meaningful chunks with a new label. However, the key difference with this organizational format is that she pulls out major themes only from Interview Questions 1 and 2 to answer the first research question. For example, perhaps there was a clear pattern that leaders believed collaboration was a key component of their effective leadership style. Then she pulls out major themes from Interview Questions 3 and 4 to answer the second research question. After the major themes are identified, then rich, thick descriptions with supporting evidence and quotations are reported.

Here is an example of findings reported around research questions adapted from a former student's master's thesis:

An analysis of the data yielded from the student and staff questionnaires revealed findings within the areas of the research questions. Student and staff participants' responses to the questionnaires were grouped to correspond to the research questions and then categorized for major themes or patterns.

Research question 1 asked what factors of communication (whether verbal or nonverbal) triggered negative behavioral outbursts or promoted positive and effective communication in classrooms serving students with emotional disturbances (ED) and learning disabilities (LD). The data revealed that the verbal factors of communication that triggered students' behavioral outbursts were yelling, especially once the student was already upset. Other factors included students feeling like they were not being understood or listened to, not getting help with their assignments, and negative peer interactions in the classroom. The nonverbal factors of communication that triggered students' negative behavioral outbursts were slamming books down and making angry faces.

The data revealed various verbal factors that promoted positive behavior and effective communication in classrooms serving students with ED and LD. Some of these factors were taking the time to discuss classroom issues with the students in a calm voice, giving the students some extra chances, the implementation of classroom reward systems, explaining the lessons thoroughly when needed, and positive peer interactions. The nonverbal factors that promoted positive behavior and effective communication were allowing the students space when their behaviors were escalating.

The questions on the students' questionnaires that corresponded to this research question were questions 1, 4, 7, 8, and 10.

Question 1 asked what the staff should or should not do to help when the students were having a particularly rough day. Most students responded that yelling would only escalate their behavior, and that the teachers should either speak to them about whatever the problem was in a calm voice or give them some extra chances. For example, one male Caucasian student in the 11th grade said, "They should tell me to cool down or give me a break outside. They shouldn't get on my back when I am mad." A few students felt the need to be left alone when they were having rough days. For example, one female African American student in the 12th grade said, "[If I am having a bad day] they shouldn't do anything because I will still get mad."

Question 4 asked for the reasons behind the students' best and worst behaviors. Most students attributed their best behavior to factors outside of the classroom such as having a good night sleep, a good breakfast, good weather, or positive experiences with friends prior to class. For example, one male Caucasian student in the 11th grade said, "I woke up on the right side of the bed and played with my brother. That made me happy." Other participants reported that on days when their behaviors were at their best, they were connected to factors inside the classroom such as classroom rewards, having lessons explained to them well, or positive student interactions. For example, one male African American student in the ninth grade said, "[The day my behavior was at its best] was the day I hit level 5."

With regard to negative behavior, a few students attributed the behavior to factors outside of the classroom such as showing up in a bad mood. Most attributed their negative behavior to factors inside the classroom such as the teacher yelling at them, not being understood or listened to, not getting help with assignments, or negative peer interactions. For example, one male Caucasian student in the 11th grade responded, "When my teacher always yells and gets in my face and I get mad and punch the walls." Another male Latino student in the 11th grade reported, "They don't even listen to me, and they act like I wasn't even there. That's why I had the worst behavior in Mrs. C.'s class because I don't get any help with my work." (Kendall, 2006)

Validity of Findings

Regardless of the format that is chosen to report findings, an important component of reporting qualitative data is to ensure their validity. Validity in this context is about the quality of the findings, which is different than the validity with regard to quantitative measures that was mentioned in Chapter 7. For qualitative studies, validity refers to the accuracy and credibility of the findings (Creswell & Creswell, 2018). In other words, are the findings plausible and trustworthy? You increase the validity of a qualitative study by applying strategies to reduce factors that threaten the credibility of your conclusions. For example, personal bias (subjectivity) is a validity threat because your own experiences, assumptions, goals, and beliefs will influence how you analyze, interpret, and present the data. There are many strategies available to increase validity, and you should apply those that are specific to the validity threats in your study. Some recommended strategies include being upfront and honest about your own personal biases, having extensive time and opportunities for data collection, checking back with participants for accuracy (i.e., member checking), and providing rich and thick descriptions (Creswell, 2013). A commonly used method to increase validity is triangulation. Triangulation is "the combination of methodologies in the study of the same phenomenon" (Denzin, 1978, p. 291, as cited by Onwuegbuzie, 2002). **Data triangulation** is one form of triangulation where multiple methods of data collection are used to study one phenomenon. The different methods act as a "check" on the others to support a single conclusion or provide new information from different angles (Maxwell, 2013). For example, a researcher could use multiple data collection methods such as observations, interviews, and written documents. The point is not to combine the data but rather to find the intersections, conflicts, or connections among them. In doing so, the researcher is able to confirm, dispute, or corroborate findings between data sources and have a holistic picture of the phenomenon.

Mixed Methods Data

For mixed methods research studies, the researcher collects both quantitative and qualitative data. Therefore the data analysis procedures will depend on the specific mixed methods research design and the research questions. For example, in some mixed methods designs, the quantitative and qualitative data analyzed separately because the data collection was done in different phases. There are also separate research questions for the quantitative and qualitative data. In the convergent design, the quantitative and qualitative data may be merged together for data analysis. The results are reported in a single joint display, which combines both quantitative and qualitative data. This integration allows for a richer understanding of the research problem and response to the research question than separate quantitative and qualitative results (Creswell & Plano Clark, 2018).

SUMMARY

Chapter Four is a significant chapter in the thesis because it reports the major results and findings of the study to the reader. Chapter Four may also be one of the most satisfying chapters to write because after all the months of data collection and data analysis, you finally get to share all that was discovered. Whether you are reporting quantitative, qualitative, or both types of data, it is critical to be as detailed and comprehensive in your descriptions as possible. This will enhance the validity, quality, generalizability, or transferability of the results. In this chapter, you are also laying the foundation for the final discussion and conclusions, which are the focus of Chapter Five, Discussion, of your thesis. This will be the topic of the next chapter of the book. Here is a summary of the most critical points from Chapter 8:

- Depending on the research questions and design, the presentation of the results can be in narrative, numerical, tabular and/or graphic format, or a joint display.

- Before reporting the results, make sure that all your data have been organized and analyzed.

- In descriptive statistics, measures of central tendency, such as the mean, median, and mode, tell you the "average" score in a distribution.

- Measures of variability, such as the range or standard deviation, tell you how close or spread apart (i.e., dispersed) the scores are in a distribution.

- Inferential statistics use sample group data to make assumptions about the general population.

- In experimental studies, tests of significance are used to determine if observed mean differences between groups or conditions represent a real difference or were due to chance.

- The null hypothesis, H_0, represents the "chance" theory, meaning any observed differences are due to chance, and the treatment has no significant effect on the dependent variable.

- One of the ways to report findings from narrative data is to organize them around the major themes and patterns that *emerge* during data analysis.

- Another way to organize the narrative findings is around the research questions where items from the data collection instruments help to answer the research question(s).

- There are several ways to increase the validity of a qualitative study, such as being upfront and honest about your own personal biases, having extensive time and opportunities for data collection, member checking, providing thick descriptions, and data triangulation.

RESOURCES

Common Obstacles and Practical Solutions

1. A common obstacle that students face in writing Chapter Four is being overwhelmed with the amount of results to report. Words that come to mind are "How do I make sense of all these data?" If you have quantitative data, the best way to overcome this obstacle is to report the results in chunks. First, look at the total data set. Then examine the data to see which method would make the most sense to report in terms of organization (usually by each measurement instrument or research question). Next, decide whether you should report the data with descriptive statistics, inferential statistics, or with visual representation such as figures and graphs. Definitely get help from your chairperson if you do not understand the results from the data analysis. Then report the results from one measurement instrument or research question, and have your chairperson review it before you go on to do the rest.

2. Another common obstacle faced by students is finding the major themes and patterns in the qualitative data. Although the major themes and patterns do emerge from the data, sometimes it is not obvious as to what they are. Words that come to mind are "How do I tie all these together?" After coding the data for specific topics, you need to step back and look at the data from a broader perspective. Sometimes, you have to recode the data into larger categories. Using multiple highlighting colors to code or physically cutting and grouping "like data" together may also help find the themes and patterns. You may also want to invest in a computer software program to help you with the data analysis. One thing to always keep in mind is the purpose of the study and the research questions. If you use these as your guiding principles, this will help make sure you do not get lost in all the trees.

Reflection/Discussion Questions

When you report your data in Chapter Four, it is important to understand the differences in how to organize the results (depending on the type of data collected) so that it is meaningful to the reader. This is also important for replicability purposes in case someone is interested in confirming or corroborating the results. The following reflection/discussion questions will help guide you through the reporting process.

1. Pick one quantitative measurement instrument that you used in data collection and discuss what type of statistics you would use to report the results. Will you analyze data using descriptive or inferential statistics? Which measures of central tendency and variability will you report? Does your study require an independent-samples t test, a paired-samples t test, or another statistical test?

2. Pick one qualitative measurement instrument that you used in data collection and discuss how you are going to analyze the narrative data. Are you going to select a software program and if so, which one? What is the definition of a "thick description"? Give examples of what information you could provide in the thick description to increase validity.

Try It Exercises

The following exercises are designed to help you write Chapter Four. In Activity One, you will calculate the descriptive statistics for a given data set. In Activity Two, you will identify the inferential statistics that will be used to report the data. In Activity Three, you will report the findings from one measurement instrument that you used to collect data.

1. Activity One: For this activity, use your knowledge of descriptive statistics.

   A researcher conducted a study on the effects of an online course to teach nursing students how to provide proper drug dosage calculations for their critical care patients. The students were randomly assigned into two groups: online course (Group A) or traditional course with instructor (Group B). The following data set represents their posttest scores on a drug dosage calculation test. With a partner, identify the descriptive statistics for each set of scores.

Group A:	3	4	4	9	1	15
Group B:	3	17	12	4	3	3

   - What are the mode scores for Groups A and B?
   - What are the median scores for Groups A and B?
   - What are the mean scores for Groups A and B?
   - What are the range scores for Groups A and B?
   - Which group do you think has a larger standard deviation?
   - Report the findings for each group in APA format.

2. Activity Two: For this activity, use your knowledge of inferential statistics.

   Now the researcher wants to know if there was a statistically significant mean difference between the two groups. With a partner, identify the inferential statistics using the scores from Activity One.

   - What test of significance should the researcher use to analyze the mean difference?
   - Write a null hypothesis for the research study.

- What should the researcher set the significance (alpha) level at, and what does this mean?
- If the *t* score is 4.52 and the probability value is .03, should the researcher reject or retain the null hypothesis?
- What is the researcher's final conclusion about the online course?
- Report the findings in APA format.

3. Activity Three: For this activity, focus on the data from one measurement instrument that was used during the study.
   - Pick one measurement instrument that you used to collect data such as a test, survey, interview questions, and so on.
   - Decide the best way to report the data. If you collected numerical data, decide whether to report descriptive or inferential statistics. If you collected nonnumerical data, decide whether you want to report the major themes/patterns from the entire data set or want to connect specific items to corresponding research questions.
   - Prepare a draft report of the results and have a partner or your chairperson review it before proceeding with the other data.

Key Terms

data triangulation 189
descriptive statistics 171
independent-samples *t* test 179
inferential statistics 178
mean 172
measure of central tendency 171
measure of variability 173
median 172

mode 172
null hypothesis 179
paired-samples *t* test 181
range 174
standard deviation 174
t test 178
thick description 184
Type I error 180

Suggested Readings

Ali, Z., & Bhaskar, S. B. (2016). Basic statistical tools in research and data analysis. *Indian Journal of Anaesthesia, 60*(9), 662–669. Retrieved from http://doi.org/10.4103/0019-5049.190623

Bazeley, P. (2011). Integrative analysis strategies for mixed data sources. *American Behavioral Scientist, 56*, 814–828. Retrieved from https://doi.org/10.1177/0002764211426330

Bazeley, P. (2013). *Qualitative data analysis: Practical strategies.* London, UK: Sage.

Creswell, J. W., & Plano Clark, V. L. (2018). *Designing and conducting mixed methods research* (3rd ed.). Thousand Oaks, CA: Sage.

Denzin, N. K., & Lincoln, Y. S. (2018). *The SAGE handbook of qualitative research* (5th ed.). Thousand Oaks, CA: Sage.

Guetterman, T. C., Fetters, M. D., & Creswell, J. W. (2015). Integrating quantitative and qualitative results in health science mixed methods research through joint displays. *Annals of Family Medicine, 13*(6), 554–561. doi:10.1370/afm.1865

Moseholm, E., Rydahl-Hansen, S., Lindhardt, B. O., & Fetters, M. D. (2016). Health-related quality of life in patients with serious non-specific symptoms undergoing evaluation for possible cancer and their experience during the process: A mixed methods study. *Quality of Life Research*, 1–14. doi:10.1007/s11136-016-1423-2

Teddlie, C., & Tashakkori, A. (2009). *Foundations of mixed methods research: Integrating quantitative and qualitative approaches in the social and behavioral sciences.* Thousand Oaks, CA: Sage.

Web Links

Atlas.ti

https://atlasti.com/qualitative-data-analysis-software/

https://atlasti.com/quantitative-software/

MAXQDA

https://www.maxqda.com/

MSU Library

https://libguides.lib.msu.edu/c.php?g=96626&p=626739

NVivo

https://www.qsrinternational.com/nvivo/home

OxfordLipGuides

https://ox.libguides.com/c.php?g=422947&p=2888387

QDA Miner

https://provalisresearch.com/products/qualitative-data-analysis-software/freeware/

References

https://www.basketball-reference.com/players/c/curryst01.html

Reporting Statistics in APA Style

http://www.ilstu.edu/~jhkahn/apastats.html

Reporting Statistics in APA Style: A Short Guide to Handling Numbers and Statistics in APA Format

http://my.ilstu.edu/~mshesso/apa_stats.htm

SPSS

https://www.ibm.com/analytics/spss-statistics-software

https://www.spss-tutorials.com/spss-data-analysis/

Top 16 Qualitative Data Analysis Software

https://www.predictiveanalyticstoday.com/top-qualitative-data-analysis-software/

Top 52 Free Statistical Software

https://www.predictiveanalyticstoday.com/top-free-statistical-software/

Using SPSS to Understand Research and Data Analysis

http://wwwstage.valpo.edu/other/dabook/home.htm

How to Write Chapter Five, Discussion

Say not, "I have found the truth," but rather,
"I have found a truth."

—Kahlil Gibran

If you have completed Chapter Four and are ready to write Chapter Five, this means that you have finished reporting all your results and findings—fantastic! Conducting research and writing the master's thesis have been like running a marathon. You now realize how much work is involved in conducting research and how tedious (and rewarding) it can be at times. In addition, you have learned about the ethics involved throughout the research process. Chapter Five is the last chapter of the thesis. Like the last 6.2 miles of a marathon, it may be the most difficult chapter to write. Chapter Five requires you to think differently about your study than in previous chapters. You are called on to use all your research skills, and in addition, you need to use the skills of reflection and interpretation. Sometimes readers will read Chapter One and then skip to Chapter Five for a quick check on the conclusions. Thus, you will need to demonstrate what you have learned as a researcher as well as what you learned in your research.

This chapter will focus on how to write the Discussion chapter of the thesis. Chapter Five is a vital component of the master's thesis. This is where you will make the final interpretation of the results that were reported in the previous chapter. However, this is more complex than writing a summary. This chapter needs to be written so that the results are interpreted in a meaningful way, and the implications are made clear to the reader. As you prepare to write Chapter Five, ask yourself, "So what? What do these findings really mean, and how do they help me understand the research problem?" Remember that in conducting your research, the end goal was not to collect data and report the results. Rather, the goal was to identify a research problem (reflecting personal and professional interests) and explore solutions and in the process to increase understanding of a particular phenomenon. Keep in mind that your readers share your interest in the research questions.

As you write this chapter, keep in mind who will be your intended audience. Who will be reading the completed thesis? Will it be your thesis committee and family members? Will you be presenting the thesis to a larger group of faculty and students? Will you be presenting the thesis at a local or national conference and perhaps preparing it for publication in a peer-review journal? Depending on your intended audience, you may need to tweak or add some parts to the chapter so that it is meaningful and comprehensible. For example, if you will be presenting to a group or at a conference, find out what the presentation guidelines are so that you can organize your chapter in the same way. If you are planning to publish the thesis, find out the journal's criteria now so you can align your chapter with their guidelines. It is easier to do this now as you write the chapter rather than go back and revise it later.

Preparation and Organization

There are several tasks that need to be completed before you begin to write. First, make sure that all the results and findings have been edited and clearly reported in Chapter Four. This will make the writing process go much faster since you will be following the organizational structure of Chapter Four. Once all the results are in final form, make an appointment with your chairperson. Although you have already discussed the findings, you will need another meeting to help you with the interpretation and conclusions of the findings. Aside from yourself (and some unsuspecting friend or partner), your chairperson is the person most familiar with your research study. With this knowledge, she will be able to ask you guiding questions to "draw out" the interpretations and conclusions related to the results. Think of it as a friendly Vulcan "mind-meld." However, before meeting with your chairperson, review Chapter Four and frame in your mind what you believe to be the key findings.

Chapter Five Sections

Once you have met with your chairperson and discussed the final interpretations, you can start to write Chapter Five. Chapter Five starts on a new page in the thesis and is divided into five main sections: (a) *Introduction*, (b) *Discussion*, (c) *Limitations*, (d) *Recommendations for Future Research*, and (e) *Conclusions* (see Figure 9.1 for major sections in Chapter Five). Check with your chairperson before you start writing for how he wants you to organize the sections in Chapter Five. If you remember the research synthesis structure from the literature review, the sections in Chapter Five are very similar to the discussion section of a research article. Although they are written and discussed separately, the sections may be intertwined. Collectively, they form the discussion of the study. If writing a master's thesis is like telling the "story" of your research study, this is the resolution or conclusion of the story. As most narrative stories go, there are usually "lessons learned" embedded in the conclusions. To guide you in writing Chapter Five, I first discuss how to write each section in general. Then I provide examples of written work adapted from former students' completed master's theses.

Introduction

Like every chapter of the thesis, this one begins with an introduction (this section usually does not have a level heading). In the *Introduction*, remember to use purposeful redundancy to connect this chapter seamlessly to the previous ones. The *Introduction* should include a broad statement

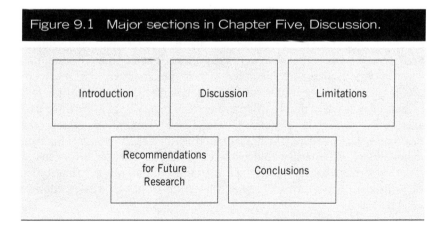

Figure 9.1 Major sections in Chapter Five, Discussion.

Introduction	Discussion	Limitations

Recommendations for Future Research	Conclusions

of the general problem. This is similar to a recap of the issues raised in Chapter One of the thesis. Then include a reminder of the purpose and design of the study. The *Introduction* should be concise and can be short.

Here is an example *Introduction* section adapted from a former student's master's thesis:

> Students with Asperger Syndrome (AS) typically have challenges that primarily affect reading comprehension. Children with AS tend to exhibit high vocabulary and decoding skills but have low reading comprehension (Gillberg, 1991). This challenge, coupled with an increased emphasis on standardized testing, has put pressure on educators to identify strategies to aid in the development of reading comprehension for students with AS.
>
> Various studies have sought to identify the causes behind this reading comprehension deficit. One theory is that children with AS have difficulty creating gestalt imagery when they are reading (Bell, 1991). Research has also shown that a correlation may exist between reading comprehension and one's motivation to read. Since children with AS tend to have circumscribed interests surrounding one or two topics, they are less likely to be motivated to read outside of their limited interests. This could also possibly contribute to their lower reading comprehension skills.
>
> The purpose of this quantitative study was to increase the reading comprehension of students with AS by using graphic novels that incorporate both words and images. The researcher also sought to determine whether the students' motivation to read was influenced by reading the graphic novels. (Gomes, 2008)

Discussion

The second section in Chapter Five is the *Discussion* (this section usually does not have a level heading). One way to organize this section is to use the three parallel ladders strategy. Write the discussion of the results or findings in the *same* order they were reported in Chapter Four. For example, if you reported quantitative data for various measurement instruments in Chapter Four, then the discussion for each measurement instrument would be written as a subsection in Chapter Five (see Figure 9.2 for the three parallel ladders strategy for Chapters Four and Five). Similarly, if you reported qualitative data by major themes or patterns, then the discussion for each major theme or pattern would be a subsection in Chapter Five. Finally, if you reported qualitative or mixed methods data by research questions, then the discussion for each research question would be a subsection in Chapter Five.

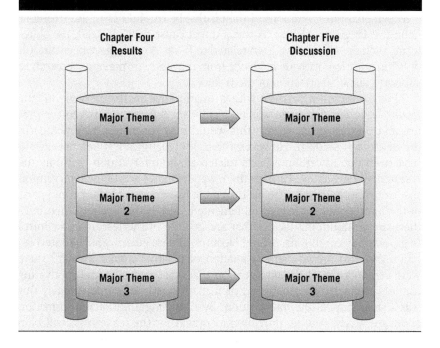

Figure 9.2 The three parallel ladders strategy for Chapters Four and Five.

Chapter Four
Results

Chapter Five
Discussion

Major Theme
1

Major Theme
1

Major Theme
2

Major Theme
2

Major Theme
3

Major Theme
3

In the discussion for each subsection, include a summary of the major findings and a brief interpretation of the findings. This section is usually difficult for students because for the last four chapters, you were asked to minimize your personal interpretations of the findings. I usually receive first drafts of this section that look exactly like what was reported in Chapter Four because students do not feel like they have anything new to add or permission to discuss their interpretation of the results. Remember, you have already reported the results in Chapter Four, so you do not need to repeat verbatim that information here. Instead, report a brief summary or synthesis of the major results. The summary should help answer the research questions.

After the brief summary of the major results, provide an interpretation of the results. For this process, ask yourself, "What factors from the study could have contributed or influenced these results?" This is where the interpretation part comes in except that the interpretation is not based on pure conjecture. Instead, it is based on your knowledge of what occurred during the research study or supported by previous research. As the primary researcher, you have more information about the study than anyone else because you have spent a considerable amount of time and energy at the research site interacting with or observing the participants. Therefore, your interpretations should help explain, increase understanding, or add a different perspective to the results. However, since they are still considered personal interpretations of the results, be careful not to use strong or definitive language such as "A was a direct cause of B"; instead, use softer forms such as "A may have been related to B" or "A could have been a result of B." In addition, provide evidence from the study or previous research to support your interpretation of the results.

For example, in a study with a quantitative math intervention, the results indicated that there was no significant difference between the pretest and posttest mean scores (this would be a major result to include in the discussion section). However, the lack of significant differences could have been due to certain aspects related to the intervention that only the researcher knew about. Perhaps there were certain parts of the intervention that were not sensitive to the measurement instrument. Maybe certain parts of the intervention were not implemented with 100% fidelity. Oftentimes there are confounding factors that are outside of the researcher's control (e.g., weather conditions, school closures, illness, absence). The interpretation can also provide an explanation of positive results. Perhaps there were certain parts of the intervention that were engaging and motivating to the participants that increased their math scores, but unfortunately this was a small part of the intervention. By providing additional information about the study, you are providing a context for the reader that will help her understand and interpret the results. However, be sure that the interpretations are supported by data from the study or previous research. This is where it is helpful to refer back to any field notes or journals and/or logs that you kept during the study.

Here is an example of the *Discussion* section from a quantitative study from a former student's master's thesis:

> The Teaching Each other About Meaning (TEAM) intervention was designed to assess the effects of peer-mediated instruction on the inferential reading comprehension of elementary school students with emotional disturbance who are performing at a variety of reading levels. While the students were chronologically in the 3rd through 7th grades, they were performing approximately at the 1st- and 2nd-grade reading levels. After working together in their peer-mediated-instruction teams, students demonstrated some improvements in the areas of Basic Skills (decoding) and Reading Comprehension skills on the Woodcock Reading Mastery Tests-Revised (WRMT-R).
>
> Mean gains in grade equivalency and percentile rank were statistically significant from pretest to posttest. The mean gain in standard scores was not statistically significant. Through the

TEAM intervention, students were exposed to interesting and varied grade-level passages, articles, and stories that were read aloud by the researcher. Students then had to refer back to the text to extract information for the various skills taught to them during Collaborative Strategic Reading (CSR). Documenting this information on the CSR learning logs may have helped them learn and remember new words. However, as the intervention took about three months to complete (and was not focused on decoding), it is difficult to determine whether the gain on the Basic Skills subtest was due to the intervention or to the increased language arts instruction that was conducted over the intervention period.

On the Reading Comprehension subtest, four of seven students made gains in grade equivalency, percentile rank, and standard scores for reading comprehension. This may have been related to the CSR tasks. The Preview task not only helped the students generate interest in the text but also allowed them to connect to their previous knowledge about the subject matter. The Click and Clunk task helped the students break down and interpret the meaning of unfamiliar words they encountered. The Get the Gist task helped the students determine the main idea of what they read. However, there were no statistically significant results for grade equivalencies, percentile ranks, and standard scores for the Reading Comprehension cluster. The WRMT-R questions may not have assessed the specific types of reading comprehension skills taught through CSR. In addition, the reading comprehension subtests required that the students read the information independently (as opposed to having it read to them). They may have been difficult for the students since the items were read aloud to them during the TEAM intervention. (Hess, 2008)

Here is an example of the *Discussion* section of major themes from a qualitative study from a former student's master's thesis:

The major communicative factors that triggered negative behaviors were peer "put-downs" and "horse play." Based on the observations, the "put-downs" and "horse play" started off as playful and friendly. However, they may have been the antecedent behavior to verbal and physical altercations between students. For example, two African American male students, both in the 9th grade, were observed using verbal put-downs and laughing until one student said something about the other student's mother. That was when one of the students stood up and began posturing at the other, threatening the student with bodily harm. In another instance, two African American male students, one in the 9th grade and the other in the 11th, were observed "horse playing." Another student who was observing (a female African American student in the 12th grade) began laughing and said to the 11th-grade student, "He just dipped you!" The 11th-grade student then began to get rough with the 9th-grade student, and as the situation escalated, the two students needed to be separated from each other.

The communicative factors that promoted positive behavior and effective communication were using clear language, helping students with their work, and one-on-one interaction. This could possibly be due to an increase in clarity of expectations. Clear communication and direct instruction may have been more successful in promoting positive behavior than ambiguous or negatively affective language because students were observed engaging in more positive behaviors during structured/supervised times. For example, the psychologist never reported having behavior problems when conducting assessments with students in a one-on-one situation. Furthermore, negative behaviors were not observed when the students were given clear instructions during the one-on-one interviews for the data collection of this study. Conversely, when the class was observed returning from lunch, only two out of five students were given an assignment. The three students who did not receive an assignment began to engage in verbal put-downs, and the two students who did receive assignments stopped working after five minutes and began to observe the other three students. (Kendall, 2006)

Limitations

The third section is *Limitations* (this section typically has a level heading). In this section, you will discuss the limitations and weaknesses of the study. In Chapter One, there was a section on limitations; however, those were the limitations based on the design of the study. Now that you have completed the study, you are aware of additional limitations that occurred during the study. Remember that all research studies have limitations or weaknesses; as you become a more experienced researcher, you will find ways to reduce the limitations, but you can never get rid of them altogether. Thus, having limitations or weaknesses does not mean that you did a bad job on your study. This just means that in research you are rarely able to control all the variables or situations. What you are unable to control becomes the focus of your limitations. The best way to handle limitations and weaknesses in a study is to be honest and upfront about them. Concealing, falsely reporting, or not reporting the limitations would be considered unethical.

There are several benefits to discussing the limitations of the study. First, you can learn from them. One way to prepare for this section is to ask, "If I had to do the study again, what would I do differently?" This could be a variety of things including changing the sampling plan, adapting the measurement instruments, using different materials, changing the timeline, taking more detailed notes, having more or fewer research sites, asking different questions, and so on. By reflecting on the things that you would do differently, this helps you grow as a researcher and ensures you will not make the same mistakes on your next study! This also helps you become a "critical consumer" of the research literature as you begin to identify similar limitations/weaknesses in other studies.

Another benefit of the limitations section is that other researchers will learn from them. By sharing the dos and don'ts, this will allow the next researcher to modify his study before it is conducted to correct for these limitations. For example, perhaps for a quantitative study, the next researcher should plan for a longer intervention period. Perhaps for a qualitative study, the next researcher should allow for more time and fewer interview questions to obtain more in-depth responses from the participants.

In addition, the limitations may also help provide possible explanations for disappointing or unexpected results. For example, perhaps many students were unexpectedly absent or pulled out of class during an intervention, or there were substantial behavioral problems that interfered with the teaching. Perhaps there were an inordinate number of weather-related issues that interfered with data collection (this has actually happened to me!). These would be limitations that could affect the study's results. However, do not use the limitations section as a justification or excuse for conducting unethical or low-quality research. There is no tolerance for blaming participants or covering up unwanted results.

Finally, when describing the limitations of the study, it is not sufficient to list them. The purpose of the limitations section is to allow the reader to make a judgment on how the limitations impacted the research. Thus, you need to explain what the limitation was and *why* it was a limitation. In other words, how did the limitations affect the validity of the results? Remember that there are many different kinds of validity; there is the validity or trustworthiness of the results for qualitative studies and internal validity (variables within the study) and external validity (applicability outside the study) for quantitative studies. Consider limitations as little caution signs for the reader when extrapolating from the results.

Here is an example from the *Limitations* section of a former student's master's thesis:

> Although the TEAM intervention helped the students improve their inferential reading comprehension skills and their social skills, there were several limitations to the study. The first limitation was related

to the sample and sample size. The sample size was very small—the self-contained classroom in the nonpublic school consisted of 10 students at the beginning of the intervention. During the study, three students were discharged from the school due to extreme behaviors. A second limitation was that the students were generally placed at this school because they were unsuccessful in public school. The students were all diagnosed with emotional disturbance (ED), but some had dual diagnoses of learning disability or mild mental retardation, while others had minimal issues with learning. Therefore, both of these limitations have an impact on external validity and make the results difficult to generalize to other students with disabilities in special education settings.

Other limitations were related to the implementation of the intervention. First, there were problems with the scheduling. There were typically only two sessions per week; therefore, there was a lot of time between lessons, and the students may not have been able to retain information during the gaps in lessons. Furthermore some of the students with ED displayed extreme behaviors such as disruptions, tantrums, and crises during several of the lessons, which caused some students to be removed from the classroom by staff escort. This also meant less staff was present in the classroom to monitor and assist the peer tutoring teams. In addition, due to behavioral issues such as extreme tantrums, pullouts due to therapy sessions, or classroom disruptions, the researcher was not able to maintain the same student teams throughout the program. Therefore, partners were reassigned on a regular basis. The above limitations affect the internal validity of the results—with a greater number of sessions in a more condensed time frame, consistency of partners within a team, and the appropriate number of staff present, the results may have more accurately reflected the impact of the intervention. (Hess, 2008)

Recommendations for Future Research

The fourth section is the *Recommendations for Future Research* (this section typically has a level heading). There are several methods that you can use to write this section. First, you can tie the recommendations for future research to the issues that were identified in the limitations section. In other words, which procedures should be changed by the next researcher? With this method, the recommendations are based on the weaknesses from your study. For example, perhaps you would recommend adding another measurement instrument such as an observation protocol for data triangulation. This will help the next researcher modify her study to strengthen it. Another method to consider is to suggest recommendations on how your study could be continued or expanded. Remember that your study added to an existing body of research, so your suggestions should also build from the previous research. In other words, what are the next steps to extend the findings that were produced in the study? This will help the next researcher identify gaps that still exist in the literature. For example, perhaps you would recommend implementing the intervention with a different sample group such as adults or a more diverse sample. By including these two types of recommendations, you are making a major contribution to your field in terms of moving the research base forward and launching the next line of studies.

Here is an example of *Recommendations for Future Research* section from a former student's master's thesis:

> Based on the results of the study, there are several recommendations for future research. First, some of the limitations outlined in this study may be minimized or eliminated in a revised implementation of the Student Choice treatment. To improve or verify the accuracy of the data collection, interrater reliability could be used to cross check the number of off-task behaviors exhibited and verify the portion of the instruction in which they occurred. Second, to identify which of the components of the Student Choice treatment had the largest impact on the decrease or increase of off-task behaviors, each of the components could be introduced separately. In addition, to determine whether the number of exhibited off-task behaviors remains consistent for longer than three weeks, the treatment phase should be extended. Third, this study did not measure student satisfaction and perceptions toward the increase in choices and decision-making opportunities. Future studies should employ a student survey or interviewing procedure to measure student perceptions toward the Student Choice treatment. Finally, this study only measured the impact of the Student Choice treatment on the off-task behavior of students with learning disabilities. Future studies could implement the treatment and measure the impact on students with other disabilities such as emotional/behavioral disorders or attention deficit disorders. (Rau, 2006)

Conclusion

The last section of the chapter is the *Conclusion* (this section typically has a level heading). In this section, you will identify at least three critical conclusions based on the results of the study. One way to think about this is to ask, "What are the three main lessons learned from the study?" Your conclusions are like a synthesis of the major findings. For example, perhaps one of the major conclusions from a study on cyberbullying was that the middle school students' level of psychological health was positively related to time spent with adult mentors and caretakers. The conclusions may also include unintended but significant discoveries that were made as a result of the study. However, base the conclusions on the findings of the study, and avoid overstating or overgeneralizing the findings (i.e., do not claim that you discovered the fountain of youth). If appropriate, you may also reference previous research that either substantiates or contradicts your conclusions.

After you have identified each major conclusion, discuss the implications of the conclusion. The implications are recommendations for how to bridge the "research to practice" and can be in the form of actions, policies, or procedures. For example, one implication from the study above would be for adult mentors and caretakers to set aside a period of "sacred" time during the week to spend with the middle school students. These implications are critical because the reader has some guidance for how to actualize and benefit from the conclusions.

Here are four different examples of *Conclusion* sections from various students' master's theses. For each example, there is an advance organizer, which states the major conclusions, and then a discussion around one of the conclusions with implications.

1. Three major conclusions can be made from this study (Gomes, 2008). The first conclusion is that using the graphic novels may have improved the reading comprehension of some students with Asperger's (AS) because they provided the students with visual images. The second conclusion is that using graphic novels may not be effective for students who have very low levels of reading comprehension. The third conclusion is that the students' motivation and amount of time spent reading was increased after reading the graphic novels, possibly translating to increased reading comprehension.

    The first conclusion is that reading graphic novels improved the reading comprehension of some students who had low reading comprehension and high decoding skills. Other studies have noted the correlation between reading comprehension and decoding but have not yet identified the root cause of poor reading comprehension skills for students who have high decoding skills. In schools with students with AS and other autism spectrum disorders, using graphic novels may help bridge the gap between high decoding and low reading comprehension, allowing these students to be successful in an academic environment. On a broader scale, similar results may be found for students exhibiting like characteristics in a general education setting.

    If this gap exists because these students are not creating visual images when reading, graphic novels may provide students with the visualizations needed to comprehend the text. Though this may not be universally effective for all students with AS, using graphic novels in a Language Arts class could be a strategy that teachers can use to help some students with AS. Teachers may also want to consider incorporating visual images into other aspects of teaching outside of Language Arts. Using visual images to correspond with written directions may help with a student's comprehension of the directions. Additionally, visual images could be used to illustrate historical events or to explain a scientific process rather than just relying on text.

2. The results of this intervention led to four major conclusions (Irey, 2008). The first conclusion is repeated reading was an effective strategy in terms of improving reading pace although not for decreasing errors for students with learning disabilities (LD) or who are English learners (EL). Error correction with corrective feedback was effective in decreasing errors although its effect on reading pace was minimal, and prosody instruction appears to have had a minimal effect on rate and a moderate effect on decreasing errors. The second conclusion is that the intervention was successful in increasing the student's reading comprehension. The third conclusion is that the students' prosody skill levels improved through fluency instruction. The fourth conclusion is that students' attitudes toward reading improved after the intervention.

   Several fluency strategies were used in this study. Each appears to have strengths and weaknesses in terms of student achievement. Repeated readings were found to have a significant effect on reading rate but not for error correction. However, error correction and corrective feedback can be added to repeated readings to strengthen the intervention. The addition of prosodic instruction did not greatly affect reading rate, but it did serve to decrease the number of errors made.

   Students will be well served by teachers who select the most appropriate strategy for the needs of each student. The time and effort required by implementing error correction and corrective feedback would not serve the needs of a student who makes minimal errors but needs to increase his rate of reading. Conversely, a student who reads at an appropriate pace but makes multiple errors would not benefit from an intervention of only repeated reading. By determining the appropriate strategy to address each individual's needs, educators will be able to provide all students the opportunity to reach his or her full academic potential.

3. Several conclusions can be made based on the results of this study (Hess, 2008). One of the conclusions is that students with emotional disturbance (ED) benefit from direct instruction in

social skills. Another conclusion is that peer-mediated instruction is an engaging and effective method for delivering reading comprehension instruction. A third conclusion is that students with ED appeared to perform better in the program when staff was facilitating the team's activities.

The results of this study indicated that students with ED benefited from explicit instruction and modeling of social skills. When a new social skill was introduced through the TEAM intervention, the students listened to an explanation of the skill and how to use it, discussed the skill and how it was relevant to them, watched and participated in teacher modeling of examples (and non-examples) of the skill, practiced with a peer, and then implemented the skill in the program. Many programs designed to incorporate cooperative learning relating to reading skills do not have a sufficient emphasis on the social skills involved in working together as a team. As students with ED often have difficulty with peer interactions, they need explicit instruction in how to teach, learn from, and cooperate with their peers. The results of this study indicated that student behaviors did improve as a result of the TEAM intervention. Therefore, students with ED would benefit from direct instruction in social skills prior to (and during) peer-mediated instruction or cooperative grouping. Explicit social skills instruction in the classroom could help educators minimize disruptive behaviors and foster more positive communication between peers.

4. The present study illuminated some salient findings within the area of effective communication in classrooms serving students with emotional disturbance (ED) and learning disabilities (LD) (Kendall, 2006). First, the power of verbal and nonverbal communication in a classroom setting to influence behavior either positively or negatively by specific means was revealed. The greater implication of this finding is that classrooms serving students with ED/LD often place the fault and blame of students' negative behaviors on the student rather than considering factors such as tone of voice, levels of ambiguity, body tension, and other forms of communicative intent of the educators. On the other hand, the root of all conflicts cannot rightfully be placed on the communication styles of the educator. A deeper awareness of the way educators come across within a cultural framework of the population they serve could only benefit in preventing the conflicts and misunderstandings between both educators and students that often invariably lead to negative behavior blowouts. Teachers and educators may consider getting additional training in cultural sensitivity to avoid these misunderstandings with the populations that they serve.

Second, it was revealed by the student and staff participants in the study that students with ED and LD wanted more individualized assistance with academic tasks, and furthermore, students' behavior was positively impacted by prolonged, individualized help. Currently, in high school special education classrooms for students with ED, teachers may often focus more on students' behavior than academics. This may not be that irrational being that recurring negative behavior can be a major impediment to student learning. However, it could be argued that when students do not receive academic instruction at their instructional level combined with individualized help, this could be a causal factor for frustration, acting out, and incomplete assignments. The greater implication for this finding was that behavior needed to be analyzed on a deeper level than prevalence. Understanding the causal factors of negative behaviors may be a more effective tool for analysis than simply recording the occurrence of negative behaviors. Therefore, when students act inappropriately, teachers should be aware of the antecedent events and consider a causal framework for the negative behavior.

After you have completed the conclusion section, it is typical to have one last closing paragraph. You are probably thinking, "She's not seriously expecting me to write one more sentence! What more could I possibly say?" The closing paragraph is typically your final thoughts and reflection on the entire study. As these will be the last sentences in the thesis, they should leave a lasting and profound impression on the reader.

SUMMARY

Chapter Five is perhaps the most significant chapter in the thesis because it provides interpretations and conclusions of the major findings from the study. Chapter Five may also be one of the most difficult chapters to write because it involves synthesizing the results to draw out the "lessons learned." In this chapter, you are also providing the implications or applications of the findings for the reader. In the next chapter, I discuss the APA editorial style and other formatting issues to help you complete the master's thesis and get it ready for printing and binding. Here is a summary of the most critical points from Chapter 9:

- Chapter Five can be divided into five main sections: (a) *Introduction*, (b) *Discussion*, (c) *Limitations*, (d) *Recommendations for Future Research*, and (e) *Conclusions*.

- One way to organize the discussion section is to use the three parallel ladders strategy and write the discussion of the results in the same order they were reported in Chapter Four.

- The interpretations of the results should help explain, increase understanding, or add a different perspective to the results.

- All research studies have limitations or weaknesses. As you become a more experienced researcher, you will find ways to reduce the limitations, but you can never get rid of them altogether.

- There are several benefits to discussing the limitations of the study: (a) learn from your mistakes, (b) help other researchers learn from your mistakes, and (c) provide possible explanations for disappointing or unexpected results.

- When describing the limitations of the study, explain what the limitation was and *why* it was a limitation.

- One method to write the recommendations for future research section is to connect the recommendations to the issues that were identified in the limitations section.

- Another method to write the recommendations for future research section is to offer suggestions on how your study could be continued or expanded based on previous research.

- Base the conclusions on the findings in the study; avoid overstating or over-generalizing the findings.

- The implications of the conclusions are recommendations for how to bridge the "research to practice" and can be in the form of actions, policies, or procedures.

RESOURCES

Common Obstacles and Practical Solutions

1. A common obstacle that students face in writing Chapter Five is interpreting the findings. Words that come to mind are "What does this really mean?" The best way to overcome this obstacle is to review your journal notes (I hope you kept those updated!). The notes will remind you of the procedures that were used during the study and perhaps shed light on situations or events that were irregular or unexpected. In addition, definitely meet with your chairperson. You have been so immersed in reporting the minute details that sometimes it is difficult to tie them back to the research questions and purpose of the study. Speaking with your chairperson or someone familiar with your study will help you make these connections.

2. Another common obstacle faced by students is finding the major conclusions from the study. Although you have reported a summary of the major findings and interpretations, sometimes the overall conclusions are not so obvious. Words that come to mind are "What is the bigger lesson here?" One thing to always keep in mind is the original purpose of the study and the research questions—ultimately, did you find what you were looking for? The major conclusions could be related to one of the research questions or focus of the study. However, sometimes a major conclusion could be something that you found but were not looking for at all. These unanticipated conclusions are sometimes even more beneficial than confirming preset hypotheses because they expand your perspective and knowledge about the research topic beyond what was expected or indicated in the research literature.

Reflection/Discussion Questions

When you discuss your study's findings in Chapter Five, it is important to understand the differences in reporting results versus making interpretations about the results. The following reflection/discussion questions will help guide you through the discussion process.

1. What are different kinds of limitations and weaknesses that could exist in a quantitative, qualitative, or mixed methods study? Give examples of limitations that may have occurred in your study. Discuss how these limitations affect the internal/external validity or quality of the results.

2. What are the differences among making interpretations, conclusions, and implications about a study's findings? Give one example of each and discuss how they are interrelated.

Try It Exercises

The following exercises are designed to help you write Chapter Five. In Activity One, you will outline the first four major sections of Chapter Five and begin to flesh out the components. In Activity Two, you will write an outline of the conclusions section.

1. Activity One: For this activity, focus on the results or findings that were reported in Chapter Four.
   - Based on your research design, you will create an outline of three major sections in Chapter Five (e.g., discussion, limitations, and recommendations).
   - For each section, write at least three bullet points (they do not have to be complete sentences) of what you will include to answer these questions:

A. Summarize the major findings. What interpretations could be made around these findings?

B. What were some of the limitations? How do the limitations affect the internal/external validity or quality of the findings?

C. What recommendations do you have for future research?

- Meet with your chairperson to discuss the bullet points before writing each section.

2. Activity Two: For this activity, focus on the synthesis of the major findings.

- Write one conclusion (one paragraph) based on a synthesis of the major findings.

- Write one implication of the conclusion (one paragraph).

- Meet with your chairperson to discuss the conclusion and implication before moving on to the next two conclusions.

Key Terms

external validity   205
internal validity   205

purposeful redundancy   199

Suggested Readings

American Educational Research Association. (n.d.). *Standards for reporting empirical social science research in AERA publications*. Retrieved from http://journals.sagepub.com/doi/abs/10.3102/0013189X035006033

Denzin, N. K., & Lincoln, Y. S. (2018). *The SAGE handbook of qualitative research* (5th ed.). Thousand Oaks, CA: Sage.

Plano Clark, V. L., & Creswell, J. W. (2008). *The mixed methods reader*. Thousand Oaks, CA: Sage.

Şanlı, Ö., Erdem, S., & Tefik, T. (2013). How to write a discussion section? *Turkish Journal of Urology, 39*(Suppl. 1), 20–24. Retrieved from http://doi.org/10.5152/tud.2013.049

Web Links

American Psychological Association (Discussing Your Findings)
http://www.apa.org/gradpsych/2006/01/findings.aspx

Free Management Library: Analyzing, Interpreting and Reporting Basic Research Results
http://managementhelp.org/businessresearch/analysis.htm

USC Research Guides: The Discussion
https://libguides.usc.edu/writingguide/discussion

10

Wrapping It All Up

There are three rules for writing the novel.
Unfortunately, no one knows what they are.

—W. Somerset Maugham

A hearty congratulations for completing the text of your master's thesis! You should feel really proud of yourself. Now that you have completed the bulk of the work, we will focus on putting on the final touches and wrapping it all up! Yes, every muscle and joint in your back aches from all the sitting, and you have blisters on your fingertips from all the typing. Your vision is fuzzy, and you feel light-headed from staring at the computer screen. But wait! What is that sound you hear? No, those are not voices in your head; those are the screams from your loved ones on the sidelines cheering you on! In fact, if you wipe away the sweat, you can actually see the finish line! Now is not the time to slow down but rather to regroup and reenergize for the last leg of the race. Depending on how much formatting you have completed up to this point, this may take a bit of time, so keep the momentum going knowing there are loved ones waiting for you on the other side of the finish line!

This chapter includes the style and format of the thesis using the sixth edition of the *Publication Manual of the American Psychological Association* (APA, 2010). As mentioned, the APA style is commonly used in various social science disciplines such as education, psychology, sociology, business, economics, nursing, and social work. The American Psychological Association uses the APA style to publish all its books and journals. Two other common style forms are the Modern Language Association (MLA) style and the University of Chicago style. Check with your institution or department to find out which style form is required for your thesis. Typically, the style form requirements are included in documents made available from the graduate school or your department. However, confirm with your chairperson that you are following the correct form.

When referring to a particular style such as APA, publishers are focusing on the *editorial* style in addition to the writing style. This includes rules and guidelines on how to format level headings, citations, references, tables, figures, statistics, and so on. By following a particular style, the publisher ensures that the printed material is consistent and uniform (think of it like a common language). While this common language is important to publishers, it is of equal importance to academic disciplines and institutions of higher education for many of the same reasons. Keep in mind that style forms do change. When this occurs, the changes are published through revisions or addendums of the APA manual (check to make sure you are using the most current version). Updates and electronic resources are also posted on the APA website (http://apastyle.apa.org).

There is quite a bit of information in the publication manual, which can be overwhelming at first glance. However, much of it may not apply to the master's thesis. Therefore, in this chapter, I focus on only those sections that are most relevant to the typical thesis. Depending on your discipline, you may have some rather unique formatting needs and will need to refer to the APA manual for specific queries. At the end of this chapter, I also make suggestions on other formatting issues that are not in the APA manual that I have found to be useful for the master's thesis.

Preparation and Organization

There are several tasks that need to be completed in preparation for the final formatting process. First, make sure you have all the sources that were cited in the text or know where to find them (we discuss how to format the citations and references later). This is often the task that requires the most work if you have not been keeping track of the sources throughout the writing process or using a reference management software program. Second, make sure that you have all the data available in an easy-to-read format. These will be needed to prepare tables and figures. Third, make sure that all the text has been edited in Chapters One through Five. Since you will be developing a table of contents based on the existing document, the text needs to be in its final draft to determine the appropriate level headings and page numbers. Finally, prepare clean blank photocopies of all the materials and measurement instruments that were used, including the Institutional Review Board (IRB) cover letter, consent forms, intervention materials, surveys, tests, interview questions, observation protocols, and so on (see Appendixes A, B, and C of this volume for samples). These will be included as the appendixes in the thesis. Doing these preparation and organizational tasks first will make the formatting process much quicker and less stressful for you in the end.

APA Style

Once you have completed all the necessary preparation tasks, you can start the final editorial process in APA style. I highly recommend that you have a copy of the most recent APA publication manual (or the electronic version) handy at all times. The manual has over 200 pages of rules, guidelines, and examples. However, I do not recommend reading the manual from cover to cover (unless you are having trouble sleeping). Instead, it is a great tool that you can refer to for specific style elements. The sixth edition manual is divided into eight chapters. Chapter 1 focuses on different types of articles and ethical considerations for publishing. Chapters 2 and 8 focus on preparing manuscripts and the publication process for academic journals. I highly recommend reading these chapters when you are ready to submit your thesis for publication to a journal in your field. Chapters 3 and 4 focus on the writing style aspects such as the style, grammar, and mechanics. I do not focus on these two chapters as much (except for the APA heading style), but I do recommend that you read them because there are some very good writing strategies and examples for language usage and grammar (see Appendix D in this volume for additional writing tips). Chapter 3 also has suggestions on how to reduce bias in your writing. Chapters 5 and 6 of the APA manual focus on the editorial style aspects such as formatting tables and figures, citations, and references. There are numerous examples of reference examples in Chapter 7.

In this chapter, I focus on specific editorial style sections of the APA manual. I discuss briefly how to format the following elements since these are most relevant to the master's thesis and often confusing to students: (a) headings, (b) citations, (c) references, (d) tables, and (e) figures. Since presenting statistics was covered in Chapter 8 of this volume (see Chapter 4 in the APA manual), I do not review that information here. To guide you in this process, I first discuss the APA style rules in general. Then I provide examples. I have also listed numerous resources at the end of the chapter to assist you with applying APA style.

In addition to covering APA style, I discuss the final format sections of the master's thesis that I have used with my graduate students. These are not necessarily in APA style. These include the appendixes and a section that I call the *front pages*. The front pages include the title and signature pages, acknowledgments, abstract, table of contents, and lists of tables and figures. Check with your chairperson or program to see if there are formatting rules and guidelines for the appendixes and front pages.

Levels of Heading

One element of APA style is determining the levels of heading to use in the thesis. This is like solving a Rubik's cube—very difficult to solve initially, but once you are proficient, it becomes routine. The **levels of heading** refer to the organizational structure or hierarchy of the sections. They inform the reader of the importance of the sections and whether they are main sections or subsections. Sections that are of equal importance are on the same number level heading, while subsections would be on a different number level heading. In the sixth edition of the APA manual, the heading style was immensely simplified, so now it is much easier to determine how many levels of headings you need and how to format them.

In APA style, there are five possible levels of heading (see Figure 10.1). Keep in mind that the number of level headings is different from the number level heading. Huh? The *number of* level headings refers to the quantity of level headings you use. The maximum number of level headings is five. The *number level* heading refers to a specific heading location. There are five different locations, and the headings can be at Level 1, 2, 3, 4, or 5. Note in Figure 10.1 that the number level headings are in numerical order; the top level heading is Level 1, then Level 2, and so on. A good way to determine how many levels will be required in your thesis is to look at your initial outline. How many sections and subsections are there in each chapter? Are there larger sections that could be divided into smaller subsections?

In Figure 10.2, there is an example with five levels of heading from Chapter One of a sample thesis. As you read down the levels, each descending level acts as a subheading for the previous level (i.e., Level 2 is a subheading for Level 1, Level 3 is a subheading for Level 2, and so on). Note that even though Levels 3, 4, and 5 headings end with a period, the heading does not have to be a complete sentence. When you have multiple levels of heading, you can have as many of the same number level headings

Figure 10.1   Five levels of heading in APA style.

(Level 1)   **Centered, Boldface, Uppercase and Lowercase Heading**

(Level 2)   **Flush left, Boldface, Uppercase and Lowercase Heading**

(Level 3)   **Indented, boldface, lowercase paragraph ending with a period.**

(Level 4)   ***Indented, boldface, italicized lowercase paragraph ending with a period.***

(Level 5)   *Indented, italicized, lowercase paragraph heading ending with a period.*

Figure 10.2   Five levels of heading from sample Chapter One.

(Level 1)   **Chapter One, Introduction**

(Level 2)   **Statement of the Problem**

(Level 3)   **Students with disabilities.**

(Level 4)   ***Students with learning disabilities.***

(Level 5)   *Reading comprehension difficulties.*

as necessary. These show that the sections are of equal importance. For example, you can have three Level 4 headings as subheadings to one Level 3 heading. In Figure 10.3, there is an example with four levels of heading from Chapter One of a sample thesis that also has multiple subheadings at the same number level. Note how the Level 3 heading, *Students with disabilities*, has two subheadings at Level 4, and the same is true for the Level 3 heading, *Bilingual learners*. In this figure, I have also indicated where you would start to write the text. Obviously, you would not include the labels

Figure 10.3 Four levels of heading from Chapter One with multiple subheadings.

Chapter One, Introduction (Level 1)

You would indent and start writing the text on the next line. Notice how the heading is centered and boldface with upper and lowercase font (like a book title).

Statement of the Problem (Level 2)

You would indent and start writing the text on the next line. Notice how the heading is flushed left and boldface with upper and lowercase font (like a book title).

Students with disabilities (Level 3). You would start writing the text here after the period and keep wrapping around underneath the subheading like this. Notice how the heading is indented and boldface with upper and lowercase font (like at the beginning of a sentence).

***Students with learning disabilities* (Level 4).** You would start writing the text here after the period and keep wrapping around underneath the subheading like this. Notice how the heading is indented, italicized, and boldface with upper and lowercase font (like at the beginning of a sentence).

***Students with autism* (Level 4).** Notice how this is on the same (equal) level as the previous Level 4 heading.

Bilingual learners (Level 3). Notice how this is on the same (equal) level as the previous Level 3 heading.

***Spanish-speaking bilingual learners* (Level 4).** Notice how this is on the same (equal) level as the previous Level 4 heading.

***Other-language bilingual learners* (Level 4).** Notice how this is on the same (equal) level as the previous Level 4 heading.

Background and Need (Level 2)

Notice how this is on the same (equal) level as the previous Level 2 heading.

of each level in your thesis—those are included here to help you see the different levels and how they relate to one other.

For the master's thesis, it is rare that you would need five levels of headings; three or four levels are more common. Check with your chairperson regarding how many levels of headings is recommended. I typically advise students to use three levels of heading because large sections can be divided into smaller subsections, which makes the text more reader friendly. In addition, with three levels, you can use the three parallel ladders strategy. For example, the title of the chapter is at Level 1 (e.g., Chapter One, Chapter Two), the main sections in the chapter are at Level 2 (e.g., *Statement of the Problem*, *Purpose of the Study*, *Procedures*), and the subsections for each main section are at Level 3 (e.g., *Problem area number one*). In Figure 10.4, there is an example with three levels of heading from Chapter One of a sample thesis. Note that both the *Statement of the Problem* and *Background and Need* sections have multiple Level 3 subheadings. These would be the three subsections for the three parallel ladders strategy.

Citations in Text

The next element in APA style is how to cite sources (referred to as *works*) in the text of the thesis. This is extremely important for several reasons. First, readers may want to read the source document, and they will need an accurate citation. Second, including citations from the research literature adds credibility to support your claims. Third, you should give appropriate credit to the work that you are citing. If you do not give appropriate credit to the original work, this is considered a form of plagiarism,

Figure 10.4 Three levels of heading from sample Chapter One.

Chapter One, Introduction (Level 1)

Statement of the Problem (Level 2)

    Reading difficulties. (Level 3)

    Math difficulties. (Level 3)

    Behavioral difficulties. (Level 3)

Background and Need (Level 2)

    Reading strategies. (Level 3)

    Math strategies. (Level 3)

    Behavioral interventions. (Level 3)

which is a very serious offense akin to stealing. Citations of works are necessary when you use a direct quote or paraphrase someone else's words, ideas, or research findings. Be very careful when paraphrasing, because simply changing the order of the words or substituting a few words can still be considered plagiarism (see the website on plagiarism, http://www.plagiarism.org). Academic institutions have a zero tolerance for any form of plagiarism, and this can result in not receiving your degree or having it revoked (not to mention any legal or monetary penalties).

Direct Quotes

One of the items that you *must* cite is a direct quote. However, I would recommend using direct quotes sparingly and only if paraphrasing the original work would not capture the essence of the message. Since a page number is required for direct quotes, it is always preferable to have a PDF reproduction of the written material if possible. If you are quoting a lengthy passage (e.g., more than 500 words) from copyrighted material, you may need to get permission from the copyright holder. If you cite a direct quote, put the exact words in quotation marks and write the author's last name, year of publication, and page number of where the quote is located in parentheses at the end of the quote. Here is an example:

"I am only using this direct quote because I could not paraphrase it" (Bui, 2020, p. 14).

Paraphrasing

Another case in which items must be cited in the text is when you paraphrase ideas, words, or findings. There are multiple ways to do this, depending on the number of authors, type of author, number of works, source of the material, and so on. I give common examples of how to reference a citation in the text for different numbers of authors or works. For specific queries or other circumstances, please refer to the APA manual or website.

One Work, One Author

A common citation is one work by one author. This consists of the author's last name and the year of publication. There are two different formats. The first format is when the author is the subject of the sentence. When this is the case, the year of publication is put in parentheses. Note that the verb "argued" is in the past tense to indicate that the research has already been conducted. Here is an example:

Bui (2020) argued that having a dog as a companion extended people's life spans.

The second format is used when the citation is at the end of the paraphrased sentence or paragraph to support the text. When this is the case, the author's last name and year of publication are separated by a comma and put in parentheses. Here is an example of the second format:

> Having a dog as a companion may extend a person's life span (Bui, 2020).

One Work, Multiple Authors

If there are multiple authors (between two and five) for one work, they are listed similarly with their last names and year of publication. If the authors are listed as subjects in the sentence, separate the names with commas and spell out the word "and" between the second to last and last author. The year of publication is in parentheses after the listing of the authors. If the citation is at the end of the sentence, put the authors' names in parentheses, separate them with commas, and use an ampersand (&) between the second to last and last author. After the last author, put a comma and the year of publication. Here are examples of multiple authors in both formats:

> Bui and Meyen (2020) argued that having a dog as a companion extended people's life spans. Having a dog as a companion may extend a person's life span (Bui, Rodriguez, & Meyen, 2020). **[three authors]**

Keep the listing of the authors in their original order from the article even if it is not in alphabetical order. This is critical because authors are usually listed in a particular order based on their contribution to the manuscript. If there are three, four, or five authors, you can shorten the citation to reduce space (after the first full citation) by using "et al." (which means "and others") after the first author's last name and then the publication date. If there are six or more authors for one work, you would automatically use the "et al." format. For example,

> Bui et al. (2020) argued that having a dog as a companion extended people's life spans. Having a dog as a companion may extend a person's life span (Bui et al., 2020).

Two or More Works

There will be times when you need to cite two or more works with a variety of single or multiple authorships for the same idea. In this case, you would keep the individual authors in the order that they appear in the work and then list the works in alphabetical order by the first author's last name. The works are separated with semicolons. Here is an example:

> Several studies have indicated that having a dog as a companion may extend the life span (**Bui**, 2020; **Garcia**, 2017; **Meyen** & Brewster, 2018; **Nguyen**, Edwards, Alia, & Jackson, 2019).

Note how the works are listed in alphabetical order, but within each work, the authors are listed as they would appear in a separate citation.

Reference List

All the works that are cited in the text (excluding a few exceptions) will be included in the reference list at the end of the thesis. Therefore, it is imperative that they match! In other words, if the work is cited in the text, it must be in the reference list, and vice versa. In addition, the citation in the text (e.g., spelling and order of the authors, year of publication) will be exactly the same as the citation in the reference list. Thus, be very careful not to miss any references in either location, and you should also compare them to make sure they are identical. The reference list is intended to give credit to the source and allow readers to retrieve the sources that were cited in your thesis. This means providing as much specific information as possible about the author, year, title, source, and retrieval location (for online sources). Include the **digital object identifier** (DOI) if one is assigned. The DOI is a unique code of letters and numbers that provide a link to the article's location on the Internet (think of it as a tracking device). Typically, the DOI can be found on the first page of the article and should be copied exactly as it is written. If you retrieved the periodical online and there is no DOI, you can list the URL home page for the journal. If the URL is very long and you need to continue the address on the next line, do not put in a hyphen; separate before a punctuation mark such as a slash or period. After you have listed the URL in the reference list, test it to make sure that it works! The different ways to list references are so numerous that Chapter 7 (30 pages!) in the APA manual is devoted to this cause. Thus, it would be impractical to discuss every possible configuration you might encounter. Please refer to the APA manual for specific queries. If you have been using a reference manager software program, most of the hard work is done for you!

Order and Format

APA has strict rules about how to order and format the reference list. The references are listed in alphabetical order by the last name of the first author, name of the group, or title of the work when there is no author provided. In general, the listing follows typical rules for alphabetical order (see APA manual for exceptional cases). For example, the author/group/ title starting with A would precede those starting with B, and so on. The APA manual recommends double spacing in the reference list for a journal manuscript, but single spacing is allowed within references (use a double space between references) for the thesis. Check with your chairperson to see if single or double spacing is preferred for your thesis.

There are a few general formatting rules. First, list each reference using a hanging indent. A **hanging indent** is when the first line is flushed all the way to the left margin and the rest of the lines in the reference are indented one-half inch. This makes it easier to read down the list to find specific references and helps separate the references from each other. Second, in addition to listing the last name, always include the first and middle initials (if given) of the author's full name. This helps distinguish between authors with the same last name. Third, list the publication year in parentheses or "n.d." if no date is provided. Finally, use sentence capitalization to write the title of the work. **Sentence capitalization** is when only the first word of the title and proper nouns are capitalized (like in a regular sentence). Unlike the citations in the text, the titles do not have quotation marks around them in the reference list.

In Figures 10.5–10.9 there are many examples of different types of references that you could use in a master's thesis. In Figure 10.5, there is a sample reference list. Notice how there are many different types of

---

Figure 10.5   Condensed sample reference list.

Becker, L. B., Vlad, T., Huh, J., & Prine, J. (2001). Annual enrollment report: Number of students studying journalism and mass communication at all-time high. *Journalism & Mass Communication Educator, 56*(3), 28–60. Retrieved from http://www.grady.uga. edu/annualsurveys/Enrollment_Survey/Enrollment_2000/Enrollment2000.pdf

Creswell, J. W. (2013). *Qualitative inquiry and research design* (3rd ed.). Thousand Oaks, CA: Sage.

Ethical principles: The Belmont Report. (n.d.). Retrieved from Duke University, Office of Research Support website: http://www.ors.duke.edu/irb/regpolicy/ethical.html

Gillberg, C. (1991). Clinical and neurobiological aspects of Asperger syndrome in six family studies. In U. Frith (Ed.), *Autism and Asperger syndrome* (pp. 122–146). Cambridge, UK: Cambridge University Press.

Niolin, R. (2001). *Families and substance abuse*. Retrieved from http://www.psychpage. com/family/library/familysubstanceabuse.htm

Ponterotto, J. G., & Grieger, I. (2007). Effectively communicating qualitative research. *The Counseling Psychologist, 35*(3), 404–430. doi:10.1177/0011000006287443

---

references, including a journal article, book, book chapter, and online source. In Figure 10.6, there are different examples of journal articles from a reference list. Notice how they are listed in alphabetical order by the author's last name. In Figure 10.7, there are different examples of books and book chapters from a reference list in alphabetical order. Notice when it is an edited book or when there are different editions of the books. In Figure 10.8, there are examples of different online journal articles and documents from a reference list in alphabetical order. Notice how the citation leads to the specific URL web address. In Figure 10.9, there are examples of different websites and webpages from a reference list in alphabetical order. Notice how some of the web pages do not have publication dates listed. These are just a sampling of possible references; if you have some that do not fit into these categories, be sure to check the APA manual or website.

Tables

Tables are another element of APA style that students often have difficulty with in the thesis. Since there are 42 pages devoted to how to format tables in the APA manual (Chapter 5), I can definitely sympathize! A table is an alternative method to communicate ideas, words, or findings in the thesis. Number tables are typically used to portray data from a quantitative study (e.g., results in Chapter Four), and word tables are sometimes necessary for findings from a qualitative study. Researchers will also sometimes include a table to describe participants' demographic data (e.g., methods in

---

Figure 10.6   Examples of journal articles in a reference list.

Hallinger, P., & Snidvongs, K. (2008). Educating leaders: Is there anything to learn from business management? *Educational Management, Administration, & Leadership, 36*(1), 9–31. doi:10.1177/1741143207084058 **[two authors with DOI]**

O'Mahony, S., Blank, A., Simpson, J., Persaud, J., Huvane, B., McAllen, S., et al. (2008). Preliminary report of a palliative care and case management project in an emergency department for chronically ill elderly patients. *Journal of Urban Health, 85*(3), 443–451. Retrieved from http://www.ncbi.nlm.nih.gov/pmc/articles/PMC2329741/?tool=pubmed/ **[more than six authors with URL]**

Proctor, E. K. (2008). Notation of depression in case records of older adults in community. *Social Work, 53*(3), 243–253. doi:10.1093/sw/53.3.243 **[one author with DOI]**

Smith, L., Foley, P. F., & Chaney, M. P. (2008). Addressing classism, ableism, and heterosexism in counselor education. *Journal of Counseling & Development, 86*(3), 303–309. doi:10.1002/j.1556-6678.2008.tb00513.x **[three authors with DOI]**

Figure 10.7 Examples of books, reference books, and book chapters in a reference list.

American Psychological Association. (2010). *Publication manual of the American Psychological Association* (6th ed.). Washington, DC: Author. **[association as author, sixth edition]**

Borgatta, E. F., & Montgomery, R. (Eds.). (2001). *Encyclopedia of sociology* (2nd ed., Vols. 1–5). New York, NY: Macmillan Reference. **[edited reference book, second edition]**

Fraenkel, J. R., & Wallen, N. E. (2009). *How to design and evaluate research in education* (7th ed.). New York, NY: McGraw-Hill. **[two authors, seventh edition]**

Heer, D. M. (2001). International migration. In E. F. Borgatta & R. Montgomery (Eds.), *Encyclopedia of sociology* (2nd ed., Vol. 2, pp. 1431–1438). New York, NY: Macmillan Reference. **[chapter in edited reference book, second edition]**

Kemmis, S., & Wilkinson, M. (1998). Participatory action research and the study of practice. In B. Atweh, S. Kemmis, & P. Weeks (Eds.), *Action research in practice: Partnerships for social justice in education* (pp. 21–36). New York, NY: Routledge. **[chapter in edited book]**

Figure 10.8 Examples of different online journal articles and documents in a reference list.

Davidson, G., Devaney, J., & Spratt, T. (2010). The impact of adversity in childhood outcomes in adulthood: Research lessons and limitations. *Journal of Social Work, 10*(4) 369–390. Retrieved from http://jsw.sagepub.com/content/10/4/369.refs **[URL directly to article]**

Institutional Review Board for the Protection of Human Subjects manual. (2008). Retrieved from University of San Francisco website: http://www.usfca.edu/uploadedFiles/Destinations/School_of_Education/documents/IRBPHS/irbManual.pdf **[no author, document on university website]**

Neighborhood. (n.d.). In *Merriam-Webster* online dictionary. Retrieved from http://www.merriam-webster.com/dictionary/neighborhood **[online reference material, no author, no date, URL to source's home page]**

Sleeter, C. (2008). An invitation to support diverse students through teacher education. *Journal of Teacher Education, 59*, 212–219. Retrieved from http://jte.sagepub.com/ **[URL to journal home page]**

U.S. Department of Health and Human Services. (1979). *The Belmont Report*. Retrieved from http://www.hhs.gov/ohrp/humansubjects/guidance/belmont.htm **[government report, organization as author, URL directly to report]**

About graduate education in the U.S. (n.d.). Retrieved from http://www.educationusa. info/pages/students/researchgrad.php#.UCXnUZH4LB1**[webpage, unknown author, no date]**

Criminological transition in Russia. (n.d.). Retrieved from Indiana University website: http://newsinfo.iu.edu/news/page/normal/3876.html **[webpage on university website, author unknown, no date]**

Niolin, R. (2001). *Families and substance abuse*. Retrieved from http://www.psychpage. com/family/library/familysubstanceabuse.htm **[webpage, author and date provided]**

U.S. Department of Health and Human Services. (n.d.). *U.S. public health service syphilis study at Tuskegee*. Retrieved from Centers for Disease Control and Prevention website: http://www.cdc.gov/tuskegee/timeline.htm **[webpage on government agency website, organization as author, no date]**

Chapter Three). When considering whether or not to include a table in the thesis, you should first decide if it is necessary. Sometimes it is more effective to present information in text format (and will save you a lot of time and effort). However, there are a few occasions when it is recommended to use a table. First, the table should increase efficiency for the reader. Sometimes presenting information in the text, especially when there are a lot of data, can be dense or rambling, and the reader can get lost in all the words. A table is a great way to convey information in a more efficient manner. Second, the table should supplement the text rather than duplicate it. In other words, the information in the table should extend or enhance the information that is in the text. If the table matches exactly what is in the text, then decide which is more efficient and select only one approach. Third, the table should allow for easy comparison between groups or participants. For example, in quantitative studies, sometimes you will have pre- and posttest scores or scores from different groups. In qualitative studies, you might have quotes to support a major theme. Presenting this information in the text might be too cumbersome and confusing for readers to keep track of which group performed better or who said what, so a table is a great way to show comparative data between participants and groups.

If you have decided to include a table, follow the three "C" rules for design: comprehensibility, clarity, and consistency. The first rule is comprehensibility. Since a table is a communicative tool, the reader should be able to understand it instantly. In other words, the table should be able to stand on its own. The reader should not have to guess what table headings or data in the body represent or refer back to the text to understand the table. The second rule is clarity. For the table to stand on its own, it is critical that the title, headings (e.g., for rows and columns), and data clearly convey the information. All uncommon abbreviations should be spelled out in the title or explained in the notes. The table should be easy to read and not distracting with superfluous information. Finally, the last rule is consistency. The presentation of the table needs to be consistent within and between tables. This means using similar formatting for titles and headings, being consistent with terminology, and expressing values in the same manner (e.g., decimal points, unit of measurement).

Formatting a table in APA style is like measuring happiness: There are many different ways to do it, and it depends on the message that you want to convey. There is no one best way, but if you follow the three Cs you will create a table that is organized and efficient for the reader. In the next few sections, I provide a few general tips on how to refer to and format a table. For queries on specific types of tables, please refer to the APA manual (there are many different sample tables in Chapter 5).

Tables in Text

When discussing a table in the text, number the table in the order that it appears. For example, the first table that you refer to in the text would be Table 1, then Table 2, and so on. Then give a brief description of what the table entails. Here are two examples:

The participants in the study were very diverse. Table 1 displays the participants' demographic data.

The participants in the study were very diverse (see Table 1 for participants' demographic data).

You can also highlight some of the major findings of the table, but remember that the text and table should not be redundant.

Placement and Spacing

APA has recommendations for where to place tables and what type of spacing to use in the body of tables. In a manuscript for publication for a journal, the table is placed at the end of the manuscript text. However, for student theses and dissertations, APA allows the table to be included within the text close to where it was first mentioned. A short table can share the page where it was mentioned, while a long table would be on the next page by itself. I prefer students to put tables at the end of the thesis for readability purposes; check with your chairperson to see where you should place the tables.

Table 1   Students' Mean Scores by Ethnicity on the Arc's
Self-Determination Scale

Autonomy			Self-Regulation		Psych. Empowerment	
Ethnicity	Pretest	Posttest	Pretest	Posttest	Pretest	Posttest
African American	59	59	29	62	62	75
Boys	49	59	40	60	58	77
Girls	69	73	29	75*	65	79
American Indian	40	30	43	43	75	75
Boys	49	59	40	60	58	77
Girls						
Asian American	50	66	33	33	75	81
Boys	49	59	40	60	—	—
Girls	69	73	24	75*	65	79
Caucasian	46	67	95	71	94	94
Boys	49	59	40	60	58	77
Girls	69	73	29	75	65	79
Latino/Hispanic	92	83	52	81*	88	88
Boys	49	59	40	60	58	77
Girls	69	73	34	75*	40a	79*

Note. Psych. = Psychological. Maximum score = 100. A dash indicates that the score was not available. Adapted from "Transition from School to Work," by Y. N. Bui, 2006, *Journal for Educators, 84,* p. 81. Copyright 2006 by the American Association of Educators.

aThree students did not complete the entire subscale.

*p <.05

Regarding spacing for a manuscript for publication, everything in the table is double-spaced. Again, APA makes some adjustments for student papers and allows single-spacing for table titles and headings. I prefer students to use double spacing because it makes the table easier to read. I also want students to use the regular APA rules so that they will be prepared to publish their work! Ask your chairperson if you should use single- or double-spacing in tables.

Title

Regarding selecting a title, it should be evident from the title what data are being presented in the table; this follows the rule of comprehensibility. However, the title should not be too general or detailed. For example, the title "Participants' Responses" is too vague because it does not tell the reader what the responses were from. The title, "Participants' Responses to the Online Qualtrix Survey to Measure Employees' Satisfaction With Changes in Their Health Plan, Manager's Leadership Style, and Growth Opportunities" is too long and detailed. The title, "Participants' Responses to Satisfaction Survey" is just right.

Headings and Body

The way to format headings within a table is probably the most difficult part to master; these follow the rule of clarity. Remember to organize the table to minimize distractions and maximize comprehension. In addition, if the purpose of the table is to compare data, align the two sets of data closely together. In a table, there are columns and rows. The column is vertical (up and down), and the row is horizontal (left to right). However, there are no visible vertical lines in the table. Every column and row must have a heading, and they are written in sentence capitalization. While it is not important for you to memorize APA's names of headings, it is important to understand how the headings help organize the table and facilitate comprehension.

Table 1 presents an example of an APA table. Notice a few important details of this table. The **stub head** is Ethnicity, but it can be any category that can be broken into groups such as grade, political party, gender, and so on. The **stubs** are the row headings, which are the major independent variables (groups) under the stub head. You can also have a subordinated stub, such as gender (a subgroup of the independent variable). There are also headings to identify the items that are listed vertically in each column. In this example, the **column spanners** are Autonomy, Self-Regulation, and Psychological Empowerment, which are the subscales within the Arc's Self-determination Scale (Wehmeyer & Kelchner, 1995). The **column head** identifies the items in just one column (Pretest and Posttest). Note that the pretest and posttest scores are placed next to each other for easy comparison.

Next let's discuss the cells, the points of interaction between a row and a column. The data in the cells make up the body of the table. There are several rules to follow for the cells. The key rule is consistency. However you decide to display the data, it should be consistent within the columns. For example, if you round a score in one item to two decimal points (which is usually recommended), then all the scores in that column should be rounded to two decimal points. In addition you cannot change the unit of measurement within a column. If there is a cell where the data are not applicable, then leave the cell blank. For example, the cells for American Indian girls for the "Autonomy Pretest and Posttest Scores" are left blank because there were only American Indian boys in the study. If there is a cell where the data were not obtained or reported, then insert a dash in the cell and write an explanation in the notes. For example, this table has dashes in the cells for the "Psychological Empowerment Pretest and Posttest Scores" for Asian American boys because they did not complete that particular subscale.

Notes

APA allows you to write notes to explain certain items within the table. There are three kinds of notes, and they are listed in this order at the bottom of the table: (a) general, (b) specific, and (c) probability. **General notes** are those that explain information relating to the entire table such as abbreviations or symbols. To include a general note, write the italicized word "*Note.*" at the bottom of the table followed by the notes. The notes are written in a slightly smaller font size than the rest of the table and do not have to be in complete sentences. If the table was adapted or reprinted from another source, this also needs to be indicated in the general notes. If you are reprinting a table or adapting parts of a table from a copyrighted source, you must first obtain permission from the copyright holder. The original source is then cited in the general note. After the general notes, you can list specific notes. **Specific notes** are those pertaining to an individual column, row, or cell. These are labeled with a lowercase letter superscript in the cell and explained in the specific notes (after the general notes). Finally, the probability notes are listed after the specific notes. The **probability notes** indicate the results of statistical tests for hypothesis testing. An asterisk (*) is placed in the cell, and $*p < .05$ or $**p < .01$ is written in the probability note to identify the alpha level. In Table 1, there are examples of the three different kinds of notes at the bottom of the table, although it is not required to have all types of notes in one table.

Figures

In addition to tables, it is sometimes helpful to include figures in the thesis. A figure can be a chart, graph, map, photograph, or drawing. Figures are a great way to show nonlinear relations, patterns of results, concepts, or ideas that are difficult for the reader to "see" from text descriptions. As mentioned, there are many different kinds of figures, and each one serves a different purpose. However, before including a figure, make sure that it is necessary. The decision rules for whether or not to include a figure are similar to those for a table regarding efficiency over text format and text enhancement. If you decide to include a figure in the thesis, be sure to follow the three Cs of comprehensibility, clarity, and consistency. The figure should be easy to understand (stand on its own), easy to read, and consistent in appearance.

Since there are many different types of figures you could include, I provide a few general rules. They are very similar to those for tables. For queries on specific types of figures, please refer to the APA manual.

Figures in Text

When discussing a figure in the text, number the figure in the order that it appears. For example, the first figure you refer to in the text would be Figure 1, then Figure 2, and so on. Then give a brief description of what the figure entails. Here are two examples:

Figure 1 displays the pattern of students' off-task behaviors in minutes during the 2-week program.

The students' off-task behaviors steadily decreased over the 2-week program (see Figure 1).

You can also refer to some of the major highlights in the figure, but remember that the text and figure should not be redundant.

Placement, Size, and Font

In a manuscript for publication, the figures are placed at the end of the manuscript after the tables with a separate page listing the captions. However, for student theses and dissertations, APA allows the figure to be included on the next page after it was first mentioned in the text. I prefer students to put figures at the end of the thesis; however, check with your chairperson to see where you should place the figures.

Regarding size and font, all the elements of the figure must be legible. The smallest font size is 8 point, and the largest is 14 point. The figure should also fit on the page (landscape or portrait) although APA has dimension rules for publication purposes. APA also recommends a sans serif font (without serifs) like Arial. Serifs are the small features added to strokes (which can clutter up the figure). Another thing to consider is the shapes that are used in the figure. APA recommends using circles and triangles (open and solid) because other combinations of shapes, such as squares and diamonds, can look too similar. If there is a legend to help explain the lines and points in a graph, this must be included within the margins of the graph.

Captions and Legends

For a thesis, the figure caption, or title, is placed below the figure itself. The caption is labeled Figure 1 (or whatever number figure it is), italicized with a period, and flushed to the left margin. The description of the figure follows this label using sentence capitalization. The caption should be detailed enough (but not overly detailed) so that the reader can understand the figure without having to refer to the text. The caption does not have to be a complete sentence, although it ends with a period. Following the description, you can add any necessary notes such as explaining symbols, abbreviations, and reprints from other sources. Use the same notes format APA recommends for tables.

Graphs

One common type of figure used in the master's thesis is graphs. Graphs are typically used to show relationships between two variables, comparisons of data, percentages/proportions, or patterns over time. There are many different types of graphs including scatter plots, line graphs, bar graphs, pictorial graphs, and circle (pie) graphs. A legend is located within the graph and explains any symbols used in the graph. In many graphs, there is an x axis (horizontal line) and a y axis (vertical line). The independent variable is represented on the x axis, and the dependent variable is represented on the y axis. Most computer spreadsheet programs (e.g., Microsoft Excel) can generate the graphs for you. In Figure 10.10, there is an example of a graph in APA style.

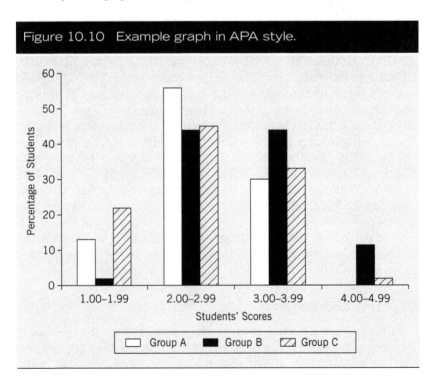

Figure 10.10 Example graph in APA style.

Final Formatting

Appendixes

Appendixes are a critical part of the thesis because they allow you to include detailed information about the study and procedures that would not be appropriate to include in the five chapters. Some items that I require students to include in the appendixes are the Institutional Review Board (IRB) cover letter and blank consent form(s), sample lessons and/or intervention materials, and measurement instruments. I require these items because they are critical to understanding the design and results of the thesis. An advantage of putting these items in the appendix is that they do not have to be computer-generated by you. For instance, if you used a commercial assessment tool or instructional materials, you could photocopy parts of these (with permission from the copyright holder) as examples.

APA does have rules to follow for appendixes in a manuscript for publication, but I do not follow them all because I want to allow for greater flexibility in the thesis. Check with your chairperson for how she wants you to include appendixes in the thesis.

Appendixes in Text

The APA rule for referring to appendixes in the text is similar to tables and figures. When mentioning an appendix in the text, label the appendix in the order that it appears; however, use capital letters instead of numbers. For example, the first appendix you refer to would be Appendix A, then Appendix B, and so on. Then give a brief description of what the appendix entails. Here is an example:

> The researcher obtained parental consent prior to contacting the students for participation in the study (see Appendix A for informed parent consent forms).

Placement and Cover Pages

The appendixes are typically placed at the very end of the thesis after the tables and figures. For a manuscript for publication, APA requires that page numbers extend into the appendixes. I do not require students to continue the page numbers for the appendixes in the thesis. This allows for flexibility in photocopying items from other sources. However, since the individual items do not have page numbers, make sure that each item has an appropriate heading for easy identification.

Figure 10.11   Sample cover page for appendix.

Appendix B: Measurement Instruments

- Student satisfaction survey
- Student observation protocol
- Teacher interview protocol
- Caregiver interview protocol

To identify and label the appendixes, each one begins with a cover page on a separate page. The cover page lists the title of the appendix and the items within the appendix (i.e., you can have more than one item in a single appendix). On the cover page, use a larger font for the title of the appendix and then list the items in a smaller font. The title is centered near the top of the page and the items are below the title, flushed left with bullet points. In Figure 10.11, there is an example of a cover page. Note that there are four different measurement instruments included in this appendix. These items would be inserted after the cover page in the order that they are listed.

Front Pages

Remember when I promised in Chapter 1 that I would pull you through the finish line if I had to? Well, look at where you are today! If you are ready to prepare the front pages of the thesis, this is like the last 385 yards of the marathon. You can almost touch the finish line, and your loved ones are on the other side taking pictures and chanting your name! Savor this moment. As soon as you complete the front pages, you are truly done. I promise. The front pages include the title and signature pages, acknowledgments, abstract, and table of contents. These are not in APA style, so check with your chairperson for how he wants you to proceed with these items. Each institution will have its own formatting requirements for these front pages.

Title Page

The title page is the cover page for the entire thesis. On this page, you need to identify the title of the thesis, institution, name of the degree, your name, and date. The title of your thesis should be between 10 and 12 words and encompass the essence of your study. There is a sample title page in Figure 10.12 (adjust the spacing on your page to make it look aesthetically pleasing).

Title in Heading Capitalization [Centered and Bold]

A Thesis Presented to the Faculty of the College of Education [Name of College]

San Francisco State University [Name of University]

In Partial Fulfillment of the Requirements of the Degree of

MASTER OF ARTS [DEGREE TITLE]

in

SPECIAL EDUCATION [DEGREE AREA]

by

Yvonne N. Bui [Your Name]

May 15, 2020 [Date thesis will be signed]

Signature Page

The next page is the signature page; this is where your chairperson and committee members will sign the thesis. Remember, the thesis is not official until it has been approved and signed by your chairperson and committee members. On this page, leave space and lines for your chairperson and committee members to sign (add more lines if necessary). There is a sample signature page in Figure 10.13 (adjust the spacing on your page to make it look aesthetically pleasing).

Acknowledgments

The next page is the Acknowledgments. This is really the best page in the entire thesis because you get to acknowledge and thank every person who supported you along the way. Do not forget to acknowledge your chairperson and committee members, family, friends, pets, the local coffee barista, me, and so on. The title of this page is "Acknowledgments" (in British spelling, it is "Acknowledgements"), and it is centered at the top of the page. This page is also where you begin the page numbers in roman numerals (e.g., i, ii, iii, iv). I prefer page numbers at the bottom of the page in the center. However, APA style is upper right-hand corner for manuscripts, so check with your chairperson to see if she has a preference.

Abstract

The next page is the abstract. The abstract is a brief (usually between 150 to 250 words) summary of the thesis. While it is brief, the abstract should also be comprehensive in describing the purpose, participants, methods, and major findings/results/conclusions. The title "Abstract" is centered, but the text is flushed to the left margin. There is an example of an abstract in Figure 10.14.

Figure 10.13   Sample signature page for thesis.

Title in Heading Capitalization

In Partial Fulfillment of the Requirements of the

MASTER OF ARTS

in

SPECIAL EDUCATION

By

Yvonne N. Bui

SAN FRANCISCO STATE UNIVERSITY

May 15, 2020

Under the guidance and approval of the committee, and approved by all its members, this thesis has been accepted in partial fulfillment of the requirements for the degree.

Approved:

_____   _____

Chairperson   Date

_____   _____

Committee Member   Date

Figure 10.14   Sample abstract that summarizes the study.

Abstract

The purpose of the study was to measure the effects of a comprehensive writing program for students with and without learning disabilities (LD) in inclusive general education classrooms. The program included prewriting, narrative text structure, writing strategies, and process writing. The study was conducted in five 5th-grade classrooms with 113 students (14 students with LD). A quasi-experimental comparison-group design was used; three experimental classes received the intervention, and two comparison classes received traditional writing instruction. Measures included writing indicators as well as state writing competency test scores. The students in the experimental group made significant gains from pretest to posttest on most writing measures. Students in the comparison group made gains on some measures, but the effect sizes were smaller.

Table of Contents

The next few pages are the table of contents. The table of contents is extremely critical because it is a road map to the entire thesis. Therefore, make sure the page numbers and headings match exactly what is in the text of the thesis. I typically advise students to create the table of contents at the end after all the final, final, final edits are completed (in case things shift around). The title of your thesis is at the top center and every letter should be capitalized. Then the front pages are listed on separate lines starting with the Acknowledgments, Abstract, and Table of Contents.

Lists of Tables and Figures

The next items in the table of contents are List of Tables, List of Figures, and List of Appendixes. These are recommended if you have more than one table, figure, or appendix, because it makes it easier for the reader to find the information embedded in the text or at the end of the thesis. The List of Tables and List of Figures are lists of the titles and page numbers of individual tables and figures. The List of Appendixes lists the titles of the appendixes but there are no page numbers.

The next page is the first page of Chapter One. This page starts the Arabic numerals (1, 2, 3, etc.) that extend into the references, tables, and figures. After each chapter heading, list all the Level 2 and Level 3 headings with their corresponding page numbers. Slightly indent each subheading within the chapter. Do not list Level 4 headings. After the chapters, the last item on the table of contents is "References" with the corresponding page. Figure 10.15 is a sample of a condensed Table of Contents.

Final Tips and Checklist

The final tips and checklist are to ensure that everything is in place before you copy and bind the thesis forever. They are not in any particular order. Some of them may not apply to your situation, so when in doubt, check with your chairperson.

- Do a final grammar and spell check for all chapters.

- Match citations in text with reference list.

- Set left-hand margin at 1.5 (4 cm) for binding purposes.

- Copy thesis on heavyweight high-quality white paper.

- Start each chapter on a new page.

- Use Roman numerals (i, ii, iii) for the front pages (e.g., Acknowledgments, Abstract).

Figure 10.15 Sample condensed table of contents.

TITLE [ALL LETTERS ARE CAPITALIZED]

- Use Arabic numerals (1, 2, 3) on the first page of Chapter One and continue into the references, tables, and figures.

- Keep at least one signed copy for yourself (your chairperson and institution/program usually also get a copy).

- All text, references, and tables should be double-spaced (unless your chairperson says otherwise).

- Check the levels of heading to make sure they are correct.

- Spell out all abbreviations at first mention and put in notes in the tables and figures.

- Check that all table columns have headings.

- Obtain written permission for all copyrighted material for quotes, tables, and figures from the copyright holder.

- Cite all direct quotations with page numbers.

- List a retrieval location for online sources.

- Check all URLs to ensure they work.

Copying and Binding

After you are done with the front pages, thesis text, references, tables, figures, appendixes, and final check, you can bring it all to get copied and bound (see Final Tips and Checklist on p . 239). Check with your chairperson for the guidelines for copying and binding. At some institutions, they may ask only for an electronic copy. However, you can make as many copies as you want (they make great gifts!). If you choose a professional copy center, you should not have problems. Allow the center a few days to have the copies made, since they are usually very busy at the beginning and end of semesters. After you have the bounded (or electronic) copies signed by your chairperson and committee members, you are truly done.

CONGRATULATIONS!!! Bravo! Hooray! Yippee! Yahoo! I don't have the words to express how happy I am for you and how relieved you must be. Thank you for taking this journey with me. Now sprint across the finish line with your head held high, arms waving in the air. Then reward yourself with a nice long vacation.

Next Steps: Presenting at Conferences and Getting Published

Wait! There's more? Now that you are well-rested from your long vacation (I know you wore a hat and plenty of sunscreen), it is time to present and publish your master's thesis! You have spent months (years?) researching and writing the thesis, so why not put in a bit more effort and present your thesis and publish it in an academic journal. I promise you will love the way your name looks in print. Plus since your study is filling a gap in the existing research, it is important that you disseminate your work! Chapters 2 and 8 in the APA manual are completely devoted to the publication process (with a great checklist at the end of the chapter), so I give you a few tips and a lot of encouragement.

The first step is to submit a proposal to present your research at a professional conference in your field. This is critical because it will allow you to get feedback from the peers in your discipline. You cannot go back and change your methodology, but perhaps there were data that could have been analyzed differently or critical implications that you missed. By presenting your study first, you have the opportunity to review the study with fresh, critical eyes. Remember that when you are presenting at a conference, you want to make sure that you are not reading from a script or verbatim from your thesis. You want to give an overview of the study, background, and methodology, and highlight the critical findings and results. Visuals or participant quotes are very helpful to help illustrate main points. Your attendees will want to know how your study impacts their work, so be sure to share some key takeaways or lessons learned.

The second step is to find the perfect journal to submit your manuscript. The perfect journal will be one that is in your field/discipline and is related to the research topic of your thesis. The journal should also be at the research level of your study, most likely at a scholarly practitioner level. You do not want to submit your manuscript to a top tiered journal unless your research methodology was very rigorous (which is really hard to do at the master's level). Once you have selected a journal that you think is appropriate, review the manuscript guidelines and read several articles so that you have a sense of the writing style and whether your study will be a good fit. Finding a good fit is critical—you can have a fantastic study but if the editor and reviewers do not believe it is good fit for their audience, they will reject it.

The third step is to read and follow directions carefully. The manuscript guidelines for author submission will be posted on the journal's webpage, and you need to follow them step-by-step. If you do not follow their exact instructions, there is a good chance that your manuscript will not be reviewed. Most journals want manuscripts submitted through an electronic portal (with all identifiable information removed) so that the review process is confidential.

The fourth step is to edit your thesis very carefully. Submitting sloppy work with grammatical or spelling errors (or not following APA style) will only upset the editor and reviewers and will reduce any chances of the manuscript being accepted. Do not simply cut and paste chunks of your thesis. You will need to rewrite the manuscript by following the journal's guidelines. Remember that you can submit your manuscript to only one journal at a time. This is partly why it takes so long for research to become published. You have to wait until the entire review process is completed before you can submit your study to another journal.

Finally, do not give up. Based on the peer reviews, the editor has the choice to *accept, accept with revisions,* or *reject the manuscript.* I will not tell you how many times my manuscripts have been rejected and about how every manuscript that has been accepted was with revisions. The positive part about being rejected is that you can read the reviewers' comments (after you give yourself a pity party) and revise your manuscript to make it stronger. Then you can submit the manuscript to another journal that might be a better fit. The key to getting published (like everything else in life) is perseverance. Do not give up if you are rejected! I know it is difficult to keep it separate, but a manuscript rejection is not a personal rejection of you! Simply find a journal that might be a better match and go through the submission process again. It can take several tries before you are successful. Obviously you know a thing or two about perseverance because you have just completed a master's thesis! Just think, after you present and publish your thesis, you can take another long vacation. You will need the energy to get ready for your next big study. . . . Did I hear you say "doctoral dissertation"?

SUMMARY

In this chapter, I discussed the editorial style rules and guidelines established by APA (2010) for citations, references, tables, figures, and other issues to help you finalize the master's thesis. I hope they helped you complete the final product. Congratulations again on completing your master's thesis, a major feat! Here is a summary of the most critical points from Chapter 10:

- The APA editorial style is commonly used in various social science disciplines such as education, psychology, sociology, business, economics, nursing, and social work.

- The *number* of level headings refers to the quantity of headings you use. The total maximum number of level headings is five. The *number level* heading refers to a specific heading location.

- Citations of works are necessary when you use a direct quote (which needs a page number) or paraphrase someone else's words, ideas, or research findings.

- Keep the listing of the authors in their original order from the source even if it is not in alphabetical order.

- If the work is cited in the text, it must be in the reference list and vice versa. In addition, the citation in the text (e.g., spelling and order of the authors, year of publication) must be exactly the same as the citation in the reference list.

- For online sources, provide the retrieval location (or DOI) in addition to information required for printed material.

- Follow the three "C" rules for table and figure design: comprehensibility, clarity, and consistency.

- Figures are a great way to show nonlinear relations, patterns of results, concepts, or ideas that are difficult for the reader to "see" from text descriptions.

- Items that may be included in the appendixes are the IRB cover letter and blank consent form(s), sample lessons/intervention materials, and measurement instruments.

- The front pages include the title and signature pages, acknowledgments, abstract, and table of contents.

RESOURCES

Common Obstacles and Practical Solutions

1. A common obstacle that students face in final editing is keeping track of the citations and references. Words that come to mind are "Where do I find all these references?" The best way to overcome this obstacle is to cite and reference as you write (rather than wait until the very end). Put the citation in the text immediately when you paraphrase or quote with the year and page numbers. Then keep a list of all the sources, even if it is not in the correct APA format. You can format the references at the end, but this will save you time searching for the references. Investing in a reference management software program will really pay off in the end!

2. Another common obstacle is preparing tables. Words that come to mind are "Do I really need this table?" First, you should decide if the table really is necessary. If it is, then keep it as simple as possible. Have a few columns (no more than three) and rows. Since printing cost and spacing is not as much of an issue in the thesis (like it is for manuscripts for publication), you can spread out your data over several tables. This will help you in terms of formatting and may make it easier for your reader to decipher the tables.

Reflection/Discussion Questions

When you are doing the final formatting for the thesis, it is important to understand the APA style editorial rules and guidelines. The following reflection/discussion questions will help guide you through the editorial process.

1. What is the difference between the number of level headings and a number level heading? Looking through an outline, how would you use different levels of heading in your thesis to help organize the topics and subtopics for the reader?

2. Why is it important to provide citations and references for the sources that you use? What are the different types of sources (print and online) that you used in your thesis? Do you have all the information that is required to provide a complete citation?

3. After you have completed the master's thesis, it is time to think about how to present it at a professional conference and have it published in a peer-reviewed journal. Think about possible conferences and peer-reviewed journals in your discipline that would be a good fit to submit a manuscript.

Try It Exercises

The following exercises are designed to help you edit and format the thesis. In Activity One, you will create a reference list for various sources. In Activity Two, you will create a table using demographic data from the participants in your study.

1. Activity One: For this activity, create a condensed reference list from five of your in-text citations (try to list a variety). Be sure to identify the type of work and then include all necessary information in your reference. Have a partner check them to make sure they are correct!

2. Activity Two: For this activity, create a table based on your participants (e.g., demographic data, test scores, qualitative quotes). Have a partner check it to make sure it is comprehensible, clear, and consistent.
   - Include the stub column, one column spanner, and two column heads.
   - Include at least one stub (row header).
   - Insert data for at least five participants.

Key Terms

column head 231
column spanner 231
digital object identifier (DOI) 224
general notes 232
hanging indent 225
levels of heading 218

probability notes 232
sentence
   capitalization 225
specific notes 232
stub head 231
stubs 231

Suggested Readings

American Psychological Association. (2010). *Publication manual of the American Psychological Association* (6th ed.). Washington, DC: Author.

Schwartz, B. M., Landrum, R. E., & Gurung, A. A. R. (2012). *An easy guide to APA style*. Thousand Oaks, CA: Sage.

Web Links

APA Style

http://www.apastyle.org/

APA Style Resources

https://www.apa.org/pubs/apastyle/index.aspx

BibMe

http://www.bibme.org/citation-guide/apa/

Citation Machine

http://www.citationmachine.net/apa/cite-a-book

Penn State: APA Quick Citation Guide

http://guides.libraries.psu.edu/apaquickguide

Plagiarism.org

http://www.plagiarism.org/

Purdue Online Writing Lab: APA Style

https://owl.purdue.edu/owl/research_and_citation/apa_style/apa_style_introduction.html

Appendix A

Sample Institutional
Review Board Initial Application

Project Title: Bridging Cultural Themes in Educational Practices: Increasing Students' Math Performance

(1) Background and Rationale

With today's changes in demographics, there is evidence to suggest that the United States is becoming *more* culturally and linguistically diverse. Unlike 50 years ago when schools and classrooms were primarily composed of a homogeneous student population, today's schools and teachers are increasingly challenged with educating students from diverse cultural, linguistic, and economic backgrounds. By the year 2020, it is estimated that nearly 50% of school-age students in the United States will represent African American, Asian, Hispanic, or some other non-European ethnic group (Woolfolk, 2001).

The recent demographic changes have serious implications for the nation's public education system. In addition to adjusting to differences in cultural values and behaviors, classroom educators are faced with the additional challenge of teaching students who may come from cultural and linguistic backgrounds that differ from their own. Moreover, as the student population in the United States continues to become more heterogeneous, the demographics of school staff have become more homogeneous (Taylor, 2000). In other words, although most teachers are middle class and mono-cultural, and many are also monolingual, depending on the geographic region and type of district (e.g., rural, urban, suburban) they teach in, the students they serve may be from diverse cultural, economic, and linguistic backgrounds. Thus, teachers are less likely than in the 1950s to be from the same cultural and language backgrounds as their students (Santos, Fowler, Corso, & Bruns, 2000). This is even more apparent in states and regions where students from different cultures and languages are disproportionately represented in certain disability categories (Meese, 2001). For example, African American, Hispanic, and Native American students tend to be overidentified with emotional disturbances, learning disabilities, and speech/language impairments, and underidentified for gifted and talented placements (Artiles & Trent, 1994; Artiles & Zamora-Duran, 1997; Gollnick & Chinn, 1990).

Students of color also tend to perform lower on national and state standardized assessments than White students. For example, on the National

Assessment of Educational Performance (NAEP) math tests, at both Grades 4 and 8, White and Asian/Pacific Islander students scored higher, on average, than Black, Hispanic, and American Indian/Alaska Native students. Black students scored lower than both Hispanic and American Indian/Alaska Native students (NAEP, 2006). On average, students with disabilities scored 23 points lower at Grade 4 and 40 points lower at Grade 8 than students without disabilities.

Considering the disproportionate rates with which minority students are placed in special education and identified with learning disabilities (LD), there is a tiny database of empirical articles on ethnic minority students in special education journals (Artiles, Trent, & Kuan, 1997). The lack of empirical research on math instruction for minority students with disabilities over the past two decades has serious implications for researchers and educators. By not providing special educators with information and training in effective math practices for minority students with LD that are empirically supported, we are only increasing the probability of cultural dissonance and academic frustration and failure for these students. Thus, the purpose of this study is to increase the mathematics performance of students with disabilities from culturally and linguistically diverse backgrounds. This will be accomplished by integrating African American cultural themes of *communalism, movement,* and *orality* into the math instruction as a means to align the students' home and school cultures.

(2) Description of Sample

The research study will examine and measure the effectiveness of an intervention, Bridging Cultural Themes in Educational Practices, in an elementary classroom in an urban school district. The research will be conducted at one public elementary school in (name of city) in the (name of district) School District. This district was targeted because of its urban climate and high proportion of low-income students with disabilities representing culturally diverse populations. One fourth- through sixth-grade class (special education day class) in a school where the principal and teacher have shown significant interest and support for the project will be selected for participation. The class is made up of 12 boys with emotional disturbance or learning disabilities. Ten of the students are African American, and two are Latino. Two of the students are fourth graders, six of the students are fifth graders, and four of the students are sixth graders.

(3) Recruitment Procedure

Once the district and principal have given their permission to conduct the study, the researcher will then ask the classroom teacher to send home consent forms to the students' parents, informing them about the study

are successful, these themes could be used and integrated with research-based math instruction for students with disabilities. Following integrated instruction within the three cultural themes, students will be expected to achieve the following outcomes: increased math performance on informal math assessments and increased student satisfaction.

(9) Costs to Subjects

There are no financial costs to the participating students. All the supplies needed for instruction will be provided to the students by the researcher. All the BCTEP instruction will be delivered during normal instruction time during the school day.

(10) Reimbursement/Compensation to Subjects

Student participants will not be reimbursed or compensated for participating in this study. The classroom teacher who participates will be given a small honorarium for her time (e.g., during informal meetings) and help with collecting consent forms.

(11) Confidentiality of Records

All data from the study will be kept confidential and the subjects' identities will not be revealed before, during, or after the study. The students' names will be removed from the pre- and posttest data, and they will be assigned numbers to ensure confidentiality. Data will be kept by the researcher in a locked file away from the school site. Computerized data will be inputted into a password-protected laptop computer that will also be removed from the school site. Only the researcher and her assistant will have access to the data.

_____   _____

Signature of Applicant   Date

Appendix B

Sample Cover Letter

Dear Sir or Madam:

[introduction] My name is (insert your name) and I am a(n) (insert your role) in the Department of (insert your department/school) at (insert name of college/university).

[purpose] I am writing to you to request your consent for your child to participate in a research study that I am doing to investigate the effectiveness of an intervention called Bridging Cultural Themes in Educational Practices (BCTEP) on students' math performance.

[description of study] This intervention integrates the African American cultural themes of communalism, movement, and orality with standards-based mathematics instruction for students with disabilities. For example, students will work in interdependent groups (i.e., communalism) to solve math problems together. Movement will be integrated during the math instruction through dance, rhythm, and music. Orality will provide the opportunity for students to participate in the mathematics instruction through various forms of spoken language (e.g., call and response). The intent of this intervention is to match the classroom environment and teaching practices with the students' home culture to minimize conflicts and maximize achievement for students with disabilities from culturally diverse backgrounds.

[procedures] If you allow your child to participate, your child's classroom teacher, (insert name of teacher), will teach a math curriculum on fractions for 8 weeks (50 minutes per day) using standards-based math materials by integrating the African American cultural themes. Before and after the study, your child will take math tests and a satisfaction survey to measure the effects of the intervention. A mini math test will also be given after every lesson.

[confidentiality] Rest assured that I will take steps to maintain confidentiality of your child's records by keeping all data materials, including teacher reports and academic records, in a locked filing cabinet at my home. All records will remain confidential, and your child's participation or nonparticipation will in no way negatively affect the quality of education your child receives, or the quality of services you receive as a parent of a child attending the researcher's school.

[cost/benefit] There will be no cost to your child for participating. At your own request, I will provide you with a copy of the completed study at no cost. There will be no payment available to you for your child's participation; however, it is my feeling that your child will benefit greatly from the math instruction and teachers will also be informed of effective math instruction.

[informed consent] Participation in research is voluntary. You are free to decline your child's participation in this study, or withdraw from it at any point. (Insert name), principal of (insert name of school), is aware of this study, but she is not requiring that your child participate in this research and your decision as to whether or not to participate will have no influence on the quality of education your child will receive at (insert name of school), nor will your child's participation or nonparticipation influence future interactions between him/herself and school personnel.

[contact information] Thank you for your consent and assistance with this study. If you have any questions, please feel free to contact me by phone at (insert phone number) or by e-mail at (insert e-mail address) or by regular mail at (insert mailing address).

Sincerely,

(insert your name)

(insert your title)

Appendix C

Sample Informed Consent Form

PARENT INFORMED CONSENT FORM
(INSERT NAME OF COLLEGE/UNIVERSITY)
CONSENT TO BE A RESEARCH SUBJECT

Purpose and Background

(Insert name, role, school/college, university) is doing a study to investigate the effectiveness of Bridging Cultural Themes in Educational Practices (BCTEP), an intervention that integrates the African American cultural themes of communalism, movement, and orality with standards-based mathematics instruction for students with disabilities.

My child is being asked to participate because he/she is a student in the special education classroom in which the teacher has voluntarily agreed to participate in the study.

Procedures

If I allow my child to be a participant in this study, the following may happen:

1. The classroom teacher will teach my child math strategies daily (50 minutes) for 8 weeks using standards-based math materials that integrate African American cultural themes.
2. (Insert name) will have access to my child's relevant documents/educational records (which will remain confidential).
3. My child will complete a math test before and after the study is completed.
4. My child will complete a satisfaction survey about math before and after the study is completed.
5. My child will complete a mini math test after each lesson is completed.

Risks or Discomforts

1. It is possible that some of the questions on the satisfaction survey may make my child feel uncomfortable, but he/she is free to decline to answer any questions or to stop participation at any time.

2. Participation in research may mean a loss of confidentiality. Study records will be kept as confidential as is possible. No individual identities will be used in any reports or publications resulting from the study. Study information will be coded and kept in locked files away from the school site at all times. Only study personnel will have access to the files.

Benefits

There will be no direct benefit to me for letting my child participate in this study. However, it is likely that my child will improve his/her math performance and increase his/her satisfaction with school and math. Other benefits include minimizing the probability of cultural misunderstandings and therefore maximizing achievement for students from culturally diverse backgrounds who have special needs.

Costs/Financial Considerations

There will be no financial costs to me or to my child as a result of taking part in this study.

Payment/Reimbursement

There will be no payment for my child's participation in this study. However, my child will receive school supply materials at no cost to the school or me.

Questions

I have talked to (insert your name and chairperson) about this study and have had my questions answered. If I have further questions about the study, I may call him/her at (insert phone number) or e-mail him/her at (insert e-mail address).

If I have any questions or comments about my child's participation in this study, I should first talk with the researchers. If, for some reason, I do not wish to do this, I may contact the Institutional Review Board for the Protection of Human Subjects (IRBPHS), which is concerned with protection of volunteers in research projects. I may reach the IRBPHS office by calling (insert phone number), by e-mailing (insert e-mail address), or by writing to the IRBPHS at (insert school address).

Consent

I have been given a copy of the "Research Subject's Bill of Rights" and I have been given a copy of this consent form to keep.

PARTICIPATION IN RESEARCH IS VOLUNTARY. I am free to decline to be in this study or to withdraw my child from it at any point. My decision as to whether or not to participate in this study will have no influence on my or my child's present or future status as a student or employee at (insert name of college/university).

My signature below indicates that I agree to have my child participate in this study.

_____   _____

Student's Name   Student's Teacher

_____   _____

Signature of Parent/Guardian   Date of Signature

(PLEASE KEEP ONE COPY OF THE CONSENT FORM FOR YOUR RECORDS)

Appendix D

Dr. Bui's Writing Tips and Rules From A to Z

A:

- Active vs. passive voice: Use the *active voice* so that your sentences are more concise:
  - "The dog bit the boy." (active)
  - "The boy was bitten by the dog." (passive)
- Affect vs. effect:
  - Affect is the *verb* form: "The students' reading scores were affected by the instruction."
  - Effect is the *noun* form: "There was a positive effect on the students' reading scores."
- Also: Do not start a sentence with "also"—use other transitions such as "in addition," "further," and so on.
- Always use APA format in the text and in the reference section.

B:

- Back it up: When you make a definitive statement such as, "Students with disabilities perform lower on standardized tests," you need to back this up with a citation.
- Buffers: Do not write paragraphs where every sentence ends with a citation. This makes the writing extremely choppy. You need to include buffer statements in between the citations where you are connecting the information or expanding/commenting on it in some way.

C:

- Chairperson: Communicate frequently with your chairperson. When in doubt, or if you get stuck, make an appointment to see him. Do not hide from your chairperson, especially if you are not making steady progress.
- Citations in text use APA format.

- Colons: Only use them sparingly and when you're making a long list. Then number the items.
  - "The intervention included the following components: (a) blah, (b) blah blah, (c) blah blah blah, and (d) final blahs."
- Commas: Do not go crazy with your use of commas.
  - Use them with lists: "preferences, attitudes, and behavior."
  - Use them in between compound sentences: "The students increased their scores, and the teachers improved their instructional methods."
  - Use them after dependent clauses: "When the students were grouped by disability, there was a difference in their scores."

D:

- Data are always plural. Say, "Data are" or "data were."
- Don't (do not) use contractions in the thesis at all—spell them all out.

E:

- Edit, edit, edit. Read your writing aloud to make sure it makes sense. Then have someone else read it before you turn it in to your chairperson.
- Et al.: This can only be used if you have listed all the authors the first time or if there are six or more authors (see APA). If you are going to use it, then it should be "(Bui et al., 2020)."

F:

- Fluency: Use transitions and segues so your writing is not choppy (see buffers).
- Fragments: Sentence fragments are incomplete sentences, such as "While they were taking the test," or "Because they had a disability."

G:

- Graphs (all figures) follow APA format.

H:

- Headings: Use three level headings if you want to organize using the three parallel ladders strategy.

I:

- "It" is a pronoun—do not start your sentence with "It."

J:

- Jargon: Terms that are uncommon should be briefly defined in the text. Longer definitions belong in the definition of terms section in Chapter One.

K:

- Keep paragraph structure intact. Start the paragraph with a good topic sentence and then make sure all the sentences within the paragraph fit the topic sentence.

L:

- Label all the acronyms the first time they appear: "students with learning disabilities (LD)"—after that, you can use the acronym alone, "students with LD."

M:

- Match the subject with the appropriate pronoun: "The *student's* score and *her* attitude." "The *students'* scores and *their* attitudes."

- Multiple works: When you have multiple works, group them together in alphabetical order—"Students of color are overrepresented in special education (Bobbett, 2014; Bui, 2018; Edwards, 2015; Hawk & Lee, 2020)."

N:

- Numbers should always be spelled out when they start a sentence. Spell out numbers under 10 and use figures to express numbers 10 and above.

O:

- Organizational structure: Be sure to structure your chapters using the three parallel ladders strategy.

- Outline: Before you write, you should create an outline of the topic sentence for each paragraph. Then you can see if your paper has funneled correctly in the Introduction and if you have the three related areas in the *Statement of the Problem* and the *Background and Need.*

P:

- Pace yourself: Set a writing goal for yourself every day whether it is a time goal or a completion goal. Do not wait 2 weeks before the thesis deadline. This is not something you can "wing" at the last minute.

- Paraphrase; do not plagiarize.

- Possessives:
  o For singular, the apostrophe goes before the "s"—"The teacher's class had eight students."
  o For plural, the apostrophe goes after the "s"—"The teachers' classes had a total of 50 students."

Q:

- Quotes: Use quotes sparingly, and if you do, you need to cite the exact page number from the source.

R:

- References: Look to see how APA formats citations in the text and in the reference list.

- Rhetorical questions: Do not ask rhetorical questions in the text.

- Run-on sentences: Break "long" sentences into shorter ones. This does not mean you should only write simple sentences. However, if your "sentence" is longer than four lines, it is probably a run-on sentence.

S:

- Save: Press the "save" button every time you finish writing a sentence or paragraph—this will keep you from having a nervous breakdown when your computer freezes.

- Segues and transitions: Make sure to segue between paragraphs. Headers are not transitions.

- Semicolons: Semicolons are used to separate independent clauses: "The students' behavior was atrocious; the teacher sent them to the principal's office." If you are not certain of whether or not to use a semicolon, use a period instead.

- Soften your language: Unless you have evidence to back it up (with a citation), you should soften your statement so it is not so definitive.

- o "Students' low motivation causes them to have poor self-esteem"—strong statement, needs a citation.
- o "Students' low motivation may negatively affect their self-esteem"—softer, does not need a citation.

T:

- Tense: 95% of the thesis will be in the past tense since most of the research has already been conducted.

- Their/there: *Their* is used to show possession—"Their behaviors were inappropriate." This is different from *there*, which indicates location—"The books are over there."

U:

- Use formal, technical language and terms. Do not use informal language, slang, or vernacular, and do not "preach" to the reader (no standing on a soapbox).

- Use "people-first" language:
  - o "Students receiving special education services"
  - o "Students with disabilities"
  - o "Students with special needs"
  - o "Students with autism"

V:

- Value judgments: Do not use words that express worth or value. For example: "There were *only* eight students in the study." "The students *finally* improved on their tests." "The mean gains from pre to posttest were *pitiful.*"

- Versions: Always date and properly label the versions of your writing—this will keep you from revising an old draft.

W:

- Write, write, and rewrite.

- Writing center: If you need writing help, get it!

X:

- Xerox copies: Have some form of copy of your writing—either in hard copy or electronic. E-mail drafts to yourself or save it on a jump drive, external hard drive, or Cloud storage provider. Computers crash all the time—you do not have to.

Y:

- You: "You" does not belong in the thesis—neither do "we," "our," "I," or "us"—always keep the writing in the third person (check with your chairperson).

Z:

- Zzzzzzzz . . . get sleep. Writing is easier when you are rested. Take frequent (but short) breaks to rest your eyes—blink a lot when you are at the computer (do not strain your eyes). Write difficult sections when you are most alert. If you are hitting a mental writing block, do a less demanding task such as typing up your references.

Appendix E

Sample Chapter One Introduction

Adapted from Williams, A. (2006). *Motivation, metacognition, and self-determination among students with learning disabilities.* Unpublished master's thesis, University of San Francisco, California.

[broad problem: national level]

The quality of public education in the United States is often judged by student academic performance. One of the four pillars of the No Child Left Behind Act of 2001 (NCLB) is stronger accountability for academic results (U.S. Department of Education, 2003). In looking at national academic performance data, there appears to be ample room for improvement. For example, the Program for International Student Assessment (PISA) reported in 2003 that 15-year-olds in the United States performed below their peers in 29 industrialized countries in the academic area of mathematics (PISA, 2003). Only 24% of 12th-grade students nationwide performed at or above the *proficient* level in writing, and average reading scale scores were lower among 12th graders in 2002 than in 1992. Given the consequences of not meeting academic standards as outlined in the NCLB, states are eager to improve students' academic outcomes.

[implications/manifestations of national problem]

Poor academic performance may lead to student discouragement and disenchantment with the public education system, which may contribute to student dropout rates. Nationally, 5% of students enrolled in high school in 1999 left school before October 2000 as reported by National Center for Education Statistics (NCES) studies. NCES also reported that in October 2000, approximately 3.8 million people between the ages of 16 and 24 were not enrolled in high school or had not completed a high school program (NCES, 2005a).

Given the level of noncompletion of high school programs, poor postsecondary outcomes at the national and state levels may be expected. According to NCES, one of the goals of public education is to provide young people with the academic skills necessary for success in a postsecondary learning environment. Students who do not complete a secondary program do not receive this academic training and will most likely be unsuccessful in a postsecondary school setting or not attempt enrollment in a college or university at all (NCES, 2005a). The Organisation for Economic Co-operation and Development calculated the first-time entry rate in postsecondary education for students in the United States to be at 42% in 2003. This was a shamefully low percentage compared to Australia, Finland, Iceland, New Zealand, Norway, Poland, and Sweden, which had first-time entry rates of 60% or more (NCES, 2005b).

Disinterest in education among adolescents in the United States is an issue that has very serious consequences, including increased risk for poor academic performance, school dropout, poor postsecondary outcomes, and criminal activity (Caraway, Tucker, Reinke, & Hall, 2003). According to Caraway et al., one third of high school seniors in 1999 felt that what they were learning in school was not important to their future. Between 1980 and 1999, the percentage of high school seniors who felt like what they were being taught in school was *meaningful and important* declined by 29%. A study reported that peer support and encouragement of antisocial behavior has been steadily increasing since 1976 (Boesel, 2001). These negative attitudes toward school relate to poor academic achievement and postsecondary outcomes.

An alternative to attending a postsecondary program after graduating or dropping out of high school would be obtaining gainful employment; however, statistics with regards to employment opportunities for youth without high school diplomas do not appear to be very encouraging. For example, in 2003, 44% of people between 16 and 24 who dropped out of high school before receiving a diploma were not enrolled in a postsecondary program or employed. Education level was cited as an important factor in youth unemployment rates (NCES, 2005a).

In addition to poor employment prospects, young people who do not complete a high school program or do not continue their education in a postsecondary environment are more likely to be involved in criminal activity. Approximately 75% of state prison inmates did not complete high school, and approximately 47% of drug offenders do not have a high school diploma or a GED (Harlow, 2003). Additionally, high school dropouts are 3.5 times more likely than high school graduates to be arrested in their lifetimes (Alliance for Excellent Education, 2003). These figures seem to support the importance of academic achievement and enrollment in high school and postsecondary programs for young people. Clearly, school personnel should sustain dropout prevention programs and encouragement of postsecondary education. If the present trends continue, a growth in the number of incarcerated and jobless youth can be expected. These national statistics are causing growing concern among educators, politicians, parents, and students across the country.

[one-step funnel: problem on state level]

States such as California are not immune to these growing national trends, and education data for California were found to be similar to national data. For example, in 2003, only 22% of eighth-grade students in California performed at or above the *proficient* level in math and reading on the National Assessment of Educational Progress (NAEP) assessment. For the 2003–2004 Academic Performance Index (API) cycle, fewer than half of the high schools in California met their API growth target as reported by the California Department of Education (2004).

[implications/manifestations of state problems]

In California, the dropout statistics were also consistent with those of the rest of the country. A 2003 study conducted by the Pacific Research Institute (PRI) showed that over 30% of California's students did not complete a high school program within 4 years (PRI, 2005). This study also noted that due to tracking challenges, this figure might actually be higher than 30%. State postsecondary enrollment figures are equally discouraging. A study conducted by the Los Angeles Unified School District found that fewer than 50% of graduating high school students in California attended college in 1998 (PRI, 2005).

[one-step funnel: specific sample group]

Students with disabilities were reported to be at an even greater risk for poor academic achievement, noncompletion of high school programs, and involvement in criminal activity than their average-achieving peers. The NCES reported in 2000 that 8% of students enrolled in public elementary and secondary schools were classified as having a learning disability (LD), emotional or behavioral disorder (EBD), or mental retardation (MR) (NCES, 2000). This means that 3.8 million young people fall into the disability categories mentioned above. Students with disabilities lag behind their peers in the areas of employment, wages, postsecondary education, and residential independence. Fewer than 20% of students with disabilities enter postsecondary education, only 55% are competitively employed, and fewer than 30% are living independently (NCES, 2005b). Moreover, students with disabilities who found employment within the first 2 years after leaving high school were earning poverty-level wages (Blackorby & Wagner, 1996). As a consequence, adults with disabilities are less successful than their average-achieving peers in finding and sustaining employment, maintaining an acceptable standard of living, and developing independence than persons without disabilities (Field, Sarver, & Shaw, 2003).

A lack of interest in school may play a role in the negative outcomes of students with LD. Students with LD and low achievers are more likely to exhibit negative attitudes and less motivation with regard to their education than higher-achieving peers (McCoach, 2000). The challenges of encouraging positive attitudes toward school and fostering student educational involvement may be more important than ever in improving outcomes for young people.

[one-step funnel: specific research problem/study]

For students with LD to realize academic success and positive postsecondary outcomes in today's educational climate, developing self-direction may become an essential part of a special education program. A successful special education program promotes positive attitudes toward education by providing students with disabilities the skills and opportunities to have a lead decision-making role in their education and adult life. Students with disabilities require instruction on the tools that lead to this self-advocacy and self-empowerment (Grigal, Neubert, Moon, & Graham, 2003). According to a 2004 report by the Northwest Regional Education Laboratory (NREL), one of the top priorities of teachers and administrators is to assist students in becoming responsible for their own learning and academic performance. High school students with LD may be able to realize academic, behavioral, and social benefits if taught a method of self-directed learning.

Appendix F

Sample Chapter One
Statement of the Problem

Adapted from Williams, A. (2006). *Motivation, metacognition, and self-determination among students with learning disabilities.* Unpublished master's thesis, University of San Francisco, California.

The challenges present in encouraging high school students with learning disabilities (LD) to become self-directed learners are related to three important components of a self-directed educational program: [**three areas**] motivation and self-efficacy, metacognition skills, and self-determination. High school students with LD lack motivation and self-efficacy, struggle with metacognition, and are often not exposed to opportunities for developing self-determination (Deci & Chandler, 1986; Shimabukuro, Prater, Jenkins, & Edelen-Smith, 1999). A motivated student would take a genuine interest not only in subject matter but also in identifying the best strategies to accomplish learning about the subject matter. This skill is referred to as metacognition. Simply stated, metacognition refers to thinking about thinking. This includes a student's ability to self-regulate and self-evaluate her learning processes and adjust her learning behavior when necessary. The last challenge in promoting self-directed learning involves supporting and encouraging aspects of the self-determination theory in classroom curricula. In the field of education, the theory of self-determination involves a student actively engaging in making decisions regarding his education with a full sense of choice (Ryan & Deci, 2000). Self-determination requires a student to know and value himself; plan, act, and experience outcomes; and learn.

Motivation and self-efficacy. [**problems in area 1**] Motivation and self-efficacy are important facets to encouraging student educational involvement because a lack of these attributes contributes to poor academic performance and postsecondary outcomes. Motivation and self-efficacy appear to be closely related in that motivation refers to a student's interest in a subject matter or task, while self-efficacy describes a student's judgment about his or her abilities concerning a specific subject or task (NREL, 2004). A student with adequate levels of motivation and self-efficacy approaches his or her education with the attitude of "I want to succeed and I can succeed." Motivated students may be said to be actively interested in what they are learning and the tasks involved in the learning process. A student may be intrinsically or extrinsically motivated to attempt or accomplish specific tasks. The effectiveness of intrinsic versus extrinsic motivation is debatable (Cameron, 2001; Deci, Ryan, & Koestner, 2001), but researchers agree that motivation plays an important role in a student's success (Linnenbrink & Pintrich, 2002; Ryan & Deci, 2000).

Motivation is a key element of a successful learning environment for students with LD. However, motivating students with LD can be difficult. Generally, the educational research community has accepted that students with LD have low levels of motivation (Adelman, Lauber, Nelson, & Smith, 1989; Wilson & David, 1994). Motivation has been said to diminish when a student is faced with repeated failure. Students with LD have had more experiences with failure than their peers without disabilities and therefore experience lower levels of motivation (Deci & Chandler, 1986).

Students with LD also had a lower sense of self-efficacy than their peers without disabilities. Attributing academic success or failure to external factors was found to be a common practice among students with LD. This lack of self-efficacy among students with LD contributed to the amount of difficulty they experienced in academic settings (Dev, 1996).

Metacognition. [**problems in area 2**] In addition to wanting to accomplish a task (motivation) and feeling as if they have the ability to accomplish a task (self-efficacy), students with LD may also benefit from knowing the best way for them to go about accomplishing a task (metacognition). Students with LD have difficulty with metacognition skills, including self-evaluation and self-regulation (Klassen, 2002). Accurately evaluating their own academic skills presents challenges to students with LD (Stone & May, 2002). This inaccurate self-evaluation may lead to difficulties for students with LD in organizing and planning assignments because the student will have trouble determining the course of action best suited to his abilities. Students with LD are challenged by analyzing task requirements, choosing and applying appropriate strategies to complete tasks, and evaluating and adjusting performance because they have a tendency to place more of their focus on lower-order processes than on the evaluative aspects of metacognitive skills (Butler, 1998). Another aspect of metacognition is making adjustments to learning. There is a connection between adjustment, learning, and achievement in that people learn by adjusting and adjust to learn (Martin, Mithaug, & Cox, 2003).

Developing an understanding of a student's own cognitive processes may be a particularly difficult aspect of metacognition for a student with LD due to difficulties she experiences with self-regulation (Price, 2002). Self-regulation involves the student being able to understand the requirements of a task or goal and to monitor progress and deadlines. When a task is attempted but not accomplished, the student must be able to self-regulate, or make academic, behavioral, or social adjustments to meet his goal (Martin et al., 2003). Students with LD, including students diagnosed with attention deficit or hyperactivity disorders, found behavioral self-regulation especially difficult due to the nature of these disorders (Shimabukuro et al., 1999). Students with LD typically have difficulties in making adjustments and transitioning, which may present another metacognitive challenge to the student (Shimabukuro et al., 1999). An understanding of one's cognitive strengths and weaknesses seems crucial for students with LD to make effective choices and decisions about their learning.

Self-determination. [**problems in area 3**] Combining motivation, self-efficacy, and metacognition skills with the development of self-determination among students with LD may improve these students' outcomes. Students who embodied the skills of self-determination had a higher rate of success both academically and in making transitions to adult life (Bremer, Kachgal, & Schoeller, 2003). The Individuals with Disabilities Education Act (IDEA) of 1997 promoted student self-determination in intent and spirit by mandating that students be involved in the Individual Education Program (IEP) and transition planning (Grigal et al., 2003). Unfortunately, rather than supporting and encouraging development of self-determination, many educational environments rely on short-term solutions such as overreliance on accommodations or overuse of course waivers. This results in high dropout rates and low postsecondary education rates among students with disabilities (Field et al., 2003).

Research indicated that students with disabilities had greater difficulty developing a sense of self-determination than their typically achieving peers (Wehmeyer, Palmer, Agran, Mithaug, & Martin, 2000). One reason for this was that the stigma attached to having a learning disability encouraged many students to deny that their disabilities existed. This denial led to nondisclosure, which limited resources available to students with LD. This lack of self-awareness also diminished the students' belief in themselves, which undermined the development of self-determination (Hoffman, 2003).

Other barriers to developing a sense of self-determination for students with LD were the attributes of learned helplessness and self-deprecation (Bos & Vaughn, 2002) and negative or unrealistic self-concepts exhibited by these students (Price, 2002). These distortions of self may inhibit a student's ability to make effective choices and decisions, which will have a negative effect on developing self-determination. Unfortunately, students with LD have greater difficulty developing a sense of self-determination than their typically achieving peers (Hoffman, 2003).

[**section summary**] As noted, students with learning disabilities have lower levels of motivation and self-efficacy, metacognition skills, and self-determination than their nondisabled peers. These shortfalls negatively impact their academic performance and may cause them to drop out of school altogether. To improve students' with disabilities chances for successful life outcomes, educators need to implement research-based strategies that will enhance their motivation and self-efficacy, metacognition skills, and self-determination.

Appendix G

Sample Research Syntheses

Adapted from Kendall, D. (2006). *The power of communication: A special day class teacher and her students' perceptions on effective communication, lesson efficacy, and teacher-student relationships within a cross-cultural framework.* Unpublished master's thesis, University of San Francisco, California.

Ideally, it can be argued that all teachers enter their classroom with their own ideas for how their students should conduct themselves behaviorally. Furthermore, each educator's personality, cultural identity, race, and manner, which play a large role in conveying these expectations, are diverse. Previous research (Sherwin & Schmidt, 2003) has indicated a need for educators and service providers to be aware of the cultures they serve, to prevent miscommunications. A study by Dennis and Giangreco (1996) investigated similar notions by exploring aspects of cultural sensitivity in standard family interviewing practices that guide, develop, and implement students' individualized education programs (IEPs). The researchers emphasized their perspectives as professionals and as members of minority groups in the United States. The purpose of this qualitative study was to listen carefully to interview responses, consult current research in the area of cultural sensitivity, and construct more culturally sensitive family interviewing practices.

The researchers in this study used criterion sampling to select the 14 participants. The three criteria that needed to be met to be a participant in the study were (a) being a member of a minority group in the United States, (b) being knowledgeable about cultural issues related to their own heritage, and (c) being knowledgeable about current common practices in educating students with severe disabilities in the United States. Participants were identified as members of the following minority groups in the United States: African American, Latino, Chinese American, Japanese American, Native American, Asian Indian, Native Hawaiian, and Native Alaskan.

The data collection process included providing each of the 14 participants with a copy of the study's protocol and asking them to read and respond to the document. The document, *Choosing Options and Accommodations for Children: A Guide to Planning Inclusive Education* (COACH), was developed in an earlier study, and expanded on the previous research by asking family members about the importance of specific current and future life outcomes (e.g., health, safety, social relationships), as well as their priorities for learning outcomes. After reading the protocol, the participants were asked to write a report and critically assess COACH from a cross-cultural perspective. Interviews were formed based on the reports, and subsequent semi-structured, recorded telephone interviews were administered.

The research was driven by three questions: (a) "What does cultural sensitivity mean in family interviewing," (b) "How do professionals approach their work in culturally sensitive ways," and (c) "How can family interviews be conducted in more culturally sensitive ways?" These variables in the form of participant interview responses were transcribed and entered into *Ethnograph* (a computerized software program) for data analysis.

The results of this study revealed that with regard to the definition of cultural sensitivity in family interviewing, the participants conveyed the need for professionals to understand each particular student's family environment, to more accurately interpret the family's future life and learning goals. With regard to professionals approaching their work and conducting family interviews in more culturally sensitive ways, participants stated that professionals needed to form positive attitudes, greater sensitivity, and respect for other schools of thought, even if they were contrary to the values they currently identify with. This is an important implication for educators who teach students from diverse backgrounds. The aforementioned work approaches and open-mindedness may prove successful for the educator who will meet with the parents of students from various cultures. Knowledge of the students and families one serves, as well as genuine sensitivity to their cultural norms, can function to alleviate misunderstandings and may help clarify communicative intent in the classroom as well as in IEP meetings.

Although the research discussed many salient and pertinent issues in the areas of cultural sensitivity, a threat to the internal validity of the study was a lack of clarity of the variables measured and, subsequently, a lack of clarity of the results. Threats to the external validity include vague descriptions of the setting and duration of the investigation of the issue. Thus, the generalizability of these findings to other groups may be limited.

Adapted from Iniguez, D. (2007). *Providing primary language support for English language learners with learning disabilities through affirming intervention models.* Unpublished master's thesis, University of San Francisco, California.

A study based on professional development was implemented to help support teachers of culturally and linguistically diverse students. Project CRISP (Culturally Responsive Instruction for Special Populations) was established to assess teachers' perspectives about multicultural education, its place in the school curriculum, and how it can affect the number of referrals for special education services (Voltz, Brazil, & Scott, 2003). Awareness of multicultural education can prepare teachers of culturally and linguistically diverse students to avoid overrepresentation and reduce referrals for special education services. This project was aimed at lowering the overrepresentation of students of color in special education and providing a meaningful theoretical framework of multicultural education for educators.

The participants were 33 teachers from large urban school districts. The ethnic background of the participants was 45% African American and 55% European American. The teachers volunteered for the study and were also paid a modest stipend. The criteria for the participants included having only elementary and middle school teachers and a collaboration of at least two teachers from the same school. In addition, the school groups had to have at least one special educator. As a result, 60.6% were general educators with an average of 9.6 years of experience, and 39.4% were special educators with an average of 11.9 years of experience. The majority of the participants were elementary educators at 85%, and 15% were middle school educators.

The participants engaged in professional development activities based on a multicultural education framework. Project CRISP was created to help teachers understand the importance of "culturally responsive pedagogy" (Voltz et al., 2003, p. 64). In addition, the influence of culture on learning styles and behavior was also integrated into the project. The foundation of the project was based on Banks's model of multicultural education (2001), which has five main components: (a) content integration, (b) knowledge construction process, (c) prejudice reduction, (d) empowering school culture, and (e) equity pedagogy.

The professional development was divided into several stages. The initial part of the project was conducted as a seminar that lasted 3 days. The seminar was organized to begin with Banks's (2001) model of multicultural education. The other activities included were hands-on activities, developing plans with same-school participants, discussions, and demonstrations. One of the final activities included goal setting for the participants. All the participants had to name at least one goal that would continue and extend the participants' learning in the areas discussed during the seminar. From the goals, teachers wrote their own ongoing professional development plan. All schools worked in collaborative teams and worked about 26 hours to accomplish their defined goals. The participants' professional development plans included action research projects, curriculum development projects, and reading groups.

A variety of measurement tools were administered to assess the effects of Project CRISP. First, the participants were administered a questionnaire as a pre- and postassessment based on a five-point Likert-type scale that included responses from (1) strongly disagree to (5) strongly agree. The postquestionnaire had two extra questions that were relevant to the effects of the project on the participants' teaching methodology that was administered 15 weeks after participants attended the seminar. In addition, all participants were interviewed over the phone as a pre- and postassessment of overall familiarity and understanding of multicultural education and the process they used to refer students for special education services. The interviews averaged about 20 minutes each. The final measurement tool used by Project CRISP was a pre- and postlesson plan analysis that required participants to deconstruct a given lesson plan by creating a culturally appropriate one.

There were several methods of data analysis for the different measures. The data for the questionnaire were analyzed by using a paired t test to determine whether the differences in pre- to postmean ratings were statistically significant. The interviews were transcribed and coded to look for frequent themes cited in the interviews by the participants. To add to the validity of the project, a trained graduate assistant concurrently coded the transcripts and the interrater reliability was found to be 78.8%. For the lesson plan analysis, the ideas were classified in the areas of content, methodology, materials, and assessments. Again, an interrater reliability was used and had a rate of 82.9%. The amount of change between the prelesson plan analysis and the postlesson plan analysis was rated on a 1–4 scale. The total mean ratings were comparatively analyzed with a paired t test.

Results from the questionnaire indicated that most teachers thought Project CRISP was effective in helping them become better teachers. The results of the prequestionnaires showed that most general educators felt comfortable and able to work with culturally and linguistically diverse families and were also familiar with the culture of their students. Yet a distinction was found in three areas: (a) meeting the needs of their culturally and linguistically diverse students, (b) identifying the differences between a learning disability and learning differences, and (c) how to teach and implement a curriculum from a multicultural standpoint. The three areas that were identified as a need were rated significantly higher (.05 level) on the prequestionnaire results. Most participants revealed that their teacher training program was inadequate in preparing them to work with a culturally and linguistically diverse student population. The postquestionnaire showed that teachers continued to feel comfortable teaching a diverse student population.

The results of the interviews were grouped in the following categories by the authors of the study: referral practices, prereferral interventions, behavior management, and teacher perceptions on the effects of Project CRISP. The questions about referral practices during the preinterview showed that 65% of general educators had referred students for special education services because of academic difficulties in math or reading. The postinterview showed similar rates, at 60%, of teachers referring students for special education services. Yet, at the postinterview, about 25% of the participants noted the need to address a variety of factors, such as home environment and communication with other educators in the referral process. The preinterview about prereferral interventions highlighted three areas that were commonly used as a response: accommodations (35%), parent collaboration (35%), and professional collaboration (25%). The postinterview noted a new category adapting the methodology for the needs of diverse students. About 54% of special educators among the participants were found to be involved with prereferral interventions. The pre- and postinterview results about behavior management found minimal differences; 53% of general educators and 45% of special educators believed students' cultural backgrounds can affect their behavior. The teacher perception results of Project CRISP were noted as making a difference in teaching methodology by 45% of general educators and 69% of special educators.

The lesson plan analysis noted the most changes in the area of content and methodology. The variation of the mean for general educators was 2.00 during the prelesson analysis and 2.44 on the postanalysis of the lesson. The variation of the mean for special educators was 1.83 during the prelesson analysis and 2.25 during the postanalysis of the lesson. There were no statistically significant changes between the pre- and postratings.

The authors of the study indicated that teachers believed they lacked the methodology and cultural understanding to adequately teach culturally diverse students before the intervention. A difference was also found in the level of confidence by special educators to work with culturally diverse students in comparison with general educators. The study also highlighted how Project CRISP was able to influence teacher reflections of classroom practices with culturally diverse students. Participants in the study also added depth to their prior knowledge.

The implications of these results indicate a need for educators to receive more training to teach a culturally diverse student population to reduce the number of referrals for special education services. This can be obtained by providing a positive school environment and workshops for educators on how to teach to different students' cultural learning styles. This current study addresses this need by providing reading instruction in the students' primary language. The authors also suggested that special educators should participate in professional development programs focused on working with culturally diverse students.

The study had several limitations as noted by the researcher. First, the length of the professional development was a weakness because the seminar only lasted 3 days, in comparison with courses at the university level, which last for several months. More time could have been valuable for the participants. Another possible major limitation of the study was that participants volunteered for the study, and there was a small sample size. The project's sample group might have been composed of participants who wanted to learn about multicultural education theories. Other teachers may not have been present at the study because of their personal biases. Future studies need to be conducted with larger sample sizes with a diverse group of educators.

Glossary

abstracting: Abstracting is a method of organizing information about an article that includes a brief summary and selected critical information about the study.

accessibility: Accessibility refers to the ability to gain access or entry to the research site and participants.

advance organizer: An advance organizer is an outline for the literature review and informs the reader of what will be addressed in the chapter.

advanced search: Advanced search (also referred to as guided search) allows the user to set specific filters to narrow the search results.

American Psychological Association (APA) style: APA style is the writing and editorial form used by the American Psychological Association to publish books and manuscripts. This style form is commonly used in various social science disciplines such as education, psychology, sociology, business, economics, nursing, and social work.

AND: The AND Boolean operator combines two or more terms so that each record contains all of the terms.

answerable research question: An answerable research question is one where the researcher is able to collect data or information (using a measurement instrument) to answer the question related to the problem.

Belmont Report: The Belmont Report is a summary of the basic ethical principles and guidelines for conducting research with human subjects.

beneficence: Beneficence is the second principle in the Belmont Report and refers to two general rules: "(1) do not harm; and (2) maximize possible benefits, and minimize possible harms."

Boolean operators: Boolean search operators are used in electronic databases and other search engines to define the relationships between words or groups of words.

chairperson: The chairperson is the faculty member who is assigned to or selected by the graduate student to advise him or her throughout the master's thesis process.

chunking method: The chunking method refers to breaking up large tasks into smaller, more manageable chunks such as writing one section of a chapter rather than the entire chapter.

column head: In an APA table, the column head identifies the items listed under one column.

column spanner: In an APA table, a column spanner is a broad heading that covers two or more columns.

Common Rule: The Common Rule is a federal policy for the protection of human subjects followed by most of the federal departments and agencies that sponsor research with human subjects.

convenience sample: In a convenience sample, the researcher selects the individuals who are available and accessible at the time.

cost-benefit analysis: In a cost-benefit analysis, researchers must weigh the potential benefits against the anticipated risks and decide whether the benefits are so great that they justify putting subjects at a certain level of risk or whether the risks are so high that the benefits are not worth the potential harm to subjects.

data coding: Data coding is a data analysis process used in qualitative research to categorize and label the major themes.

data triangulation: Data triangulation is one type of triangulation procedure where multiple methods of data collection are used to study one phenomenon.

deception: Deception occurs when the researcher omits information about the study or gives false information.

deductive reasoning: A logic/reasoning approach that moves from the general to the specific.

dependent variable: The dependent variable is the variable that is observed to see if there is a change (e.g., effect) in response to the independent variable. The researcher cannot manipulate the dependent variable.

descriptive statistics: Descriptive statistics are the basic level of statistical analysis for a data set from a sample group. Typically, reported statistics include the mean, median, mode, variance, and standard deviation.

descriptors: Descriptors are used in electronic databases to give every record a subject indexing term (i.e., controlled vocabulary or subject terms).

dictionary definition: A dictionary definition is a definition that is offered in a dictionary to define ambiguous terms related to the study or research question.

digital object identifier (DOI): The DOI is a unique code of letters and numbers that provides a link to a journal article's location on the Internet.

dissertation: A dissertation is typically the culminating requirement for a doctoral degree.

editorial style: The editorial style is a set of rules or guidelines that writers must adhere to for publishing manuscripts, books, and so on.

electronic database: An electronic database is an electronic collection of information (e.g., books, journal articles, reference materials) where an individual can research and retrieve resources. Electronic databases can be interdisciplinary or organized around a particular subject area or field.

empirically based: Empirically based research findings are those that are based on data that are produced by experiment or observation rather than opinion or theory.

example definition: An example definition is a definition that uses examples to define ambiguous terms related to the study or research question.

expanders feature: The expanders feature is the opposite of the limiters feature and broadens an electronic search by allowing the user to combine or add key terms.

external validity: External validity (outside the study) refers to whether the results of the study are applicable or can be generalized to other settings and groups.

feasibility: Feasibility refers to how realistic it will be to access data or participants and the time needed to complete the study.

Final Rule: The Final Rule is the revised Common Rule that was issued in by the U.S. Department of Health and Human Services and 15 other federal departments and agencies. The Final Rule was published in the *Federal Register* (FR) on January 19, 2017 and went into effect on January 21, 2019.

full-text (see also PDF): Full-text is when the entire resource is available either in a printable webpage format or a PDF format.

funnel writing strategy: The funnel writing strategy is analogous to a funnel where your first paragraph about the problem is broad and every subsequent paragraph narrows the topic toward a specific problem.

general notes: In an APA table, general notes appear at the bottom of the table and explain information relating to the entire table such as abbreviations or symbols.

generalizability: Generalizability refers to the extent to which the results about a sample group from a study are applicable to the larger population.

hanging indent: A hanging indent is used in the reference list. A hanging indent refers to when the first line of a reference is flushed all the way to the left margin and the rest of the lines are indented half an inch.

heading (see also levels of heading): A heading is the name of a section or sub-section used to organize the paper. A heading at the same level has equal importance. The headings are formatted depending on how many levels of headings there are in the manuscript or thesis.

heading capitalization: Heading capitalization is when all the major words are capitalized like in the title of a movie.

hypothesis: In quantitative studies, a hypothesis involves making assumptions or predictions based on probability distributions or likelihoods of events.

independent variable: The independent variable is the variable that is deliberately manipulated (e.g., cause) by the researcher to produce a change in the dependent variable.

independent-samples *t* test: The independent samples *t* test is used to determine whether the difference in means on the dependent variable between two independent groups is a real difference or one that is due to chance.

inductive reasoning: A logic/reasoning approach that moves from the specific to the general.

inferential statistics: Inferential statistics are the higher level of statistical analysis where inferences are made from a sample to a population. Inferential statistics may also include hypothesis testing and set probability levels to test for statistically significant differences between groups or treatments.

Institutional Review Board (IRB): At institutions of higher education, the IRB is a group that has been formally designated to review and monitor research applications involving human subjects.

interlibrary loan: Interlibrary loan is a service provided by libraries whereby a user of one library can borrow books or acquire photocopies of articles in journals that are owned by another library (sometimes there is a fee involved).

internal validity: Internal validity (within the study) refers to whether the changes in the dependent variable were due to the independent variable or some other variable.

interrater reliability: Interrater reliability refers to the relative consistency of the ratings of the same stimulus given by two or more independent raters (data collectors). Traditionally interrater reliability has been measured by percentage agreement, calculated as the number of agreement scores divided by the total number of scores.

justice: Justice is the third principle in the Belmont Report and refers to fairness and equity in the selection of participants and distribution of benefits.

Kefauver-Harris Drug Amendments: The Kefauver-Harris Drug Amendments increased the regulatory powers of the Food and Drug Administration so that drug manufacturers had to prove that their drug was safe and effective before marketing and selling it to the public. The act also required that subjects from medical studies give their informed consent.

keywords: Keywords are typically two to three words or short phrases that are fundamental to the research topic, problem, or questions and are used to refine the search process.

levels of heading (see also heading): The levels of heading refer to the organizational structure or hierarchy of the sections in the manuscript or thesis. Five is the maximum number of levels of heading in a manuscript or thesis.

limiters feature: The limiters feature narrows an electronic search by allowing the user to set specific limits, so the search results will only contain research with the chosen specific criteria.

literature review matrix: A literature review matrix is an organizational tool such as a table, chart, or flow chart to display the relationship or common attributes among multiple studies.

literature synthesis: A literature synthesis (also referred to as a research synthesis) is a type of article in which the results of several related studies are compared and summarized.

mapping: Mapping is a technique to visually organize research articles around a core issue, theme, author, and so on. There are different types of mapping formats (e.g., concept, mind, subject tree, content) and software programs available.

Master of Arts (MA): The Master of Arts degree is typically awarded in the disciplines of arts, sciences, social sciences (e.g., education, psychology), and humanities (e.g., history, philosophy, religion).

Master of Science (MS): The Master of Science degree is typically awarded to students in technical fields such as engineering, nursing, mathematics, and health care management but can also be in the social sciences.

master's degree: A master's degree is a postbaccalaureate degree conferred by a college or university on candidates who complete one to two years of graduate study.

master's degree program: A master's degree program is a graduate-level, postbaccalaureate program in a specific field or discipline that typically involves a culminating activity, project, or thesis.

master's thesis: A master's thesis is an empirically based research study that is an original piece of work by the graduate student.

mean: The mean is the arithmetic average and calculated by the sum of the scores divided by the number of scores in the distribution.

measure of central tendency: The measure of central tendency is the "typical" or "average" score in a distribution.

measure of variability: A measure of variability is a statistic that indicates how close or spread apart (i.e., dispersed) the scores are in a distribution.

measurement instruments: Measurement instruments are data collection tools (e.g., surveys, observations, tests) that are used to measure changes in dependent variables or variables of interest.

median: The median is the middle score in a distribution or the score that divides the distribution in half (50% above and 50% below).

meta-analysis: A meta-analysis research study is one in which the results of several related studies are analyzed and reported with statistical measures (e.g., effect sizes).

mixed methods research: A research approach that intentionally uses both rigorous quantitative and qualitative methods and draws on the strength of each to answer research questions.

mode: The mode is the most common or most frequently occurring score in a distribution.

multidisciplinary database: A multidisciplinary database is an electronic database that covers different subjects rather than just one specific field or discipline.

National Commission for the Protection of Human Subjects of Biomedical and Behavioral Research: The National Commission for the Protection of Human Subjects of Biomedical and Behavioral Research was the first national public group whose responsibility it was to identify a set of basic ethical principles and guidelines for conducting biomedical and behavioral research involving human subjects.

National Research Act of 1974 (Public Law 93-348): The National Research Act created the National Commission for the Protection of Human Subjects of Biomedical and Behavioral Research.

nonnumerical data: Studies that use qualitative approaches collect nonnumerical data to answer their research question(s). Nonnumerical data are narrative data (i.e., words).

non-refereed: A non-refereed article is one that did not go through an external review process before being published.

nonresearchable question: A nonresearchable question is a type of question where the researcher cannot collect measurable data to answer the question or the "answers" are based on philosophical, spiritual, or religious beliefs.

NOT: The NOT Boolean operator searches terms so that records with certain terms are excluded from the results.

null hypothesis: The null hypothesis, H_0, represents the "chance" theory, meaning any observed differences are due to chance, and the treatment has no significant effect on the dependent variable.

numerical data: Studies that use quantitative approaches collect numerical data to answer their research question(s). Numerical data are mathematical (i.e., numbers) data.

Nuremberg Code: The Nuremberg Code is a set of standards of ethical medical behavior that all physicians should adhere to when involving human subjects in medical experiments.

operational definition: An operational definition is a definition that describes attributes or characteristics of the term that need to be present in order to measure it.

OR: The OR Boolean operator searches terms so that at least one of the terms is present in the record.

paired-samples *t* test (also referred to as nonindependent samples and dependent samples): The paired samples *t* test is used to determine whether the difference in means on the dependent variable between two sets of related scores is a real difference or one that is due to chance.

paraphrasing: Paraphrasing is rewriting the original text into your own words (with appropriate citations) while trying to maintain the idea or essence of the original work.

PDF: The PDF format is a full-text electronic "picture" of a document and it resembles how a research article actually looks in the journal.

plagiarize: Plagiarizing refers to using another person's ideas or words without giving them proper credit.

primary sources: Primary sources are the actual or the original results of studies reported by the researcher(s) (i.e., firsthand information).

probability notes: In an APA table, probability notes appear after the specific notes and indicate whether results were statistically significant (meaning that the null hypothesis was rejected).

purposeful redundancy: Purposeful redundancy refers to intentionally reiterating main points about the research problem and study throughout the thesis.

purposive sample: In a purposive sample, the researcher selects individuals who are considered representative because they meet certain criteria for the study.

qualitative research: A qualitative research method delves into a particular situation to better understand a phenomenon within its natural context and the perspectives of the participants involved.

quantitative research: A quantitative research method includes but is not limited to research using descriptive, correlation, prediction, and control (cause-effect) methods.

random assignment: In random assignment, each participant in the sample has an equal and independent chance of being selected for the treatment group.

random sample: In a random sample, every individual in the population has an equal and independent chance of being selected.

range: The range is the difference between the largest and smallest scores in a distribution.

refereed: A refereed (also referred to as peer-reviewed) article has been submitted for external review by a panel of reviewers before being published.

reference materials: Reference materials are collections of information such as encyclopedias, handbooks, indexes, and dictionaries.

relevancy ranked: The "relevancy ranked" option shows the search term first and then lists subject terms (i.e., descriptors) that are related to the search term displayed in order of relevance.

reliability: Reliability refers to the extent to which an instrument *consistently* measures what it was intended to measure.

replicability: Replicability refers to the ability to replicate (i.e., copy) the study to verify and interpret the results or adapt and expand the study.

research question: A research question is related to the problem in a study and is the question that the researcher attempts to answer. The research question guides the type of data that will be collected or how the data should be collected.

Research Subject Bill of Rights: The Research Subject Bill of Rights is a list of rights that is guaranteed for every participant in a study.

resources: Resources are tangibles such as materials and finances necessary to conduct a study but also include nontangibles such as personal health and energy.

respect for persons: Respect for persons is the first principle in the Belmont Report and includes "two ethical convictions: first that individuals should be treated as autonomous agents, and second, that persons with diminished autonomy are entitled to protection."

sample group: The sample group is the group of participants in a study. They are the group that the researcher collects data from or about.

sampling: Sampling refers to the process of selecting participants for a study from a population.

search engine: A search engine is a computer system where information is stored and organized for easy retrieval. The most common search engines search for information on the World Wide Web through the Internet.

secondary sources: Secondary sources describe or summarize the work of others (i.e., secondhand information).

seminal article: A seminal article is an article that was significant to the topic (e.g., classic) or created a change in the field.

sentence capitalization: Sentence capitalization is when only the first word of the title and proper nouns are capitalized like in a regular sentence.

skimming: Skimming is a technique to quickly scan a research article by reading the abstract, introduction, and conclusion to get the main idea.

specific notes: In an APA table, specific notes appear after the general notes and explain information pertaining to an individual column, row, or item.

standard deviation: The standard deviation indicates how much the scores vary from the mean in a distribution.

stub column: In an APA table, the first column on the left side of the table is called the stub column.

stub head: In an APA table, the stub column's heading is called the stub head.

stubs: In an APA table, the stubs are the row headings, which are the major independent variables related to the stub head.

t **test:** A *t* test is a statistical test that is used to determine whether the observed difference between two mean scores represents a true difference or is due to chance.

terminal degree: A terminal degree is the generally accepted highest academic degree in a field of study.

thesaurus: The thesaurus contains alphabetized descriptors (i.e., subject terms, subjects) that are used in the electronic database to give every record a subject indexing term (i.e., controlled vocabulary).

thick description: A thick description is an explanation that includes both the behavior and the context in which the behavior was displayed.

three parallel ladders strategy: The three parallel ladders strategy is an organizational writing strategy. The three ladders represent sections of your thesis chapters that are aligned by topic or order (e.g., *Statement of the Problem, Background and Need*, and so on).

time: Time refers to the researcher's time that is available to devote to the study as well as the duration (length) and frequency (how often the researcher will interact with participants) of the study.

timeline: A timeline is a schedule that is created by the researcher that outlines all the necessary steps and phases to complete the study within the allocated time.

Type I error: A Type I error is rejecting the null hypothesis when it is true.

validity: Validity refers to the extent to which the instrument measures what it was intended to measure. Validity can also refer to the credibility of findings in a qualitative study.

voluntary informed consent: Voluntary informed consent is when a person has the capacity to give consent and receives sufficient and accurate information about the study (e.g., purpose, methods, risks, benefits) to make an informed decision to participate.

vulnerable populations: Vulnerable populations are children, pregnant women, prisoners, or others who may need additional protection from harm, depending on the risks involved.

References

American Psychological Association. (2010). *Publication manual of the American Psychological Association* (6th ed.). Washington, DC: Author.

Babbie, E. (2016). *The practice of social research* (14th ed.). Belmont, CA: Thomson Wadsworth.

Bayor, R. H. (2016). *The Oxford handbook of American immigration and ethnicity.* Oxford, UK: Oxford University Press.

Bell, N. (1991). Gestalt imagery: A critical factor in language comprehension. *Annals of Dyslexia, 41,* 246–260. doi:10.1007/BF02648089

Bogdan, R. C., & Biklen, S. K. (2003). *Qualitative research for education: An introduction to theories and methods* (4th ed.). New York, NY: Pearson Education.

Brown, C. F., Demaray, M. K., & Secord, S. M. (2014). Cyber victimization in middle school and relations to social emotional outcomes. *Computers in Human Behavior, 35,* 12–21.

Creswell, J. W. (2013). *Qualitative inquiry and research design: Choosing among five traditions* (3rd ed.). Thousand Oaks, CA: Sage.

Creswell, J. W. (2015). *Educational research: Planning, conducting, and evaluating quantitative and qualitative research* (5th ed.). Upper Saddle River, NJ: Pearson.

Creswell, J. W., & Creswell, J. D. (2018). *Research design: Qualitative, quantitative, and mixed methods approaches* (5th ed.). Thousand Oaks, CA: Sage.

Creswell, J. W., & Plano Clark, V. L. (2018). *Designing and conducting mixed methods research* (3rd ed.). Thousand Oaks, CA: Sage.

Creswell, J. W., & Poth, C. N. (2018). *Qualitative inquiry and research design* (4th ed.). Thousand Oaks, CA: Sage.

Denzin, N. K., & Lincoln, Y. S. (2011). *The SAGE handbook of qualitative research.* Thousand Oaks, CA: Sage.

Drew, C. J., Hardman, M. L., & Hosp, J. L. (2008). *Designing and conducting research in education.* Thousand Oaks, CA: Sage.

Ethical principles: The Belmont Report. (n.d.). Retrieved from Duke University, Office of Research Support website: http://www.hhs.gov/ohrp/policy/belmont.html

Ferretti, R. P., MacArthur, C. D., & Okolo, C. M. (2001). Teaching for historical understanding in inclusive classrooms. *Learning Disability Quarterly, 24,* 59–71. https://doi.org/10.2307/1511296

Fetters, M. D., & Freshwater, D. (2015). The 1+1=3 integration challenge. *Journal of Mixed Methods Research, 9*(2), 115–117.

Fink, A. (2014). *Conducting research literature reviews: From the Internet to paper* (4th ed.). Thousand Oaks, CA: Sage.

Fraenkel, J., Wallen, N., & Hyun, H. (2015). *How to design and evaluate research in education* (8th ed.). New York, NY: McGraw-Hill.

Gillberg, C. (1991). Clinical and neurobiological aspects of Asperger syndrome in six family studies. In U. Frith (Ed.), *Autism and Asperger syndrome* (pp. 122–146). Cambridge, UK: Cambridge University Press.

Goldstein, A. P., & McGinnis, E. (1997). *Skillstreaming the adolescent: New strategies and perspectives for teaching prosocial skills.* Champaign, IL: Research Press.

Gomes, C. (2008). *The effects of graphic novels on reading comprehension and motivation for students with Asperger's syndrome* (Unpublished master's thesis). University of San Francisco, California.

Good, R. H., & Kaminski, R. A. (Eds.). (2002). *Dynamic indicators of basic early literacy skills* (6th ed.). Eugene, OR: Institute for the Development of Educational Achievement.

Greene, J. A., & Podolsky, S. H. (2012). Reform, regulation, and pharmaceuticals—The Kefauver–Harris Amendments at 50. *New England Journal of Medicine, 367*(16), 1481–1483. Retrieved from http://doi.org/10.1056/NEJMp1210007

Henderson, L. (2007). *The relationship between expressive language and social skills* (Unpublished master's thesis). University of San Francisco, California.

Hess, L. (2008). *The effects of peer-mediated instruction on the inferential reading comprehension and social skills of elementary school students with emotional disturbance* (Unpublished master's thesis). University of San Francisco, California.

Hinduja, S., & Patchin, J. W. (2015). *2015 cyberbullying data.* Cyberbullying Research Center. Retrieved from https://cyberbullying.org/2015-data

Ho, A. (2006). *The effects of the prior knowledge expository text experiential learning (PEEL) intervention on historical content knowledge of secondary students with learning disabilities* (Unpublished master's thesis). University of San Francisco, California.

Iniguez, D. (2007). *A reading intervention study for English language learners with learning disabilities* (Unpublished master's thesis). University of San Francisco, California.

Irey, R. (2008). *The effects of fluency instruction on comprehension for third grade English learners with learning disabilities* (Unpublished master's thesis). University of San Francisco, California.

Kahn, J. (n.d.). *Reporting statistics in APA style.* Retrieved from https://my.ilstu.edu/~jhkahn/apastats.html

Kendall, D. (2006). *The power of communication: A special day class teacher and her students' perceptions of effective communication, lesson efficacy, and teacher-student relationships within a cross cultural framework* (Unpublished master's thesis). University of San Francisco, California.

Kim, J. H., & Scialli, A. R. (2011). Thalidomide: The tragedy of birth defects and the effective treatment of disease. *Toxicological Sciences, 122*(1), 1–6. Retrieved from https://doi.org/10.1093/toxsci/kfr088

Kim, W. O. (2012). Institutional review board (IRB) and ethical issues in clinical research. *Korean Journal of Anesthesiology, 62*(1), 3–12. Retrieved from http://doi.org/10.4097/kjae.2012.62.1.3

Kornhauser, M. (2006). *Fostering protective factors to promote resiliency in secondary students with learning disabilities* (Unpublished master's thesis). University of San Francisco, California.

Lane, D. (2003, July 7). *Measures of variability.* Retrieved from http://cnx.org/content/m10947/2.3/

Machi, L. A., & McEvoy, B. T. (2016). *The literature review: Six steps to success* (3rd ed.). Thousand Oaks, CA: Sage.

Maxwell, J. A. (2013). *Qualitative research design: An interactive approach* (3rd ed.). Thousand Oaks, CA: Sage.

McCoy, B. R. (2016). Digital distractions in the classroom phase II: Student classroom use of digital devices for non-class related purpose. *Journal of Media Education, 7*(1), 5–32.

McLeod, J., & McLeod, R. (1999). *McLeod assessment of reading comprehension.* Novato, CA: Arena Press.

McMillan, J. H. (2015). *Fundamentals of educational research* (7th ed.). Upper Saddle River, NJ: Pearson Education.

Mertler, C. A., & Charles, C. M. (2010). *Introduction to educational research* (7th ed.). Boston, MA: Allyn & Bacon.

Mills, G. E., & Gay, L. R. (2019). *Educational research: Competencies for analysis and applications* (12th ed.). Upper Saddle River, NJ: Pearson.

Mireles, S. (2004). *Student preferences and self-esteem with regards to the resource specialist program* (Unpublished master's thesis). University of San Francisco, California.

Modern Language Association. (2016). *MLA Handbook* (8th ed.). New York, NY: Author.

Mujis, D. (2010). *Doing quantitative research in education with SPSS*. Thousand Oaks, CA: Sage.

National Conference of State Legislatures. (n.d.). *State bullying legislation since 2008*. Retrieved from http://www.ncsl.org/research/education/bullying-legislation-since-2008.aspx

Neighborhood. (n.d.). In *Merriam-Webster online dictionary*. Retrieved from http://www.merriamwebster.com/dictionary/neighborhood

Newman, I., & Benz, C. (1998). *Qualitative-quantitative research methodology: Exploring the interactive continuum*. Carbondale: Southern Illinois University Press.

Nixon, B. (2004). *Improving reading comprehension of sixth grade students with learning disabilities using drama techniques in reading instruction* (Unpublished master's thesis). University of San Francisco, California.

Onwuegbuzie, A. J. (2002). Positivists, post-positivists, post-structuralists, and post-modernists: Why can't we all get along? Towards a framework for unifying research paradigms. *Education, 122*(3), 518–530.

Orcher, L. T. (2014). *Conducting research: Social and behavioral science methods* (2nd ed.). Glendale, CA: Pyrczak.

Plagiarism.org. (2017). *What is plagiarism?* Retrieved from https://www.plagiarism.org/article/what_is_plagiarism

Ponterotto, J. G., & Grieger, I. (2007). Effectively communicating qualitative research. *Counseling Psychologist, 35*(3), 404–430. doi:10.1177/0011000006287443

Rau, S. (2006). *The effects of increased student choice opportunities on off task behaviors of students with learning disabilities* (Unpublished master's thesis). University of San Francisco, California.

Shavelson, R. J. (1996). *Statistical reasoning for the behavioral sciences* (3rd ed.). Boston, MA: Allyn & Bacon.

Simpson, L. A., & Bui, Y. N. (2016). Effects of a peer-mediated intervention on social interactions of students with low-functioning autism and perceptions of typical peers. *Education and Training in Autism and Developmental Disabilities, 51*(2), 162–178.

Stephens, D. (2006). *Referral of Spanish speaking English language learners for special education services* (Unpublished master's thesis). University of San Francisco, California.

U.S. Department of Health and Human Services. (1979). *The Belmont Report*. Rockville, MD: Author. Retrieved from http://www.hhs.gov/ohrp/humansubjects/guidance/belmont.html

U.S. Department of Health and Human Services. (1991). *The Common Rule*. Retrieved from http://www.hhs.gov/ohrp/humansubjects/commonrule/index.html

University of Chicago Press. (2017). *The Chicago Manual of Style* (17th ed.). Chicago, IL: Author.

VandenBos, G. R. (Ed.). (2010). *Publication manual of the American Psychological Association* (6th ed.). Washington, DC: American Psychological Association.

Warr, M. (1998). Life-course transitions and desistance from crime. *Criminology, 36*(2), 183–216.

Way, N., Stauber, H. Y., Nakkula, M. J., & London, P. (1994). Depression and substance use in two divergent high school cultures: A quantitative and qualitative analysis. *Journal of Youth and Adolescence, 23*(3), 331–357. Retrieved from https://doi .org/10.1007/BF01536723

Wehmeyer, M. L., & Kelchner, K. (1995). *The Arc's self-determination scale.* Arlington, TX: The Arc of the United States.

Wendling, B. J., Schrank, F. A., & Schmitt, A. J. (2007). *Woodcock Johnson III Tests of Achievement.* Rolling Meadows, IL: Riverside.

Williams, A. (2006). *Motivation, metacognition, and self-determination among students with learning disabilities* (Unpublished master's thesis). University of San Francisco, California.

Author Index

Subject Index

CPSIA information can be obtained
at www.ICGtesting.com
Printed in the USA
BVHW050022271222
655003BV00014B/149